Legal Issues of Services of General Interest

Services of general interest have been high on the political agenda in Europe in recent years as a result of EU liberalisation measures and the case law of the European Courts. At the heart of the debate is the question of how to balance market economies with the pursuit of public policy. Of crucial concern are questions on the role of services of general interest and other public policies essential in modern society.

The aim of the Series is to sketch the framework for regulating markets and public interests in Europe and to explore the legal issues raised by developments related to services of general interest and other public policies. The Series encompasses, inter alia, analyses of EU internal market and competition law, as well as EU legislation impacting particular public policies, international and domestic law, often from a comparative perspective. Sector-specific approaches will be covered as well (for instance, health, social services, energy, education, environment and communication). Furthermore, the present Series also addresses the emergence of a European Social Union and will therefore raise issues of fundamental and theoretical interest in Europe and the global economy.

Narine Ghazaryan ·
Johan Willem van de Gronden · Simon Tans ·
Marc Veenbrink
Editors

Services of General (Economic) Interest and EU Law

State of Play and Current Challenges

ASSER PRESS

Springer

Editors
Narine Ghazaryan
Department of International
and European Law
Radboud University, Faculty of Law
Nijmegen, The Netherlands

Johan Willem van de Gronden
Department of International
and European Law
Radboud University, Faculty of Law
Nijmegen, The Netherlands

Simon Tans
Law Group
Wageningen University
Wageningen, The Netherlands

Marc Veenbrink
Department of International
and European Law
Radboud University, Faculty of Law
Nijmegen, The Netherlands

ISSN 3004-9962 ISSN 3004-9970 (electronic)
Legal Issues of Services of General Interest
ISBN 978-94-6265-722-9 ISBN 978-94-6265-723-6 (eBook)
https://doi.org/10.1007/978-94-6265-723-6

Published by T.M.C. ASSER PRESS, The Hague, The Netherlands www.asserpress.nl
Produced and distributed for T.M.C. ASSER PRESS by Springer-Verlag Berlin Heidelberg

This T.M.C. ASSER PRESS imprint is published by the registered company Springer-Verlag GmbH, DE, part of Springer Nature.
The registered company address is: Heidelberger Platz 3, 14197 Berlin, Germany

Acknowledgements

This edited volume is the result of the 6th Radboud Economic Law Conference on '*Services of General (Economic) Interest: State of Play and Current Challenges*' which took place on 7 October 2022 at the Faculty of Law, Radboud University Nijmegen. This volume follows other volumes published in the past by Asser Press as part of their series on Services of General (Economic) Interest by taking stock of the most recent influential developments in the relevant field, including the impact of digitalisation and sustainability.

We would like to express our sincere gratitude to all the participants of the conference whose insights and contributions helped shape the stimulating discussions that form the foundation of this collection. The editors would also like to express their gratitude to the Faculty of Law at Radboud University for hosting the event and providing an engaging academic environment conducive to meaningful exchange.

We are also grateful to the editorial team of Asser Press whose dedication and support were instrumental in bringing this volume to completion. We extend our sincere thanks to Ms. Charley Berndsen for her invaluable administrative support in organising the conference which laid the groundwork for this volume. We are also deeply grateful to Ms. Lisanne Kooijman, who, in her role as student assistant, provided crucial editorial support during the final phase of the publication. Her dedication and meticulous work were essential to bringing this volume to completion.

Finally, we thank all the contributors to this collection for their scholarly commitment and for sharing their research, which not only advances our understanding of the subject but also raises important questions for further investigation.

Nijmegen, The Netherlands
July 2025

Narine Ghazaryan
Johan Willem van de Gronden
Simon Tans
Marc Veenbrink

Contents

Chapter 1
Introduction: The State of Regarding SGEIs in a Rapidly Changing World

Johan Willem van de Gronden

Contents

Abstract In this introduction the aim of the present volume will be explained. The focus of the volume is on important novel issues while the lessons that can be learned will be reviewed. The developments that have taken place in the healthcare, digitalization and sustainability policies take centre stage in the analysis. It will be argued that the rapidly changing world has posed new legal questions on SG(E)Is. Answers to these questions must be found and novel and creative approaches should be developed. Solidarity remains an important value in the debate on SG(E)Is. The (EU) law on SG(E)Is should address the challenges at issue in such a way that solidarity is achieved and maintained.

Keywords Services of General (Economic) Interest · Healthcare · Digitalization · Sustainability · Concept of Undertaking

J. W. van de Gronden (✉)
Radboud University Nijmegen, Nijmegen, The Netherlands
e-mail: johan.vandegronden@ru.nl

N. Ghazaryan et al. (eds.), *Services of General (Economic) Interest and EU Law*, Legal Issues of Services of General Interest, https://doi.org/10.1007/978-94-6265-723-6_1

1.1 Introduction

In 2009, the volume *The Changing Legal Framework for Services of General Interest in Europe — Between Competition and Solidarity*[1] was published. The contributions in this volume took stock of the developments regarding such services. The volume also explored significant concepts and important principles relevant for current problems and issues. Confirming the significance of Services of General Interest (SGIs) in EU law, the 2009 volume concluded that this concept contributes to developing a framework for the functioning of public services based on the balancing of the advantages of competition and solidarity.[2]

The aim of the current volume is to measure the temperature and explore and evaluate noteworthy recent developments. Unlike the 2009 volume, no comprehensive overview is given; rather the focus is on important novel issues. In this introduction, the lessons that can be learned from these issues are reviewed, based on the contributions to the current volume. First, the relevant principles surrounding Services of General (Economic) Interest (SGEI) are addressed. Then, the developments related to healthcare, digitalization and sustainability are analysed. Over the years, many SGEI cases have risen in the healthcare sector which plays a major role in national social welfare systems. It goes without saying that the digitalisation transition has a major impact on modern societies and SGIs are not immune to this impact. For this reason, attention is paid to how this process has shaped SGIs. Given the huge challenges the world faces today, sustainability issues are high on the agenda, and it is important to analyse their relevance for SGIs. The introduction draws some conclusions at the end providing a context for the discussion unfolding in the subsequent chapters.

1.2 Certain Principles of SG(E)Is

The Treaty of Rome already contained a provision on SGEIs. According to then Article 90 (2) EEC Treaty (now Article 106 (2) TFEU), the competition and other rules of the Treaty apply to SGEIs, in so far as these rules do not obstruct the supply of these services. In other words, if such obstruction occurs competitive restraints and other restrictions could be justifiable. The concept of SGEIs features as a justification ground in this Treaty provision, which allows for balancing the need to protect the EU internal market and the public interest policies of the Member States.

The concept of SGEI has much in common with the French notion of *service public*. In French law, this notion has a very long-standing tradition: it was developed by Léon Duguit and others in the first half of the twentieth century.[3] Its purpose is not

[1] Krajewski et al. 2009.

[2] Krajewski 2009, pp. 505 and 506.

[3] See Schweitzer 2011, p. 13.

only to promote societal development but also to limit state power.[4] In French law, it is accepted that particular services of industrial or commercial nature could constitute *services public* and that such services could be supplied by private operators.[5] In German law, a similar concept has been developed: *Daseinvorsorge* (public services task), which comes down to the duty of the State to intervene on the market to ensure that its citizens have access to essential services (public services).[6] As is apparent from German case law, this concept plays an important role in the context of the social welfare state, as it is geared towards guaranteeing that the population has access to services, such as the supply of gas and electricity, district heating, as well as postal and telecommunication services.[7]

As the EU concept of SGEI is inspired by the national traditions of the Member States, in EU law access to essential services also plays an important role,[8] while such services provided by private operators could qualify as SGEIs.[9] In my view, the inclusion of the concept of SGEI in the TFEU demonstrates that values that are not directly connected with competition and trade, but are geared towards various public interest objectives must be accommodated in the functioning of the EU internal market. To put it differently, competition and trade, although being important means for European market integration, may not prevent the universal provision of key services to the citizens of the EU Member States. Viewed from this perspective, the concept of SGEI is capable of contributing to the development of EU citizenship,[10] where the notion of solidarity plays an important role as a value.[11] Guaranteeing access to, for example, health and social services contributes to solidarity between various groups of citizens (high and low income groups, groups of various generations, healthy and ill people, etc.).

Given the values at play, it was inevitable that the evolution of SGEIs would not be limited to a derogation from the EU competition and free movement rules. An important development in this respect was the entry into force of the Treaty of Lisbon, which contained a number of changes regarding SGEIs. The first change concerns Article 14 TFEU. This provision sets out that both the EU and its Member States are obliged to guarantee the proper functioning of SGEIs. This provision gives a special dimension to the concept of SGEI: it underlines the significant role of this concept and accordingly it, inter alia, serves as a source of inspiration for shaping and interpreting EU legislation. Article 14 TFEU even contains a legal basis for adopting

---

[4] Dreyfus 2009, p. 270.

[5] Dreyfus 2009, pp. 271 and 272.

[6] See Schweitzer 2011, p. 15.

[7] See Krajewski 2011, pp. 29–32.

[8] See for example Charter of Fundamental Rights of the European Union, published 26 October 2012, CFREU, Article 36.

[9] A significant feature of SGEI is that these services are of an economic nature and, therefore, fall within the ambit of EU competition law. Consequently, SGEI operators are undertakings for the purposes of Articles 101–109 TFEU and, many of them are, of course, private operators.

[10] See Ross 2007, p. 1965; Van Eijken 2014, p 138.

[11] See e.g. Ross 2007, pp. 175 and 176.

regulations, although to date none has been adopted based on this legal basis.[12] Then again, references are made to Article 14 TFEU in measures based on the internal market clause of Article 114 TFEU.[13]

The second development linked to the Lisbon Treaty concerns the Charter of Fundamental Rights of the EU, particularly its Article 36 highlighting the significance of the access of citizens to SGEIs. The point of departure in this provision is that the EU must recognise and respect the way this access is regulated in the national laws of the Member States. Consequently, the provision of SGEIs is not seen as a task to be carried out at the EU level. Rather, the EU measures should not obstruct the Member States when ensuring access to SGEIs to their citizens. As is stated in the explanation on Article 36, this principle is not new.[14] Nevertheless, underlining the importance of the role of SGEI gives a boost to the values embodied in this concept.

The third development has to do with Protocol No. 26 on SGI. This protocol, similar to Article 36 of the Charter of Fundamental Rights of the EU, stresses the competences of the Member States to provide the services their citizens should have access to. Remarkably, it also refers to the general concept of SGIs and, by doing so, it explains that SGEIs are part of this overarching concept. This means that SGIs concern both non-economic and economic services. The latter category includes SGEIs: the word economic refers to the nature of the activities concerned (triggering the application of, for example, the EU competition rules), while the word general reflects the public interest characteristics of the services.[15] In other words, SGIs consist of non-economic SGIs and SGEIs. The evolution surrounding the SGEI debates has led to the creation of the overarching notion of SGIs. It is striking that the Protocol on SGI does not only emphasise the discretionary nature of the Member States' competences, but also introduces a set of principles applying to SGEIs, such as high level of quality, safety, affordability and universal access.[16] Thus, by doing so, their status as principles of EU law is acknowledged.

What do non-economic SGIs and SGEIs have in common, however? Both categories concern services that are classified by the EU Member States as being of general interest and that are subjected by them to public service obligations.[17] Moreover, both types of services concern the entrustment of a task that should be performed in the general interest.[18] In order to give some guidance, the Commission has adopted

[12] Van de Gronden and Rusu 2024, p. 486.

[13] Ibid.

[14] See Explanations relating to the Charter of Fundamental Rights, published 14 December 2007 (OJ C 303, pp. 17–35), Explanation on Article 36—Access to services of general economic interest.

[15] See e.g. Van de Gronden and Rusu 2024, p. 486.

[16] See Consolidated version of the Treaty on the Functioning of the European Union, signed on 13 December 2007, published 26 October 2012, TFEU, Protocol No. 26, Article 1.

[17] See Communication from the Commission of 20 December 2011 to the European Parliament, the Council, the European Economic and Social Committee and the Committee of the Regions: A Quality Framework for Services of General Interest in Europe, COM(2011) 900 final, p. 3.

[18] See Neergaard 2009, p. 21.

relevant communications and other soft law documents.[19] These documents are not binding but it is undeniable that (some) authority may be assigned to the interpretations and views given in these documents. For example, in the Quality Framework for Services of General Interest in Europe the Commission sets out the definitions of various basic concepts.[20]

As already stated, no general EU measure (based on Article 14 TFEU) harmonizing the provision of SGEI has been adopted yet. Sector-specific EU laws containing a couple of provisions on these services, however, have seen the light of day. For example, Articles 84–92 of Directive 2018/1972 oblige Member States to ensure that all consumers have access to broadband internet access and to voice communication services.[21] Another example is provided by Articles 27–29 of Directive 2019/944, according to which Member States have to guarantee access to electricity for all household customers.[22]

In addition, special attention must be paid to the EU state aid rules. Many Member States finance the provision of SGEIs in order to guarantee access for all (or a specific group of citizens) to these services. These national policies may lead to issues under Article 107 TFEU, which precludes Member States from granting state aid to undertakings, if this aid leads to competition distortions and to effects on the trade between Member States. Since the famous *Altmark* judgment, the role of SGEIs has increased in EU state aid law.[23] In this ruling, the CJEU held that financial compensation given to a SGEI operator does not constitute state aid if the following conditions are met:[24] (1) the operators concerned must be entrusted with the discharge of a Public Service Obligation (PSO—a concept identical to SGEI);[25] (2) the parameters for the compensation are established in advance in an objective and transparent fashion; (3) the compensation does not go beyond what is necessary; and (4) if the PSO discharged is not awarded through a public procurement procedure, the benchmark for the level of the compensation is constituted by the costs of a well-run-company.

The approach developed in *Altmark* has given the Member States some leeway in financing SGEIs. Conversely, it has also complicated the application of the EU state aid rules to SGEIs. The reason for this is that it has moderated the clear divide between the ban on state aid in Article 107(1) TFEU and the justification grounds in Articles 107(2), 107(3) and 106(2) TFEU. It should be noted that Article 106(2)

---

[19] See for example the following website: https://commission.europa.eu/topics/single-market/services-general-interest_en#documents.

[20] A Quality Framework for Services of General Interest in Europe, above n. 17, pp. 3 and 4.

[21] Directive (EU) 2018/1972 of the European Parliament and of the Council of 11 December 2018 establishing the European Electronic Communications Code (Recast), published on 17 December 2018, Directive 2018/1972.

[22] Directive (EU) 2019/944 of the European Parliament and of the Council of 5 June 2019 on common rules for the internal market for electricity, published on 14 June 2019, Directive 2019/944.

[23] CJEU, *Altmark Trans*, Judgment, 24 July 2003, C-280/00.

[24] Ibid., paras 89–93.

[25] CJEU (GC), *BUPA*, Judgment, 12 February 2008, T-289/03, para 96.

TFEU is geared specifically towards accommodating SGEI concerns. In EU state aid law, the divide between the ban and the exceptions is of special interest, as the Commission has the sole power to decide whether the conditions of Articles 107(2), 107(3) and 106(2) TFEU are fulfilled (subject to review by the Union Courts).[26] As a result, Member States must notify a state measure in advance to the Commission in order to benefit from these exceptions. If they fail to do so and implement the state aid measure without prior permission of the Commission, the standstill provision is violated,[27] which triggers the obligation to recover the unlawfully granted state aid.[28]

In *Altmark*, the need to provide SGEIs is part of the assessment carried out under the ban on giving state aid, and, accordingly, the aim of a particular state aid measure is considered together with its effect on competition and the trade between Member States. It is clear from the outset that this approach comes with an advantage: the national measures, financing SGEIs and satisfying the *Altmark* conditions, do not fall within the scope of the standstill provision of Article 108(3) TFEU and, accordingly, do not need to be paid back in absence of notification to the Commission. Nonetheless, this has given rise to certain issues of interpretation. These issues concern, inter alia, whether in a particular case it can be established that all conditions set out in *Altmark* are met. If one (or more) of these conditions are not satisfied, and no notification has been made, the aid given should be paid back, which could undermine the continuous provision of the SGEIs concerned.

In order to clarify the issues at play, but also to elaborate on the CJEU findings in *Altmark*, the Commission has adopted four measures:[29] the *De Minimis* SGEI Regulation,[30] the PSO Decision,[31] the PSO State Aid Framework[32] and the SGEI Communication.[33] According to the *De Minimis* SGEI Regulation, aid given to finance the provision of SGEIs not being in excess of EUR 750,000 over any period of three years is not subject to the notification obligation. In other words, aid below this threshold is deemed to be of minor importance, which justifies the exemption from

---

[26] See TFEU, above n. 17, Article 108.

[27] See TFEU, above n. 17, Article 108(3).

[28] See e.g. CJEU, *SFEI v La Poste*, Judgment, 11 July 1996, C-39/94, paras 39 and 40.

[29] See also the following Internet site of the Commission: https://competition-policy.ec.europa.eu/state-aid/legislation/sgei_en.

[30] Commission Regulation (EU) 2023/2832 of 13 December 2023 on the application of Articles 107 and 108 of the Treaty on the Functioning of the European Union to de minimis aid granted to undertakings providing services of general economic interest, published on 15 December 2023.

[31] Commission Decision of 20 December 2011 on the application of Article 106(2) of the Treaty on the Functioning of the European Union to State aid in the form of public service compensation granted to certain undertaking entrusted with the operation of services of general economic interest, PSO Decision (OJ L 7, pp. 3–10).

[32] Communication from the Commission, European Union framework for State aid in the form of public service compensation (OJ C 8, pp. 15–22).

[33] Communication from the Commission on the application of the European Union State aid rules to compensation granted for the provision of services of general economic interest (OJ C 8, pp. 4–14).

the obligation to notify. The PSO Decision also contains a carve-out from this obligation. This 'safe harbour' concerns specific categories of SGEIs, such as specific services supplied by hospitals, small- and medium sized enterprises and providers operating in social sectors. The PSO Decision sets out various conditions (*inter alia* dealing with the act of entrustment and the calculation of the compensation given) that must be satisfied.[34] In the PSO State Aid Framework, established by a communication (soft law), the Commission explains how it will exercise its power to apply Article 106(2) TFEU to national measures financing SGEIs. If such measures do not fulfil the conditions set out in *Altmark*, in the *De Minimis* SGEI Regulation and PSO Decision, it must be concluded that they amount to state aid. Upon notification by the relevant Member State the Commission could exempt the measures at issue on the basis of Article 106(2) TFEU. The SGEI Communication (also soft law) provides guidance on all steps that must be taken for assessing national aid granted for the SGEI financing. It also offers an overview of all relevant issues at play.

All in all, the developments surrounding the state aid and SGEIs have given rise to a comprehensive but also complex set of rules and measures. From time to time, it will be daunting for the Member States and their public authorities, tasked with the implementation of SGEI policies, to navigate these rules and measures. This will also depend on the relevant policy field characterised by its specificities and market conditions. As stated in the introduction, below the policies regarding healthcare, digitalization and sustainability will be discussed.

1.3 Healthcare and SG(E)Is

It goes without saying that SGEIs play an important role in healthcare: it is crucial that patients have access to services supplied by hospitals and other healthcare providers. As explained by Heidi Suorsa, these services could qualify as SGEIs, if the provision thereof is entrusted by the Member States to (public or private) operators and if they are of an economic nature.[35] Moreover, the interplay between healthcare services and EU law is a delicate matter, since pursuant to Article 168(7) TFEU the organisation and delivery of these services belong to the competences of the Member States, as is stressed by Mary Guy in her contribution. She points out that, as a result, the relationship between national healthcare policies and the EU competition rules should be viewed from a constitutional point of view. An important point in this regard is that the principle of subsidiarity is a great tool for explaining the tensions between the EU and national level.[36]

From this perspective the difference between non-economic SGIs and SGEIs is of significance. If a healthcare service constitutes a non-economic SGI, competition rules (including EU state aid law) do not apply, leaving considerable room

[34] See PSO Decision, Articles 4–7.

[35] See Chap. 4, Sect. 4.3.2 of Suorsa's contribution to the present volume.

[36] See Chap. 2, Sects. 2.3.1 and 2.4 of Guy's contribution to the present volume.

for manoeuvre to the Member States. In *Dôvera*, the CJEU ruled that the healthcare insurance scheme of Slovakia was of non-economic nature, although it was managed by private insurers.[37] The reason for this was that the management of this scheme was predominantly based on solidarity. Consequently, EU competition law allows Member States to assign great value to solidarity when setting up national healthcare policies. This is confirmed by the judgments of the General Court and the CJEU in *Case Regina Apostolorum*, where it was decided that the principle of solidarity is not only capable of carving out bodies managing healthcare schemes from the competition rules but also making providers of healthcare services such as hospitals immune from these rules.[38]

Moreover, economic healthcare activities are not necessarily fully subject to EU competition law. As far as these services qualify as SGEIs, certain competition distortions may be justifiable, for instance in so far as these distortions are needed with a view of the supply of these services. As stated by Mary Guy, an important case in point is the *BUPA* ruling, where the General Court found that state aid granted to a provider of a supplementary health insurance scheme was permitted on the basis of the *Altmark* approach.[39] It is apparent from the *Brussels Hospitals* case, that also Article 106(2) TFEU could be a ground for allowing aid given in the healthcare sector. These judgments show, that in cases concerning healthcare services of an economic nature, the concept of SGEI triggers a review process, in which the need to give access to care and competition concerns are balanced. In other words, solidarity considerations are accommodated in the application of the competition rules to healthcare.

Part of competition law is the merger control regime. Daniel Clark explores how SGEI concerns should weigh in when hospital mergers are assessed. He demonstrates that the current EU merger control framework is unable to accommodate these concerns sufficiently.[40] He also discusses a specific provision of Dutch competition law, according to which a merger amounting to market problems could be approved on the ground that this is necessary for the provision of SGEIs.[41] In his view, such a provision could be helpful in reconciling the public interest objectives with competition concerns. At the same time, having discussed the South-African experience, he also points out that incorporating public interest concerns in a merger control test comes with the risk of political influence.[42] If a competition authority is tasked with the duty to weigh up such interests in an assessment, procedural safeguards must be in place to ensure and protect the independence of this authority.[43] Another lesson that could be learned from South-African competition law is to specify the

[37] CJEU, *Dôvera*, Judgment, 11 June 2020, Joined cases C-262/18 and C-271/18.

[38] CJEU (GC), *Case Regina Apostolorum*, Judgment, 2 June 2021, T-223/18 and CJEU, *Case Regina Apostolorum*, Judgment, 27 April 2023, C-492/21.

[39] CJEU (GC), *BUPA*, Judgment, 12 February 2008, T-289/03.

[40] See Chap. 3, Sect. 3.2.3 of Clark's contribution to the present volume.

[41] See Mededingingswet (Dutch Act on Competition), Article 41 (3).

[42] See Chap. 3, Sect. 3.4.1 of Clark's contribution to the present volume.

[43] Ibid.

public interests that should be taken into account in a merger control assessment, for instance, by naming various examples of such interests in a legislative act.[44]

It should be noted, that the national healthcare policies and the SGEIs designated by the Member States in this sector not only has been challenged in the light of EU competition law, but also has been subject to litigation based on EU internal market law. The most important example of this are cases on free movement of patients, where persons seek treatment in another Member State and subsequently claim reimbursement of the costs involved.[45] In the present volume, Heidi Suorsa has explored this intriguing subject matter, which, in fact, concerns European citizens wishing to break away from their own national healthcare system by relying on EU internal market law. She explains that the EU rules governing these matters are highly complex, while patients have to navigate two sets of rules: Regulation (EC) No 883/2004 on the Coordination of Social Security Systems[46] and the Patient Mobility Directive.[47] Another problem is that, especially when cross-border treatment costs are assessed under the Directive, there is a real possibility that part of these costs must be borne by the patient.[48] Under the Directive the level of reimbursement is determined by the tariffs of the Member State of affiliation,[49] which could lead to additional costs for patients having received treatment in another Member State, the expenses of which exceed these 'affiliation tariffs'. On the one hand, it cannot be denied that the current set of EU measures on free movement of patients does give access to cross-border healthcare services that qualify as SGEIs. On the other hand, the current legal framework falls short of providing a clear and comprehensive set of rules.[50] Moreover, it should be stressed that the reimbursement of cross-border healthcare costs may be restricted by a prior authorisation scheme.[51] Member States are entitled to have such schemes in place for, inter alia, hospital care.[52] As already stated, many services (of economic nature) provided by hospitals could be considered as SGEIs. Accordingly, as Member States may introduce authorisation schemes to

[44] See Chap. 3, Sect. 3.4.2 of Clark's contribution to the present volume.

[45] See e.g. CJEU, *Raymond Kohll v Union des Caisses de Maladie*, Judgment, 28 April 1998, C-158/96; CJEU, *Nicolas Decker v Caisse de Maladie des Employés Privés*, Judgment, 28 April 1998, C-120/95; CJEU, *B.S.M. Geraerts-Smits v Stichting Ziekenfonds VGZ and H.T.M. Peerbooms v Stichting CZ Groep Zorgverzekeringen*, Judgment, 12 July 2001, C-157/99; CJEU, *V.G. Müller-Fauré v Onderlinge Waarborgmaatschappij OZ Zorgverzekeringen and E.E.M. van Riet v Onderlinge Waarborgmaatschappijen ZAO Zorgverzekeringen*, Judgment, 13 May 2003, C-385/99 and CJEU, *A v Veselības ministrija*, Judgment, 29 October 2020, C-243/19.

[46] Regulation (EC) No 883/2004 of the European Parliament and of the Council of 29 April 2004 on the coordination of social security systems, published on 30 April 2004.

[47] Directive 2011/24/EU of the European Parliament and of the Council of 9 March 2011 on the application of patients' rights in cross border healthcare, published on 4 April 2011, Patient Mobility Directive.

[48] See Chap. 4, Sect. 4.5.1.2 of Suorsa's contribution to the present volume.

[49] See Patient Mobility Directive, above n. 47, Article 7(4).

[50] See Chap. 4, Sect. 4.6 of Suorsa's contribution to the present volume.

[51] See Chap. 4, Sect. 4.4.1 of Suorsa's contribution to the present volume.

[52] See Patient Mobility Directive, above n. 47, Article 8(2).

control the outflux of patients seeking hospital treatment abroad, free movement of many SGEIs in healthcare could be restricted by them.

On the basis of the analysis carried out in this section, one can conclude that the concept of SG(E)I has had an important impact on the application of the competition and internal market rules to healthcare. It has moderated the effects of this application considerably, as great weight has been attached to the level of solidarity in finding to what extent Articles 101, 102 and 107 TFEU should apply to national healthcare matters. As rightfully pointed out by Mary Guy, the concept of SG(E)I has been instrumental in applying Article 168(7) TFEU, which deals with national competences, to cases, in which national healthcare measures have been contested in light of EU law. Accordingly, although EU law has shaped the national health care policies to a certain extent, the concept of SGEI has protected the national competences considerably in this respect. From this perspective, it could be argued that the concept of SGEIs has a constitutional dimension, when it comes to the division of competences between the EU and its Member States. Admittedly, the COVID-19 crisis has triggered the initiative to set up the European Health Union.[53] However, to date this has not led to a major change in the division of competences between the EU and its Member States.[54]

1.4 Digital Services and SG(E)Is

The digital sector has been subject to profound changes the last decades. In response to these developments, the EU has considered the digital transition as one of its policy priorities.[55] Digitalisation plays a major role in many areas of society. For example, a modern citizen needs to possess a smart phone in his dealings with the government, commercial enterprises, etc. Many services supplied in the digital realm are essential for functioning in the society of the 21st century. This begs the question whether essential services of digital nature could be qualified as SGEIs. It is apparent from the analysis carried out in Sect. 1.2 of this introduction, that such a qualification supposes that the task to supply the service at issue is entrusted by the State to an operator. The point is, however, that the concept of SEGI is developed in the utility sectors/network sectors (post, energy, transport, etc.), and also in the social welfare state (healthcare, social housing, etc.). In these sectors, it is common that the State intervenes by designating SGEIs and tasking specific providers with the duty to supply these SGEIs. In their case law, the Union Courts have even been willing to derive SGEI missions from universal service obligations.[56] This is not surprising,

[53] See Chap. 2, Sect. 2.3.2 of Guy's contribution to the present volume.

[54] Ibid.

[55] See, for example, the following website: https://reform-support.ec.europa.eu/what-we-do/digital-transition_en.

[56] See CJEU (GC), *BUPA*, Judgment, 12 February 2008, T-298/03, paras 174–208 and CJEU, *AG2R*, Judgment, 3 March 2011, C-437/09, para 17.

as such obligations concern requirements that are designed in order to ensure that particular services are made available to consumers and users.[57] In my view, this comes down to entrusting the task to provide the services concerned by the state to operators in an implicit way: the universal obligations make clear that these operators must give access to all or to a particular group. Although, there is no explicit act of entrustment, the State has made clear that certain enterprises have the duty to provide significant services to users.

To date, in many countries SGEI interventions are not undertaken by the State, when it comes to digital services. Many of these services are the result of private initiative, which stands in sharp contrast with the utility sectors and the social welfare industry, where the State plays a major role traditionally. From the EU perspective, it should also be noted that most of the Big Tech enterprises, providing (core) digital services, are based outside of Europe (the USA and China mostly). It is, therefore, difficult to oblige these companies to provide some of their services to everyone at affordable prices—especially now that the competence to adopt SGEI acts of entrustment lies with the Member States rather than the EU. Another issue is that SGEIs had emerged in sectors that were originally state-dominated and were subsequently (gradually) subjected to market forces through privatisation and liberalisation. Designating essential services as SGEIs can be seen as a response to the need to balance competition benefits and public interest concerns.[58] As already stated, digital services are the result of private initiative and do not originate from a state-dominated environment. Consequently, when digital services began to be developed and offered on the market, no questions were raised as to whether some of them should be considered SGEIs. Such questions have become relevant at a later stage of the developments surrounding the digital markets, namely when businesses, consumers, citizens and public authorities have become (heavily) reliant on (certain) digital services.

Does the foregoing mean that the concept of SGEI is not suitable to be incorporated in the rules dealing with digital services? It is apparent from the contributions by Gerbrandy and Lalikova that this question should be answered in the negative. Gerbrandy bases her analysis on the term public services, which is defined by her as services that all citizens should have access to, in order to be able to live a full life as a citizen.[59] She explains that Big Tech companies have set-up platforms that provide a myriad of services.[60] They have gained much (market) power and should be considered as gatekeepers, as they control the access to many key digital services.[61] In her view, (some of) the services provided by Big Tech companies should be regarded

[57] See A Quality Framework for Services of General Interest in Europe, above n. 17, section 1.

[58] For example, in the Quality Framework for Services of General Interest in Europe it is stated that the concept of universal services obligations is "...an essential component of market liberalization of service sectors, such as electronic communications, post and transport." See A Quality Framework for Services of General Interest in Europe, above n. 17, section 1.

[59] See Chap. 5, Sect. 5.2 of Gerbrandy's contribution to the present volume.

[60] See Chap. 5, Sect. 5.3 of Gerbrandy's contribution to the present volume.

[61] Ibid.

as public services given their significance in modern society and, accordingly, intervention by the State could be needed, not only for market failure reasons, but also for reasons of another nature, such as the need to tackle misinformation, disinformation and other nefarious practices.[62] In fact, Gerbrandy calls for reconsidering the reasons that justify State interventions by pointing to non-market values. In my view, this line of reasoning is of great interest for how the concept of SGEIs in relation to digital services is perceived. In the approach adopted by Gerbrandy, imposing a SGEI mission could be a progressive course of action, even if the supply of the digital service concerned, such as access to search engines, is not put under pressure, but the way it is supplied causes collateral damage to society.

Once the duty to supply a service—Gerbrandy refers to as a public service—is imposed by a EU Member State on one or more companies, such a task is likely to qualify as SGEIs for the purposes of EU law. As already was pointed out, the entrustment by the State to supply particular services is a key element for establishing SGEIs. The relevance of Big Tech companies for public services/SGEIs is illustrated further by Gerbrandy by shedding light on their activities performed in sectors, such as health and education,[63] and on the growing dependence of many governments on Big Tech services.[64] As many of the tasks performed by governments are of non-economic nature, it could even be argued that Big Tech is capable of influencing the provision of non-economic SGIs.

Lalikova, drawing on the EU experience with regulating network sectors (public utilities),[65] focuses on the services offered by search engines with special attention to Google Search. Her finding is that compelling grounds exist to qualify such services as public services and impose universal service obligations on providers, such as Google.[66] In my view, this would mean that search engine services would be SGEIs for the purposes of EU law. Lalikova presents various arguments for her view on the search engine services. For example, she points out that the continuity of the provision of these services is of great interest, as search engines give access to information of public importance.[67] Also guaranteeing some kind of basic access could be needed in the event that a subscription-based model would be introduced by companies, such as Google.[68] It is also apparent from her analysis that affordability is an issue: users pay through their data and it should be avoided that an excessive amount of data is given to search engine providers.[69]

In the light of the contributions by Gerbrandy and Lalikova, it can be argued that SGEIs are capable of playing an important role in how the EU and its Member States respond to the significant impact that digital services—particularly those provided by

---

[62] See Chap. 5, Sect. 5.4.1 of Gerbrandy's contribution to the present volume.
[63] See Chap. 5, Sect. 5.4.2 of Gerbrandy's contribution to the present volume.
[64] See Chap. 5, Sect. 5.4.3 of Gerbrandy's contribution to the present volume.
[65] See Chap. 6, Sect. 6.2.2 of Lalikova's contribution to the present volume.
[66] See Chap. 6, Sect. 6.5 of Lalikova's contribution to the present volume.
[67] See Chap. 6, Sect. 6.4.1.2 of Lalikova's contribution to the present volume.
[68] See Chap. 6, Sect. 6.4.1.3 of Lalikova's contribution to the present volume.
[69] See Chap. 6, Sect. 6.4.1.5 of Lalikova's contribution to the present volume.

the Big Tech companies—have on today's economy and society. Insofar as access to these services is deemed necessary for citizens, designating them as SGEIs may be an appropriate course of action. As many of these services are provided by enterprises having their headquarters outside the EU, an explicit act of entrustment could be problematic. However, it is apparent from the case law, as mentioned earlier, that SGEI missions could be derived from universal service obligations. On top of this, as pointed out by Lalikova, these obligations offer very clear and enforceable rights and results.[70] Accordingly, it could be sufficient to lay down only such obligations in legislation, prompting the duty for the providers of the digital services concerned to ensure access to all or to a particular group of users. Given the size of the Big Tech companies, the EU legislator is better placed to adopt the necessary laws in comparison with the EU Member States. The experience with the harmonisation measures adopted in sectors, such as postal services and energy, shows that the EU legislature is able to enact such laws. In my view, the EU has already taken the first steps by adopting the Digital Markets Act (DMA).[71] In this regulation, obligations are imposed on companies providing core digital platform services, in so far as these companies are gatekeepers.[72] At least, the enactment of the DMA shows that some digital services are of such a great importance that the supply of these services has to be in line with certain standards and norms. If these standards are not complied with, the Commission will not shy away from imposing large fines.[73] The goal of the DMA is, however, not to ensure access to the services regulated to all or a specific group of users. Achieving such an aim would require the adoption of laws containing universal service obligations.

1.5 Sustainability and SG(E)Is

Sustainability is a concept dominating current debates in many fields. As is apparent from the 2030 Agenda for Sustainable Development of the United Nations, the goals of sustainable development include a wide range of objectives, such as ending hunger, good education, gender equality, and combatting climate change.[74] It is not surprising that the subject of SGIs can also be related to the broader discourse on sustainable development.

[70] See Chap. 6, Sect. 6.2.2 of Lalikova's contribution to the present volume.

[71] Regulation (EU) 2022/1925 of the European Parliament and of the Council of 14 September 2022 on contestable and fair markets in the digital sector and amending Directives (EU) 2019/1937 and (EU) 2020/1828, published on 12 October 2022, DMA.

[72] See DMA, above n. 71, Article 3.

[73] In its press release of 23 April 2025 the Commission announced that it had imposed fines upon Apple and Meta of 500 million EUR and 300 EUR million EUR respectively. See Press Release of the Commission of 23 April 2025, Commission finds Apple and Meta in breach of the Digital Markets Act, IP/25/1095.

[74] See the following Internet site of the United Nations: https://sdgs.un.org/#goal_section.

In this context, in her contribution Van Zimmeren relates the sustainability issues to SGIs. (In her analysis no distinction is made between non-economic SGIs and SGEIs.) She explains that the issues at play should be regarded as 'wicked' problems. These kinds of problems are of a complex nature, which do have no definitive formulation; they may be addressed in various ways, and are closely related to other problems, etc.[75] Many SGIs are somehow connected with wicked problems, especially when sustainability issues are at play. Van Zimmeren, however, finds that hardly anything is written on this subject and makes, for that reason, a number of suggestions for developing a coherent view.[76] She encourages providers of SGIs to adopt an eco-centric or bio-centric approach to sustainability.[77] Within this approach, the goal of economic growth does not take centre stage, but is balanced with the interests of the living world in order to reduce inequality and to improve human well-being.[78] An important consideration in this regard is the extent to which the existing legal framework in place is capable of adapting to changes. Van Zimmeren points out that the EU has adopted a very ambitious framework when it comes to the Green Deal.[79] She also notes that the EU is flexible in responding to developments and changes given its multilateral governance structure: actions will be taken both at the EU level and the national level (national, regional and local authorities), while public authorities also cooperate with private actors.[80] Experimentalist approaches are helpful to take action when (rapidly) changing circumstances require so. Although the multi-level governance structure of the EU accommodates various laboratories for experimentation, according to Van Zimmeren more lessons should be learned with respect to SGIs.[81] The point is that experiments occur in specific policy fields and do not account for the wicked nature of the policy issues.[82] Van Zimmeren concludes by arguing that, especially in matters related to the Green Deal, it is of great importance to design an adaptive legal system for providing SGIs, in order to ensure that unexpected and unpredictable disturbances can be absorbed.[83]

In his contribution, Peter Wesselius focuses on the provision of SGEIs in the transportation sector. His analysis is based on two judgments of the CJEU: *Lux Express Estonia*[84] and *Concordia Bus Finland*.[85] The question at issue is whether the EU rules on the financing of SGEIs in the transportation sector do justice to sustainability concerns. It is apparent from the analysis of Peter Wesselius that compliance by the Member States with these rules will prevent violations of EU law applicable

[75] See Chap. 7, Sect. 7.2 of Van Zimmeren's contribution to the present volume.

[76] See Chap. 7, Sect. 7.3 of Van Zimmeren's contribution to the present volume.

[77] Ibid.

[78] Ibid.

[79] See Chap. 7, Sect. 7.4 of Van Zimmeren's contribution to the present volume.

[80] Ibid.

[81] Ibid.

[82] Ibid.

[83] See Chap. 7, Sect. 7.5 of Van Zimmeren's contribution to the present volume.

[84] CJEU, *Lux Express Estonia*, Judgment, 8 September 2022, C-614/20.

[85] CJEU, *Concordia Bus Finland*, Judgment, 17 September 2022, C-513/99.

to the transport sector.[86] In his view, the current EU approach to the financing of SGEI missions does not cater sufficiently for sustainability, and, as a result, an enterprise having made considerable investments in sustainability may be worse off than an enterprise not having made such investments.[87] Member States could tackle this problem by including sustainability objectives in the procurement procedures, when selecting operators.[88] *Concordia Bus Finland* is a particularly important precedent in this regard. In this ruling, the CJEU accepted that in public procurement procedures the contracting authorities are allowed to take into consideration environmental criteria, provided that these criteria are related to the subject matter of the contract.[89] In its reasoning, the CJEU referred to Treaty principle enshrined in Article 11 TFEU, according to which environmental protection must be integrated in other policies of the EU.[90] From Peter Wesselius's case study it could be derived that sustainability is acknowledged as an important value in EU law but that the design of the rules in place needs improvement.

1.6 Concluding Remarks

The experience with applying EU law in healthcare shows that the concept of SG(E)I does not only moderate the effects that the competition and the internal market rules may have on national policy. It is also capable of protecting national competences, and, as a result, this concept has a constitutional dimension in terms of the division of competences between the EU and its Member States. The developments in the digital markets demonstrate that the traditional design of SG(E)Is does not pay due consideration to the private and highly commercial nature of the key services supplied on these markets. Two problems should be identified in this regard: SGEIs are developed, in order to moderate the adverse effects of subjecting former state services to market forces, and Member States are the competent entities for adopting acts of entrustment. A redesign of SGEIs is necessary for doing justice to the private initiative origin of key digital services and to the size of the Big Tech enterprises operating in the digital realm. The sustainability debate makes clear that rethinking the manner in which SG(E)Is are provided is required. Sustainability concerns are not part of a particular SG(E)I mission often, but these concerns should dictate the way in which such a mission is implemented.

---

[86] See Chap. 8, Sects. 8.2 and 8.3 of Wesselius's contribution to the present volume.

[87] See Chap. 8, Sect. 8.4 of Wesselius's contribution to the present volume.

[88] Ibid.

[89] See Chap. 8, Sect. 8.5 of Wesselius's contribution to the present volume.

[90] See CJEU, *Concordia Bus Finland*, Judgment, 17 September 2022, C-513/99, para 45.

All in all, the rapidly changing world has posed new legal questions on SG(E)Is. It is of great interest to find answers to these questions and to come-up with novel and creative approaches. From the foregoing it is also apparent that solidarity remains an important value in the debate. The (EU) law on SG(E)Is should respond to the challenges at issue in such a way that solidarity is achieved and maintained.

References

Dreyfus M (2009) Experience in the Member States: France. In: Krajewski M et al. (eds) The Changing Legal Framework for Services of General Interest in Europe. Between Competition and Solidarity. T.M.C. Asser Press, The Hague, pp 269–290.

Krajewski M (2009) Conclusions. In: Krajewski M et al. (eds) The Changing Legal Framework for Services of General Interest in Europe. Between Competition and Solidarity. T.M.C. Asser Press, The Hague, pp 499–506.

Krajewski M (2011) Grundstrukturen des Rechts öffentlicher Dienstleistungen. Springer, Heidelberg.

Krajewski M et al. (2009) The Changing Legal Framework for Services of General Interest in Europe. Between Competition and Solidarity. T.M.C. Asser Press, The Hague.

Neergaard U (2009) Services of General Economic Interest: The Nature of the Beast. In: Krajewski M et al. (eds) The Changing Legal Framework for Services of General Interest in Europe. Between Competition and Solidarity. T.M.C. Asser Press, The Hague, pp 17–50.

Ross M (2007) Promoting Solidarity: From Public Services to a European Model of Competition? Common Market Law Review 44(4):1057–1080.

Schweitzer H (2011) Services of General Economic Interest: European Law's Impact on the Role of Markets and of Member States. In: Cremona M (ed) Market Integration and Public Services in the European Union, Collected Courses of the Academy of European Law. Oxford University Press, Oxford, pp 11–62.

Van de Gronden JW, Rusu CS (2024) Competition law in the EU, 2nd edn. Edward Elgar, Cheltenham.

Van Eijken H (2014) European Citizenship and the Constitutionalisation of the European Union. Europa Law Publishing, Zutphen.

Johan Willem van de Gronden is (full) professor of European law at Radboud University (the Netherlands) and state counsellor in extraordinary service at the Dutch Council of State.

Part I
Healthcare and SGEIs

Chapter 2
State Aid and Healthcare: Between Competition and Constitutionalism

Mary Guy

Contents

Abstract The recent state aid cases of *Dôvera* and *Casa Regina Apostolorum* demonstrate how competition and healthcare remains a contentious issue, highlighting tensions between both economic and social aspects, and EU and Member State competences. The approach taken by the EU courts typically emphasises total non-applicability of the state aid rules, although partial immunity via the Services of General Economic Interest (SGEI) mechanism is gaining greater recognition via cases such as *Brussels Hospitals* and successive Commission SGEI "packages". With the State Aid Temporary Framework—introduced in response to the COVID-19 pandemic—support for various healthcare activities was facilitated via the Article 107(3) TFEU justifications. This chapter suggests that these three aspects—from non-applicability, via SGEI, to Article 107(3) TFEU—can offer further insight into where market forces can usefully be deployed in healthcare reform, and where these may have a detrimental effect. However, further understanding can be gained from examining constitutional aspects—not only Member State competence for healthcare under Article 168(7) TFEU, but also perceptions of "competence creep" at EU level regarding national healthcare, and implications for both levels of developing a European Health Union. This chapter advances discussions in this area by juxtaposing

M. Guy (✉)
Liverpool John Moores University, Liverpool, UK
e-mail: maryjguy@gmail.com

N. Ghazaryan et al. (eds.), *Services of General (Economic) Interest and EU Law*, Legal Issues of Services of General Interest, https://doi.org/10.1007/978-94-6265-723-6_2

"competition" and "constitutionalism" perspectives, while drawing on insights from before and during the COVID-19 pandemic.

Keywords Competition · COVID-19 · European Health Union · EU · Member State · Service of General Interest · Service of General Economic Interest · State aid · Subsidiarity

2.1 Introduction

The relationship between competition and healthcare constitutes an issue which remains topical and contentious, highlighting tensions both between economic and social aspects, and within the EU and Member State interaction. The development of competition reforms in healthcare at a national level has been accompanied by a growing literature and body of case law outlining EU competition law frameworks since the early 1990s.[1] The first decade of the 21st century offered scope for examination of this in light of the consideration that it was not possible to ignore markets in healthcare.[2]

However, recent decisions such as the Court of Justice of the European Union (CJEU)'s 2020 judgment in *Dôvera*[3] and the 2023 judgment in *Casa Regina Apostolorum*[4] perhaps suggest an ongoing reluctance by the EU courts to engage with this evolving reality of markets in healthcare. While these cases largely follow an earlier generation of cases, they unfold against a backdrop of changing attitudes towards competition reforms in healthcare[5] and expansion of private sector delivery of public healthcare services. Thus recognition of the role markets can play in healthcare system modernisation appears to become more nuanced,[6] tempered by considerations that it may be more beneficial to recognise both where active application of competition law in healthcare may be useful,[7] and where markets may not be able to deliver effectively in the public interest,[8] for example, specialist healthcare services.[9]

---

[1] CJEU, *Christian Poucet v Assurances Générales de France and Caisse Mutuelle Régionale du Languedoc-Roussillon*, Judgment, 17 February 1993, C-159/91 is typically cited as among the first to engage with the interaction between EU competition policy and national healthcare systems.

[2] Szyszczak 2009.

[3] CJEU, *Commission v Dôvera zdravotná poist'ovňa, a.s.*, Judgment, 11 June 2020, C-262/18 P.

[4] CJEU, *Casa Regina Apostolorum della Pia Società delle Figlie di San Paolo v Commission*, 27 April 2023, C-492/21 P.

[5] The prominent reforms in Dutch and English healthcare enshrined in legislation in 2006 and 2012 respectively have both subsequently been reframed, scaled back, and in the English context, repealed. See further Guy 2019, 2023.

[6] Albeit reaffirming long-standing distinctions drawn between the US and Europe regarding competition in healthcare. Greaney and Odudu 2022.

[7] Nikolić 2021.

[8] Van de Gronden 2018.

[9] Van de Gronden and Guy 2021.

These recent cases also unfold against the separate backdrop of possible changes in attitude regarding the interaction between the EU and Member State levels emerging from the implementation of the Lisbon Treaty. Article 168(7) Treaty on the Functioning of the European Union (TFEU) is the current formulation of the "subsidiarity clause for healthcare",[10] and deemed more extensive than its predecessor[11] in underscoring the role for Member States in determining national health policy and healthcare system organisation—both relevant for considerations of competition. The TFEU's greater recognition of SGEI—and the role of Member States in defining these—has also developed with regard to healthcare via successive Commission SGEI "packages" and notable cases such as *BUPA*[12] and *Brussels Hospitals*,[13] yet the mechanism arguably remains elusive and not well understood.[14]

Both backdrops find reflection in responses to the COVID-19 pandemic, which, along with growing concerns about environmental destruction and the development of digitalisation, might be considered among the defining features of the first quarter of the twenty-first century. One of the Commission's responses to the COVID-19 pandemic was to introduce temporary frameworks relaxing the state aid rules based on the Article 107(3) TFEU exceptions which were—following several extensions—in operation between March 2020 and June 2022. While some decisions taken regarding the healthcare sector might be attributed primarily to a direct "crisis" response of, e.g., ensuring supply of items of personal protective equipment, other decisions also suggest a "continuity" response, indicating tensions to wider public healthcare delivery and access exacerbated by the pandemic which seem likely to persist.[15] This latter aspect, while addressed within the temporary framework by Article 107(3) TFEU exceptions, has features which suggest that the SGEI may provide a more robust exception over the longer term.[16] The balance between EU and national competence regarding healthcare has been given significant momentum by the further pandemic response of developing a European Health Union. While this evolved between 2020 and 2022 to suggest that its focus may be primarily on health security threats, calls were also made via the Conference on the Future of Europe for health to assume a "shared competence" status.[17]

---

[10] Hancher and Sauter 2012, p. 221.

[11] Treaty establishing the European Community (Consolidated version 2002), signed on 26 February 2001, published on 24 December 2002, Article 152(5).

[12] CJEU (GC), *British United Provident Association Ltd (BUPA), BUPA Insurance Ltd, BUPA Ireland Ltd v Commission*, Judgment, 12 February 2008, T-289/03.

[13] Culminating in Commission Decision (EU) 2016/2327 of 5 July 2016 on State aid SA.19864 – 2014/C (ex 2009/NN54) implemented by Belgium - Public financing of Brussels public IRIS hospitals (notified under document C(2016) 4051) (OJ L 351, pp. 68–144).

[14] Nikolić 2021 has suggested that Member States may prefer to try to exempt their healthcare systems totally.

[15] For an early evaluation, see Guy 2020a.

[16] Ibid.

[17] See Recommendation 49 in Conference on the Future of Europe, Report on the Final Outcome, May 2022, p. 64. https://www.europarl.europa.eu/resources/library/media/20220509RES29121/20220509RES29121.pdf. This would require amendment of Article 4 TFEU, and would mark

This chapter focuses on state aid as an aspect of EU competition policy with particular relevance to healthcare both at EU and national levels.[18] It aims to advance understanding of developments in this area of the past generation[19] by juxtaposing "competition" and "constitutionalism" perspectives (respectively Sects. 2.2 and 2.3) to consider key cases and policy. This discussion indicates that constitutionalism, defined here specifically with regard to differing EU-level oversight of healthcare (a national competence as noted above) may offer the more robust explanation for the approaches continued by the EU courts thus far. Section 2.4 concludes with insights emerging both before and during the COVID-19 pandemic regarding whether the operation of the state aid rules in the healthcare context can be better understood in terms of constitutionalism rather than competition given the political sensitivities which attach to the national and EU levels.

2.2 State Aid and Healthcare: A Competition Law Perspective

The applicability of the state aid rules—also the antitrust rules—is determined by the "undertaking" concept—typically defined in "functional" terms as an "economic activity",[20] which consists in "offering goods and services on a market".[21] Case law interpreting these principles in the context of healthcare initially generated a broad framework in which healthcare providers were typically seen as subject to competition rules (regardless of whether the healthcare system is taxation-funded or insurance-based),[22] but healthcare purchasers may not be, depending on the subsequent use of the purchased goods or services.[23] This may appear to suggest a contradiction insofar as providing and purchasing may be seen as two sides of the same transaction, thus both represent the requisite "economic activities" for triggering EU competition law.[24] A further, pertinent, consideration in view of this "functional" nature of the undertaking concept is that challenges arise "…from the fact that the law is being applied to not-for-profit or bodies controlled by the state."[25] These distinctions have given rise to different interpretations by the Commission and EU

---

a notable development. Currently, healthcare (system organisation) is exclusively a Member State competence under Article 168(7) TFEU, while the EU can complement Member State activity in other aspects of health (notably public health) under Article 168 TFEU.

[18] Thereby complementing the chapters by Suorsa (Chap. 4) and Clark (Chap. 3) on other aspects of SGEI and healthcare in this volume.

[19] Since the publication of Krajewski et al. 2009.

[20] CJEU, *Klaus Höfner and Fritz Elser v Macrotron GmbH*, Judgment, 23 April 1991, C-41/90.

[21] CJEU, *Commission of the European Communities v Italy*, Judgment, 18 June 1998, C-35/96.

[22] For further discussion, see Van de Gronden and Guy 2021.

[23] Van de Gronden and Rusu 2017.

[24] Guy 2019, p. 75.

[25] Odudu 2022.

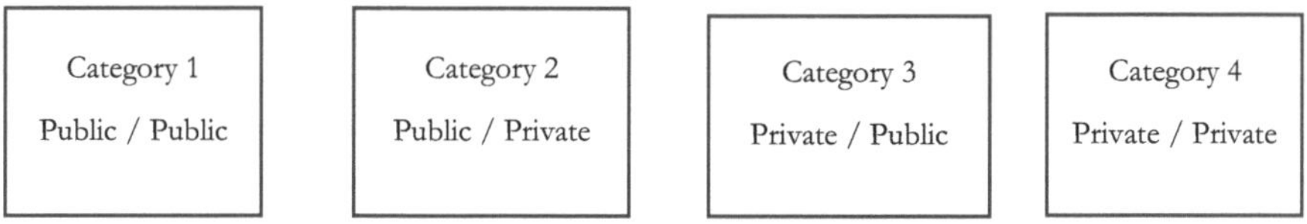

Fig. 2.1 The "four categories" of European healthcare. *Source* The author

courts being characterised as "abstract" and "concrete",[26] and "classic functional" and "attenuated functional",[27] according to how strictly the functional test is applied, and how much attention is paid to the national context/legal framework in reaching conclusions about applicability. The national context in particular also highlights tensions between competition and solidarity, which apply to the SGEI mechanism as well, which operates to provide "partial immunity" to the antitrust and state aid rules.[28]

Despite important conceptual differences between the antitrust and state aid rules,[29] the common starting-point of the "undertaking" concept, and the overall aims of avoiding distortions of competition in the internal market, mean that overall understanding of the EU's approach in these cases is shaped by both sets of rules. Nevertheless, the contours of the state aid regime with regard to healthcare have been considered better developed,[30] and this appears reaffirmed by the recent cases.

In locating where the state aid rules might become relevant in the healthcare context, it is useful to consider "four categories of European healthcare"[31] thus (see Fig. 2.1).

In essence categories 1 and 2 comprise the public healthcare system, in which public insurers or providers (category 1) or private insurers or providers (category 2) may operate. Conversely, categories 3 and 4 represent private healthcare markets which may coexist with public healthcare systems, with varying degrees of competition *between* the two. Thus category 3 typically comprises public provision, and category 4 private activity (insurance/provision), vis-à-vis *private* patients who fund their own treatment. While not intended to represent definitively all Member State healthcare systems, this typology nevertheless can provide a useful framing for aspects of national healthcare systems which are increasingly at issue in the EU courts' considerations, as any attempt to classify healthcare in terms of distinguishing the extremes of categories 1 and 4 becomes characterised by blurred lines. Thus in

26 Van de Gronden 2004.

27 Gallo and Mariotti 2017.

28 See, inter alia, Belhaj and Van de Gronden 2004; Boeger 2007.

29 For example, the consumer welfare standard underpins the antitrust rules, but arguments have been advanced for a consumer-taxpayer welfare standard to be applied regarding the state aid rules. Friederiszick et al. 2007, and for further discussion, Cseres and Reyna 2021.

30 Hancher and Sauter 2012.

31 This is adapted from the "four categories of English healthcare" identified in connection with the evolving interaction between the National Health Service and the private healthcare market which underpins competition reforms introduced in statute in England. See further Guy 2019, p. 40.

Dôvera we see private insurers challenging support for state insurers (category 2), while in *Casa Regina Apostolorum*, the focus has included not only private delivery of public healthcare (category 2), but also public hospitals treating private patients (category 3), with the underlying complaint coming from a private provider (with an implicit focus on category 4). In contrast, the SGEI packages, in emphasising hospital financing in particular, suggest an emphasis on category 1 activity (with some reference to category 2).[32]

Within the "mechanics" of EU competition law, three exception mechanisms can be identified: classification of a service of general interest (SGI) such that competition law does not apply; classification of an economic activity as a service of general economic interest (SGEI), which offers partial immunity from the applicability of EU competition law; and justifications for breaching the prohibitions on anticompetitive agreements (Article 101(3) TFEU) and on state aid (Article 107(3) TFEU). While the SGI blanket exception might be considered the most common in the EU courts' reasoning, the approaches taken with regard to the two other mechanisms also warrant examination. By linking these three exception mechanisms together, a more complete picture may emerge while reflecting recognition that individual cases may reference both Article 106(2) TFEU and Article 107(3)(c) TFEU in outlining a counterfactual,[33] or highlighting reference to SGEI in order to ground an assertion that the activities involved are indeed economic.[34]

2.2.1 SGI in Healthcare

The finding of an SGI means that activities are not economic in nature—typically purchasing activities, as noted above. Indeed it has been considered in particular that the tension between the "classic" and "attenuated" functional approaches remains unresolved[35] in the context of state aid cases.

Dôvera involved a challenge by a private health insurer to state aid granted to state health insurers, against the backdrop of the coexistence of public and private bodies

---

[32] The latter featuring in Commission Decision C(2017) final of 27 March 2017 on State aid SA.38825 Alleged State Aid to private providers of socio-sanitary services (OJ 2017 C 219, p. 1).

[33] As happened in Commission Decision (EU) 2015/248 of 15 October 2014 on the measures SA.23008 (2013/C) (ex 2013/NN) implemented by Slovak Republic for Spoločná zdravotná poisťovňa, a. s. (SZP) and Všeobecná zdravotná poisťovňa, a. s. (VZP), para 53. In contrast, the General Court in *Casa Regina Apostolorum* roundly rejected the suggested need to conduct an Article 106(2) TFEU investigation. CJEU (GC), *Casa Regina Apostolorum della Pia Società delle Figlie di San Paolo v Commission*, Judgment, 2 June 2021, T-223/18. See paras 144–151 in particular.

[34] Which formed an aspect of the complaint to the Commission in *Casa Regina Apostolorum*. In this instance, the Commission considered that including healthcare activities in the Italian SGEI reports was not evidence of the economic nature of activities. Commission Decision C(2017) 7973 final of 4 December 2017 on State aid SA.39913 (2017/NN) Alleged compensation of public hospitals in Lazio, para 76.

[35] Gallo and Mariotti 2017.

within the Slovak system of compulsory health insurance. The Commission's 2014 decision[36]—and indeed the CJEU's 2020 judgment[37]—might be considered to tend more towards the "concrete", or the "attenuated functional" approaches insofar as it emphasised how the health insurance scheme was operated, and the centrality of solidarity within this.[38] In contrast, the two grounds for appeal put forward by one of the private health insurers (Dôvera) tended towards the more "abstract" or "classical functional" approaches by referencing, inter alia, the scope for competition within the system, and the public and private health insurers' activities beyond this. It is, however, interesting to see how the General Court's response finding—that the state aid rules did apply—also appeared to align more with the "abstract" or "classic functional" approaches, by reference to a wider definition of 'competition' encompassing quality and price. The alignment appears encapsulated primarily by General Court's focus on the insurers' profit-making ability, and the striking consideration that

> [...] since it is common ground between the parties that the other [private] operators on the market in question are seeking to make a profit, so that SZP and VšZP [the state insurers], 'by contagion' would have to be considered to be undertakings.[39]

The CJEU's ultimate finding which focused, inter alia, on the solidarity-based nature of the Slovak health insurance scheme, indicated however a perspective which is consistent with the "concrete" or "attenuated functional" approaches.

The *Casa Regina Apostolorum* case involved a complaint by a religious congregation (which owns a private hospital) regarding alleged compensation of public hospitals in the Lazio Region in Italy. Here too the complainant's perspective might be considered to be in line with the "abstract" or "classic functional" approaches, given the emphasis it placed on perceptions of market behaviour by public hospitals and private hospitals delivering public healthcare services in light of successive competition reforms emphasising patient choice in the Italian healthcare system, as well as the treatment of private patients by the public hospitals.[40] In contrast, the Italian authorities—and subsequently the Commission—can be considered to take more of a "concrete", or "attenuated functional" approach,[41] by underscoring the underlying principle of solidarity within the Italian healthcare system which remained unchanged by either the "corporatisation" of public hospitals, or the treatment of

[36] See further Van de Gronden and Guy 2021.

[37] CJEU, *Commission v Dôvera zdravotná poist'ovňa*, a.s., Judgment, 11 June 2020, C-262/18 P.

[38] See Commission Decision (EU) 2015/248 of 15 October 2014 on the measures SA.23008 (2013/C) (ex 2013/NN) implemented by Slovak Republic for Spoločná zdravotná poisťovňa, a. s. (SZP) and Všeobecná zdravotná poisťovňa, a. s. (VZP), paras 85–99.

[39] CJEU (GC), *Dôvera zdrvotná poist'ová and Union zdrvotná poist'ová*, Judgment, 5 February 2018, T-216/15, para 69.

[40] Commission Decision C(2017) 7973 final of 4 December 2017 on State aid SA.39913 (2017/NN) Alleged compensation of public hospitals in Lazio, paras 12, 16, 19 and 20 in particular.

[41] The latter in particular highlighted by the clear reference to the *FENIN* judgment in Commission Decision C(2017) 7973 final of 4 December 2017 on State aid SA.39913 (2017/NN) Alleged compensation of public hospitals in Lazio, para 57.

private patients.[42] The Commission ultimately concluded that the compensation did not constitute state aid within the meaning of Article 107(1) TFEU.

On appeal,[43] the General Court rejected the claims, including that the Commission had not paid sufficient attention to the marketisation reforms indicated by the Casa Regina Apostolorum congregation. While the General Court drew on *Dôvera* (and previous case law) to make various of its points regarding the ongoing relevance of solidarity and universality, it is interesting to note that it also drew on a logic from *CEPPB*[44] (a case concerning the Spanish education system) requiring activity-by-activity-level examination, in recognising the possibility of the coexistence of both economic and non-economic activities being performed by a public hospital.[45] This "disaggregation" logic, when coupled with the *CEPPB* "three-prong test" of public financing and public interest,[46] may come to represent an alternative approach to, or mid-way point between, the "abstract"/"classical functional" and "concrete"/ "attenuated functional" approaches.

In its appeal to the CJEU,[47] the congregation raised two disputes in particular. Firstly, the General Court's reliance on *Dôvera* and application of this to the facts of *Casa Regina Apostolorum* as it did not carry out a detailed analysis of certain of the competition reforms in the Italian healthcare system, nor did it compare this with the rules governing provision of healthcare services in Slovakia. Secondly, the General Court's finding that the concept of activity on the basis of universality can preclude the applicability of the SGEI mechanism, given that such activities can be so regarded in other sectors, such as water. Strikingly, no Advocate General Opinion was provided in connection with this appeal, which both left unanswered certain questions and indicated that no new point of law was considered to be raised.[48]

The CJEU's judgment in *Casa Regina Apostolorum* further rejected the appeal claims, in a decision which is striking for two reasons. Firstly, it has been considered the first time that the "concrete" approach has been applied to healthcare providers (as distinct from healthcare purchasers/managing bodies).[49] This may appear to lend further weight to a "constitutionalism" rather than a "competition" perspective, indeed it has been considered that the judgment may signal the CJEU somehow losing interest in competition and healthcare.[50] Secondly, the lack of engagement

[42] Commission Decision C(2017) 7973 final of 4 December 2017 on State aid SA.39913 (2017/ NN) Alleged compensation of public hospitals in Lazio. See in particular paras 27–29, 37, 41, 59, 65, 75 and 78.

[43] CJEU (GC), *Casa Regina Apostolorum della Pia Società delle Figlie di San Paolo v Commission*, Judgment, 2 June 2021, T-223/18.

[44] CJEU, *Congregación de Escuelas Pías Provincia Betania*, Judgment, 27 June 2017, C-74/16.

[45] See CJEU (GC), *Casa Regina Apostolorum della Pia Società delle Figlie di San Paolo v Commission*, Judgment, 2 June 2021, T-223/18, paras 182–183.

[46] Van de Gronden 2018.

[47] CJEU, *Casa Regina Apostolorum della Pia Società delle Figlie di San Paolo v Commission*, application made on 29 October 2021, C-492/21 P.

[48] Guy 2025.

[49] Van de Gronden 2023; Van de Gronden and Rusu 2024.

[50] Van de Gronden 2023.

with the SGEI mechanism suggests a further endorsement of a "constitutionalism" approach whereby the onus is on the national authorities to engage with SGEI as this seems to trigger a different assessment process by the Commission which is more akin to "block exemptions" in antitrust. Thus distinctions have been drawn between state aid and hospital cases where the national authorities have engaged with the SGEI mechanism (such as *Czechia Hospitals*),[51] and those where they have not (such as *Casa Regina Apostolorum*).[52] In the latter, the EU-level analysis is logically focussed on questions of the existence of an undertaking unless there is a need to review suggestions of "manifest error" by a Member State in designating SGEI (as happened in the *Brussels Hospitals* case).[53]

As a final consideration of SGIs in the healthcare context, and specifically state aid cases, it should be recalled that further scope for excluding the applicability of EU competition law resides in the finding that there is no effect of the conduct on trade between Member States. An instance of where this was found was in a 2015 Commission Decision on the granting of public financing to five public hospitals in the Czech Republic.[54] Given the national (if not regional) focus of healthcare systems, it might be considered that it would not be unusual for this intra-state trade hurdle not to be crossed, at least with regard to hospital financing.

2.2.2 SGEI in Healthcare

From a competition perspective, various criticisms have emerged regarding development of the SGEI mechanism and how this has been applied in the healthcare context. These relate in part to the modifications made to utilising the *Altmark*[55] criteria as an exception to the state aid rules, and with an emphasis on Article 106(2) TFEU as a proxy for the fourth criterion—otherwise conceptualised as the tension between the "state aid" and "compensation" approaches.[56] Of particular note is the General Court's readiness to find an SGEI mission in *BUPA*,[57] a case which concerned a challenge regarding the Irish risk equalisation scheme by the then largest private provider.

---

[51] European Commission, SA.37432 (2015/NN) — Czech Republic. Brussels, 29.04.2015, C(2015) 2796 final.

[52] Guy 2025.

[53] Commission Decision (EU) 2016/2327 of 5 July 2016 on State aid SA.19864 - 2014/C (ex 2009/NN54) implemented by Belgium – Public financing of Brussels public IRIS hospitals Brussels (notified under document C(2016) 4051) (OJ L 351, pp. 68–144).

[54] Commission Decision C(2015) 2796 final of 29 April 2015 on SA.37432 (2015/NN) Funding to public hospitals in the Hradec Králové Region, as discussed in Gallo and Mariotti 2017; Biondi and Ştefan 2020.

[55] CJEU, *Altmark Trans et Regierungspräsidum Magdeburg*, Judgment, 24 July 2003, C-280/00.

[56] Gallo and Mariotti 2017.

[57] CJEU (GC), *British United Provident Association Ltd (BUPA), BUPA Insurance Ltd and BUPA Ireland Ltd v Commission of the European Communities*, Judgment, 12 February 2008, T-289/03.

This prompted concerns about the stricter approach taken to the Dutch risk equalisation scheme by the Commission,[58] the dynamic between government and market failures,[59] but also questions of competence.[60] The judgment was also considered to adopt a "jurisdictional approach", entailing that the application of Article 107 TFEU ultimately depends on the characterisation of the undertaking involved and the SGEI it performs, rather than on a substantive and in-depth (economic) assessment of whether the public service mission is discharged in a proportionate manner.[61] The General Court's approach in *BUPA*, which included a lower-intensity examination of national definition of SGEI, nevertheless appears to mark a point of reference in the evolution of SGEI both with regard to healthcare and in general.[62]

The General Court has also considered the assignation of SGEI in the context of hospital financing in the long-running *Brussels Hospitals* case. This evolved from a 2005 Commission finding of SGEI rendering payments to certain public hospitals in Brussels compatible with the internal market, to a 2009 appeal[63] in which the General Court established the procedure regarding when the Commission should conduct more in-depth assessments under Article 108 TFEU. The Commission's investigation was opened in 2014, and concluded in 2016,[64] finding that payments made to certain public hospitals in the Brussels region, while constituting state aid under Article 107(1) TFEU, were correctly classified as SGEI under Article 106(2) TFEU. This finding was made by virtue, inter alia, of their specific mission to ensure continuity (*pérennité*) of services in the face of financial difficulties—which did not also apply to private providers. By examining the context of the funding, it has been considered that SGEI considerations can also be characterised by the "attenuated functional" approach.[65] This might be considered to align the Commission's approach to SGEI in healthcare (or at least hospitals specifically) with that of the courts.

Certainly, the development of SGEI in healthcare has been cast as two phases—the first by the EU courts, as indicated above, and the second by the Commission in implementing its 2005 and 2012 SGEI packages to minimise legal uncertainty.[66] Within the SGEI packages, we see initially SGEI regarding hospitals,[67] and latterly SGEI

---

[58] See further De Vries 2011; Hancher and Sauter 2012.

[59] Burke 2018.

[60] Ross 2009.

[61] Thus a third approach to be juxtaposed with the "state aid" and "compensation" approaches. De Vries 2011.

[62] De Cecco 2013, p. 145; Skovgaard Ølykke and Møllgaard 2016.

[63] CJEU (GC), *CBI v Commission*, Judgment, 7 November 2012, T-137/10.

[64] Commission Decision (EU) 2016/2327 of 5 July 2016 on State aid SA.19864 - 2014/C (ex 2009/NN54) implemented by Belgium – Public financing of Brussels public IRIS hospitals Brussels (notified under document C(2016) 4051) (OJ L 351, pp. 68–144).

[65] Gallo and Mariotti 2017.

[66] Ibid.

[67] Commission Decision of 28 November 2005 on the application of Article 86(2) of the EC Treaty to State aid in the form of public service compensation granted to certain undertakings entrusted with the operation of services of general economic interest (notified under document number C(2005) 2673) (OJ L 312, pp. 67–73), Recital 16 and Article 2(1)(b); Commission Decision of 20 December

regarding "health and long-term care",[68] being exempt from notification requirements in the Commission's recognition that "[h]ealth and social services form an essential part of the welfare system of each Member State and are of crucial importance for citizens".[69] This might be considered reinforced by its attempt—via the 2012 SGEI package—to simplify compatibility criteria and reduce the administrative burden for Member States.[70] Nevertheless, concerns have emerged from a competition perspective that, by stipulating hospital financing already in the 2005 package, Member States were sheltered "from making tough decisions on access priorities and preferential funding.[71] The broadening of the 2012 package to include "health and long-term care",[72] was considered to prompt the need for further clarification of what might be included within this, given the various ways in which health and social care systems are organised across Member States.[73] Certainly a diversity of state aid allegations can be identified which might be considered to fall within in the health and long-term care context—for example, in connection with selling blood plasma below cost,[74] or regarding prescription of branded pharmaceutical manufacturers over cheaper generics[75]—but none of these were found to fall within the Article 107(1) TFEU prohibition. The broadened category of "health and long-term care" has, however, also required demonstration at a national level of how the 2012 package is being complied with. This has been seen in the elaboration of measures promoting social welfare services in Germany,[76] and, at a national level, by the classification of a Dutch government subsidy of non-invasive prenatal tests as SGEI.[77]

2011 on the application of Article 106(2) of the Treaty on the Functioning of the European Union to State aid in the form of public service compensation granted to certain undertakings entrusted with the operation of services of general economic interest (notified under document C(2011) 9380) (OJ L 7, pp. 3–10), Recital 11 and Article 2(1)(b).

[68] Commission Decision of 20 December 2011 on the application of Article 106(2) of the Treaty on the Functioning of the European Union to State aid in the form of public service compensation granted to certain undertakings entrusted with the operation of services of general economic interest (notified under document C(2011) 9380) (OJ L 7, pp. 3–10), Recital 11 and Article 2(1)(c).

[69] European Commission 2022.

[70] Ibid.

[71] For a critical view, see Hancher and Sauter 2013.

[72] Commission Decision of 20 December 2011 on the application of Article 106(2) of the Treaty on the Functioning of the European Union to State aid in the form of public service compensation granted to certain undertakings entrusted with the operation of services of general economic interest (notified under document C(2011) 9380) (OJ L 7, pp. 3–10), Recital 11 and Article 2(1)(c).

[73] Van de Gronden and Rusu 2013.

[74] Commission Decision C(2014) 7286 final of 15 October 2015 on State aid SA.37624 Alleged illegal State Aid to Imuna Pharm.

[75] Commission Decision C(2016) 5157 final of 11 August 2016 on State aid SA.43092 (2016/FC) Complaint of Nurse Prescribes Ltd against the UK Department of Health.

[76] Commission Decision C(2017) 7686 final of 23 November 2017 on State aid SA.42268 State Aid for the promotion of public welfare services.

[77] Court of Appeal of The Hague (Netherlands), *Gendia v Dutch Ministry of Health, Wellbeing and Sport*, Judgment, 200.225.476/01 (ECLI:NL:GHDHA:2018:3331). The facts of the case are discussed in English in Van de Gronden and Guy 2021.

The 2019 review of the 2012 SGEI package regarding health and social services has recently concluded and indicated some scope for improvement, and a need, inter alia, for further clarification on the distinction between "economic" and "non-economic" activities following cases such as *Dôvera* and *Casa Regina Apostolorum*.[78]

2.2.3 *Justifications for Prohibition Breaches in the Healthcare Context*

It has been considered that—in contrast to SGEI—the Article 101(3) TFEU exception is not broad enough to encompass general public interest considerations or special concerns relating to public services.[79] Whether this criticism—essentially of whether the competition rules can be flexible enough to accommodate specificities of the healthcare sector—also holds for the justifications associated with the state aid rules is moot. Certainly it is acknowledged that the Article 101(3) TFEU exception is more geared towards non-economic goals, while the state aid justifications have a different structure and focus, encompassing a range of aspects, such as aid having a social character and being granted to consumers,[80] and aid to facilitate the development of certain economic activities or areas.[81]

The most serviceable of the justifications for state aid in the healthcare context seems to be Article 107(3)(b) TFEU relating to promoting the execution of an important project of common European interest or to remedy a serious disturbance in the economy of a Member State. This has been used to support a pilot project for telemedicine infrastructure in Saxony in Germany,[82] and time-bounded financial support to three specialist clinics and two retirement homes in the Lazio region of Italy.[83]

This exception—and also Article 107(3)(c) TFEU, to facilitate development of certain economic activities or areas—formed the basis for the State Aid Temporary Framework (SATF), in operation between March 2020 and June 2022 as part of the Commission's response to the COVID-19 pandemic. While the aid approved under this scheme reached across the whole economy, concerns have emerged that the

[78] European Commission 2022, p. 24.

[79] Prosser 2005, p. 27. For consideration of how "non-competition goals" and public interest objectives can operate in connection with Article 101(3) TFEU in the healthcare context, see, inter alia, Hancher and Sauter 2012; Van de Gronden 2011.

[80] Consolidated version of the Treaty on the Functioning of the European Union, signed on 13 December 2007, published 26 October 2012, TFEU, Article 107(2)(a).

[81] TFEU, above n. 74, Article 107(3)(c).

[82] Commission Decision C(2013) 8441 final of 4 December 2013 on State aid SA.35679 (2012/N) Telemedicine Infrastructure in Saxony.

[83] Commission Decision C(2014) 9255 final of 10 December 2014 on State aid SA.39426 (2014/N) Rescue aid to PICFIC in A.S., health care services operator in the Region of Lazio.

SATF did not manage to adequately contribute to a real investment in quality public health services.[84]

The SATF is also relevant to the present discussion because it has produced a range of cases upon which further contours of Commission and EU courts decisions may now emerge, particularly when it is noted that these decisions can be categorised as "crisis" and "continuity" responses.[85] Examples of "crisis" responses—typically approved under Article 107(3)(c) TFEU—include where aid was approved in connection with COVID-19 R&D, and producing COVID-19 relevant products, ranging from medicines, personal protective equipment and ventilators, to data processing tools.[86] In contrast, "continuity" responses related to healthcare provision and access not directly related to treating COVID-19, which might have implications for healthcare delivery beyond the pandemic situation. Examples of "continuity" responses include the COVID-Spas programme in the Czech Republic,[87] or support for eHealth applications to facilitate healthcare access in the Netherlands during the early stages of the pandemic.[88] These were approved under Article 107(3)(b) TFEU, and while not framed in these terms, the aid approved potentially gave rise to questions about the ability of markets to deliver particular services in general, thus perhaps indicating potential SGEI candidates over the longer term, which could generate further considerations of the juxtaposition of "competition" and "constitutionalism" perspectives.

2.3 State Aid and Healthcare: A Constitutionalism Perspective

As noted above, there are both common points governing the applicability of the antitrust and the state aid rules, and divergence insofar as conceptual differences emerge between how "competition" may be understood within these. From a constitutional perspective, state aid rules occupy a distinctive place which may be defined

---

[84] Giosa 2023.

[85] Guy 2020a.

[86] See, for example, Communication from the Commission – Temporary Framework for State Aid Measures to support the economy in the current COVID-19 outbreak (Consolidated Version), sections 3.6 and 3.8.

[87] Commission Decision C(2020) 5552 final of 7 August 2020 on State aid SA.58018 (2020/N) COVID-19: Support for Health Spas and Commission Decision C(2021) 1640 final of 9 March 2021 on State aid SA.61912 (2021/N) COVID-19: Amendment of the support scheme for Health Spas (SA.58018).

[88] Commission Decision C(2020) 4982 final of 16 July 2020 on State aid SA.57897 (2020/N) COVID-19: Direct grant scheme for e-Health services at home under the Temporary Framework for State aid measures to support the economy in the current COVID-19 outbreak, which extended an application under Commission Decision C(2020) 2228 final of 3 April 2020 on State aid SA.56915 (2020/N) Direct grant scheme for e-Health services at home under the Temporary Framework for State aid measures to support the economy in the current COVID-19 outbreak.

as between the internal market and a wider European economic constitution, and within the latter, a positioning between the free movement and antitrust rules.[89] A further distinctiveness lies in the state aid regime being exclusively EU-level, with no national equivalent. Thus, concerns which may emerge in relation to the antitrust rules, might not be expected to materialise in the same way with application of the state aid rules. Examples of such concerns might include scope for divergent interpretation resulting in "Euro-national competition rules for healthcare",[90] or concerns about national enforcement of EU law,[91] parallel application of national and EU competition frameworks,[92] or compatibility of national provisions with EU law.[93]

Insofar as economic law (thus the state aid rules) can be reconciled with constitutional law by a wider framing of the former to encompass non-market values,[94] this seems to have particular relevance to discussion of healthcare, as seen in the constitutional aspects clearly arising from the three aspects outlined above. Thus total exemption from the state aid rules via a finding of non-applicability might be considered to give effect to the Member State competence of Article 168(7)TFEU regarding healthcare system organisation. Related to this, but ultimately discrete, is the partial immunity afforded by the SGEI mechanism, with the underscoring of Member State competence in assigning SGEI. This is evident particularly given the emphasis and refocusing emerging from the Lisbon Treaty regarding SGEI.[95] While this particular focus does not engage with legal and political concerns emerging from the diverse range of instruments governing SGEI,[96] it nevertheless highlights the range of actors involved and their various understandings and the potential implications of this.[97] Finally, the Article 107(3) TFEU allowances may demonstrate how far the EU recognises differing expressions of the national competence regarding healthcare system organisation, albeit via the lenses of remedying serious economic disturbances[98] (particularly in response to the early phases of the COVID-19 pandemic), or facilitating the development of certain economic activities.[99]

Allied to constitutionalism are concerns about "competence creep", with the EU institutions apparently showing an ever-greater interest in national healthcare systems

---

[89] See further De Cecco 2012, pp. 1, 17, and 31.

[90] Van de Gronden and Szyszczak 2014.

[91] Hancher and Sauter 2012, pp. 256–257.

[92] Guy 2019 regarding the Netherlands (pp. 90–92) and England (pp. 92–93).

[93] An example being "hybrid" rules for antitrust and public procurement for the English NHS: the National Health Service (Procurement, Patient Choice and Competition) Regulations (No. 2) 2013. Sánchez Graells 2015.

[94] De Cecco 2012, p. 17.

[95] To include Article 14 TFEU, Protocol No. 26 and recognition within the Charter of Fundamental Rights.

[96] For an excellent discussion, see Wehlander 2016, Chapters 6 and 10 in particular.

[97] See Wehlander 2016, and also Sauter 2014, p. 179.

[98] TFEU, above n. 74, Article 107(3)(b).

[99] TFEU, above n. 74, Article 107(3)(c).

via EU competition policy,[100] thus perhaps breaching the "subsidiarity clause" for healthcare of Article 168(7) TFEU. However, in view of the consistent line of the EU courts in finding that either the Article 107(1) TFEU prohibition does not apply, or that the activity in question is rendered compatible with the internal market by virtue of classification as an SGEI, or via one of the Article 107 justifications, it is difficult to pinpoint exactly how this "competence creep" is manifested with regard to state aid rules. This is in contrast to the free movement rules, where arguments of "Europeanisation" might be more readily articulated in view of harmonisation underpinning the Patients' Rights Directive.[101] Certainly in contrast to other manifestations of "competence creep",[102] EU-level influence on national healthcare reforms with regard to antitrust might be considered more "responsive", with varying degrees of subtlety. A clear example would be the enactment of Article 122 Dutch Health Insurance Act 2006 (*Zorgverzekeringswet*) to ensure that private health insurers were subject to Dutch (if not EU) competition law in response to the finding of non-applicability of the antitrust rules to German sickness funds in *AOK Bundesverband*.[103] A further example would be the creation of a hybrid prohibition on "anti-competitive behaviour"[104] reflecting terminology of Articles 101 and 102 TFEU introduced as part of the competition legislation governing the English National Health Service, amid concerns prior to Brexit about the reach of *EU* (sometimes as distinct from UK) competition law in this regard.[105]

In order to gain further insight into constitutionalism in this area, it is useful to examine the division of competences between the Member States and the EUin Article 168(7) TFEU and how this interacts with applying the state aid rules in the healthcare context, before considering how responses to the COVID-19 pandemic—particularly the development of a European Health Union—may now shape approaches in this area.

---

[100] This has been considered both in the wider connection with the free movement rules, and exclusively with regard to EU competition policy/state aid by lawyers and political scientists. See, respectively, Van de Gronden and Szyszczak 2011; Morton 2021, 2022.

[101] Directive 2011/24/EU of the European Parliament and of the Council of 9 March 2011 on the application of patients' rights in cross-border healthcare.

[102] See, for example, Garben 2020.

[103] See further Van de Gronden and Szyszczak 2014.

[104] Now repealed by the Health and Care Act 2022, but Section 64(2) Health and Social Care Act 2012 provided:

> 'Anti-competitive behaviour' means behaviour which would (or would be like to) prevent, restrict or distort competition and a reference to preventing anti-competitive behaviour includes a reference to eliminating or reducing the effects (or potential effects) of the behaviour.

[105] For further discussion, see Guy 2023.

2.3.1 *The Interaction Between Article 168(7) TFEU and the State Aid Rules*

Article 168(7) TFEU provides in essence:

> Union action shall respect the responsibilities of the Member States for the definition of their health policy and for the organisation and delivery of health services and medical care. The responsibilities of the Member States shall include the management of health services and medical care and the allocation of the resources assigned to them.[...][106]

Relative to its predecessor, Article 152(5) EC, it has been considered, variously, that the Member State competence regarding healthcare looked "more protected" under Article 168(7) TFEU,[107] and that the shift from the requirement that "Community action shall fully respect" to Union action merely respecting "the responsibilities of the Member States" left open more room for EU involvement.[108] While these different views are difficult to reconcile, the description of Article 168(7) TFEU as introducing a "delicate and sophisticated balance" between the EU and national competences in healthcare[109] nevertheless remains valid.

The link between Article 168(7) TFEU and the state aid rules appears most clear with the specification of the Member State competence including "the allocation of resources assigned to [health services]". However the reach of EU-level influence via other means—notably fiscal policy—may serve to influence this indirectly insofar as it can be considered that requirements for Member States to engage with fiscal constraints vary according to aspects such as membership of the Eurozone, and level of indebtedness. This was illustrated by the varying instruments implemented in the aftermath of the 2008-2009 economic downturn,[110] but could equally apply to the after-effects of the COVID-19 pandemic and varying implications for different Member States. Indeed it has been recognised by the Commission that the Resilience and Recovery Facility could benefit the health sector in many cases.[111]

Nevertheless, Article 168(7) TFEU has been characterised as a "subsidiarity clause for healthcare".[112] What the implications are for this with regard to the interaction with EU competition policy, and specifically the state aid rules, are evolving. In the case law, perhaps surprisingly little attention is paid to Article 168(7) TFEU, although it has been deemed a "wide discretion",[113] and raised with regard to arguments outlining Member State freedom to choose, for example, how to organise

---

[106] The final sentence is not directly relevant to the present discussion, but for the sake of completeness, provides "The measures referred to in paragraph 4(a) shall not affect national provisions on the donation or medical use of organs and blood."

[107] Piris 2010, p. 320.

[108] Van de Gronden and Szyszczak 2011, p. 486.

[109] Ibid.

[110] See further Guy 2020b.

[111] European Commission 2022, p. 28.

[112] Hancher and Sauter 2012, e.g. p. 221.

[113] Commission Decision C(2017) 7973 final of 4 December 2017 on State aid SA.39913 (2017/NN) Alleged compensation of public hospitals in Lazio, para 48.

health insurance,[114] and to include private medical insurance within social and health policy.[115]

A useful starting-point was outlined in terms of the causal logic of decisions having perhaps unintended, or undesired consequences. Thus, if a Member State decides to introduce competition into the healthcare system, then competition law will apply, and "[t]his effective delegation of the applicability of competition law to national authorities is in line with both the principle of subsidiarity [...] and the vesting of the primary responsibility for the organization and delivery of healthcare and medical care in Member States under [Article 152 EC]."[116] This interpretation might be further understood in terms of a wider distinguishing of subsidiarity, which frames this as concerned with promoting the efficiency of governance, rather than promoting autonomy of the Member States.[117] Certainly this might be inferred from recent case findings—notably by the CJEU in *Dôvera* and the General Court in *Casa Regina Apostolorum*—suggesting that national reforms in, respectively, Slovakia and Italy, have been insufficient to displace the solidarity basis of the healthcare systems. Whether this amounts to a streamlining of governance approaches at the EU level is moot. On the one hand, this would seem to offer an explanation for consistent case law findings that EU competition policy does not apply which may be easier to maintain than finding the existence of an "economic activity" but then establishing that there is no effect on trade between Member States. Indeed, scope for effects on trade between Member States may vary—while support to public hospitals may be confined to a single country (or even region),[118] support regarding insurance schemes may prove wider-ranging insofar as insurers may operate in more than one Member State. On the other hand, by effectively delegating responsibility for determining applicability of EU competition policy, and potential application of this at a national level, further governance complications may arise in light of the scope for divergent approaches.

2.3.2 *Developing the European Health Union—What Role for State Aid and SGEI in Healthcare?*

Section 2.2 above considered one aspect of the Commission's response to the COVID-19 pandemic, namely, the development of the SATF and how this might

---

[114] Commission Decision (EU) 2015/248 of 15 October 2014 on the measures SA.23008 (2013/C) (ex 2013/NN) implemented by Slovak Republic for Spoločná zdravotná poisťovňa, a. s. (SZP) and Všeobecná zdravotná poisťovňa, a. s. (VZP), para 64.

[115] CJEU (GC), *British United Provident Association Ltd (BUPA), BUPA Insurance Ltd, BUPA Ireland Ltd v Commission*, Judgment, 12 February 2008, T-289/03, para 164.

[116] Prosser 2010, pp. 323–324.

[117] See further Panara 2022.

[118] As noted in Commission Decision C(2015) 2796 final of 29 April 2015 on SA.37432 (2015/NN) Funding to public hospitals in the Hradec Králové Region.

further our understanding of how healthcare activities have been, and may continue to be, regarded vis-à-vis the state aid rules. A further aspect of the EU-level response has been the development of a European Health Union. This was motivated in part by perceptions that initial pandemic responses at EU level were found wanting, prompting questions about the EU's competence and whether this extended beyond the obvious source of a single Treaty provision (Article 168 TFEU). Such misconceptions were attributed in part to the political salience of Article 168(7) TFEU—that the EU-level response was necessarily constrained "because the Member States wanted it so".[119] The initial enthusiasm for "more" EU in healthcare led to suggestions that Treaty change may result,[120] and from this a suggestion that an extended public health competence would require a policy decision on how state aid rules should adapt to the new constitutional cadre.[121] The idea that the state aid rules could play an instrumental role in shaping a European Health Union was explored by parallels being drawn with healthcare exemptions modelled on the General Block Exemption Regulation in light of the Commission's experience of analysing health as an SGEI.[122] Further suggestions involved scope for EU funding of healthcare to be managed by analogy with the European Structural and Investment Funds, or via clearer links between the Member State and EU levels through the creation of networks.[123] However, the initial outlining of the construction of the European Health Union made clear that its basis would be the EU's competence to adopt incentive measures (under Article 168(5) TFEU), albeit with acknowledgement that "The European Health Union will be as strong as its Member States' commitments to it."[124]

This enthusiasm for greater EU-level competence in health became tempered over time to delegating this for discussion at the Conference on the Future of Europe,[125] and in 2021 it was played down to clarification that "[a] strong European Health Union is not about redrawing the competences of Member States".[126] However, what has emerged in 2022, is a clear call—recognised by the European Parliament[127]—for a refocusing of EU and Member State competence regarding health from the

[119] De Ruijter and Greer 2020.

[120] Nielsen N (2020) EU Commission aspires for Treaty change on health. Euractiv, 29 May 2020.

[121] Biondi and Ştefan 2020.

[122] Ibid.

[123] Ibid.

[124] Communication from the Commission of 11 November 2020 to the European Parliament, the Council, the European Economic and Social Committee and the Committee of the Regions. Building a European Health Union: Reinforcing the EU's resilience for cross-border health threats, COM(2020) 724 final.

[125] Von der Leyen 2020.

[126] Deutsch J (2021) Europe's 'health union' prepares for its first feeble steps. Politico, 1 September 2021.

[127] European Parliament resolution of 4 May 2022 on the follow-up to the conclusions of the Conference on the Future of Europe (2022/2648(RSP)) (OJ C 465, pp. 109–111).

Conference on the Future of Europe such that this becomes a shared competence by amending Article 4 TFEU.[128]

2.4 Conclusions

This chapter has sought to provide an update to considerations of how healthcare has been regarded in the context of EU competition policy in general, and the state aid rules in particular since the wider-ranging 2009 review of competition and solidarity.[129] Starting from the premise that markets in healthcare could no longer be ignored at that time,[130] it has reviewed key cases and policy developments to provide a picture of the "state of the art" in the first half of the 2020s. This has generated at least three insights.

Firstly, that, by framing the interaction between healthcare and the state aid rules in terms of a continuum of SGI, SGEI and Article 107(3) TFEU, it becomes possible to consider both competition and constitutional aspects. While these are not mutually exclusive, it is nevertheless submitted that constitutional aspects offer a way to advance ongoing discussion about the extent of applicability of the state aid rules.

Secondly, that having further understanding of how the subsidiarity principle operates in healthcare may give insights into state aid decisions as well. For example, by considering Article 168(7) TFEU in the context of the wider discussion of subsidiarity as being concerned with governance rather than autonomy, it becomes possible to understand further the tensions between EU-level and Member State competence regarding healthcare. The effect of wider EU policies—notably regarding fiscal governance in light of the 2008 economic downturn and likely also the COVID-19 pandemic—can also be shown to have an effect on national competence with regard to allocating resources to healthcare services.

Thirdly, that drawing insights from different aspects and interpretations of EU law and policy becomes inevitable in light of wider circumstances. Thus it is unsurprising that the 2019 review of the 2012 SGEI package should make copious reference to the COVID-19 pandemic. The proposals for adding healthcare as a shared competence emanating from the Conference on the Future of Europe—although not expressly mentioned by the Commission's review—might also be considered in this regard.

Finally, that there is a prevalence of state aid decisions in connection with healthcare being assessed as following the "concrete" or "attenuated functional" approaches. This indicates that this might be the intuitive approach for state aid (as distinct from antitrust) cases as these deal fundamentally with questions of government financing and organisation of national healthcare systems. However, these

[128] Conference on the Future of Europe, Report on the final outcome, May 2022. Recommendation 49, p. 64. https://www.europarl.europa.eu/resources/library/media/20220509RES29121/20220509RES29121.pdf.

[129] Krajewski et al. 2009.

[130] Szyszczak 2009.

approaches also give insights into a framework which might evolve further post-*Casa Regina Apostolorum* as approaches from *CEPPB*—a "disaggregation" logic of separating activities, if not clear recourse to the "three-prong test" —may be adopted into the healthcare context.

References

Belhaj S, Van de Gronden J (2004) Some room for competition does not make a sickness fund an undertaking. Is EC competition law applicable to the health care sector? (Joined cases C-264/01, C-306/01, C-453/01 and C-355/01 AOK). European Competition Law Review 25(11):682–687.

Biondi A, Ştefan O (2020) EU Health Union and State Aid Policy: With Great(er) Power Comes Great Responsibility. European Journal of Risk Regulation – Beyond COVID-19: Towards a European Health Union 11(4):894–902.

Boeger N (2007) Solidarity and EC Competition Law. European Law Review 32:319–340.

Burke JM (2018) A Critical Account of Article 106(2) TFEU – Government Failure in Public Service Provision. Hart, Oxford.

Cseres KJ, Reyna A (2021) EU State Aid Law and Consumer Protection: An Unsettled Relationship in Times of Crisis. Journal of European Competition Law & Practice 12(8):617–629.

De Cecco F (2013) State Aid and the European Economic Constitution. Hart, Oxford.

De Ruijter A, Greer SL (2020) EU health law and policy in and after the COVID-19 crisis. European Journal of Public Health 30(4):623–624.

De Vries SA (2011) *BUPA*: A Healthy Case, in the Light of a Changing Constitutional Setting in Europe? In: Van de Gronden JW et al. (eds) Health Care and EU Law. T.M.C. Asser Press, The Hague, pp 289–311.

European Commission (2022) Evaluation of the State subsidy rules for health and social services of general economic interest ("SGEIs") and of the SGEI de minimis Regulation {SWD(2022) 389 final}.

Friederiszick HW et al. (2007) European State Aid Control: An Economic Framework. In: Buccirossi P (ed) Handbook of Antitrust Economics. MIT Press, Cambridge, pp 625–671.

Gallo D, Mariotti C (2017) The Public Financing of Belgian Hospitals and EU Law: A Core Development in the Field of State Aid. In: Mastroianni R, Arena A (eds) 60 Years of EU Competition Law. Editoriale Scientifica, Naples, pp 173–198.

Garben S (2020) From sneaking to striding: Combatting competence creep and consolidating the EU legislative process. European Law Journal 26:429–447.

Giosa P (2023) Assessing the Use of the State Aid Covid Temporary Framework with Regard to the Healthcare and Media Sector. Journal of European Competition Law & Practice 14(5): 274–289.

Greaney T, Odudu O (2022) Introduction to Antitrust and the Provision of Healthcare in the United States and European Union. In: Orentlicher D, Hervey TK (eds) The Oxford Handbook of Comparative Health Law. Oxford University Press, Oxford, pp 311–315.

Guy M (2019) Competition Policy in Healthcare – Frontiers in Insurance-Based and Taxation-Funded Systems. Intersentia, Cambridge.

Guy M (2020a) Can COVID-19 change the EU competition law framework in health? Observatoire Social Europèen Brussels Opinion Paper No. 25, September 2020.

Guy M (2020b) Towards a European Health Union: What Role for Member States? European Journal of Risk Regulation – Beyond COVID-19: Towards a European Health Union 11(4): 757–765.

Guy M (2023) Dealing with "unworkable ideas in primary legislation": Juridifying and dejuridifying competition in the English National Health Service. Public Law 57–80.

Guy M (2025) On The Quiet Power of National Decisions: Hospitals, State Aid, and Services of General Economic Interest. Journal of Law, Medicine, and Ethics (FirstView): 1–11.

Hancher L, Sauter W (2012) EU Competition and Internal Market Law in the Health Care Sector. Oxford University Press, Oxford.
Hancher L, Sauter W (2013) This Won't Hurt A Bit: The Commission's Approach to Services of General Economic Interest and State Aid to Hospitals. In: Szyszczak E, Van de Gronden JW (eds) Financing Services of General Economic Interest – Reform and Modernization. T.M.C. Asser Press, The Hague, pp 249–272.
Krajewski M et al. (2009) The Changing Legal Framework for Services of General Interest in Europe – Between Competition and Solidarity. T.M.C. Asser Press, The Hague.
Morton AJB (2021) European Health Care Systems and the Emerging Influence of European Union Competition Policy. Journal of Health Politics, Policy and Law 46(3):468–486.
Morton AJB (2022) Re-establishing needed limits: European competition policy's role in European healthcare systems and the lessons of the *Dôvera* case. Social Policy Administration 56(3):472–484.
Nikolić B (2021) Applicability of European Union Competition Law to Health Care Providers: The Dividing Line between Economic and Noneconomic Activities. Journal of Health Politics, Policy and Law 46(1):49–70.
Odudu O (2022) Health Care Services and EU Competition Law. In: Orentlicher D, Hervey TK (eds) The Oxford Handbook of Comparative Health Law. Oxford University Press, Oxford, pp 316–348.
Panara C (2022) Subsidiarity v Autonomy in the EU. European Public Law 28(2):269–296.
Piris J-C (2010) The Lisbon Treaty: A Legal and Political Analysis. Cambridge University Press, Cambridge.
Prosser T (2005) The Limits of Competition Law – Markets and Public Services. Oxford University Press, Oxford.
Prosser T (2010) EU competition law and public services. In: Mossialos E et al. (eds) Health Systems Governance in Europe – The Role of European Union Law and Policy. Cambridge University Press, Cambridge, pp 315–336.
Ross M (2009) A healthy approach to services of general economic interest? The *BUPA* judgment of the Court of First Instance. European Law Review 34(1):127–140.
Sánchez Graells A (2015) New rules for health care procurement in the UK: a critical assessment from the perspective of EU economic law. Public Procurement Law Review 1:16–30.
Sauter W (2014) Public Services in EU Law. Cambridge University Press, Cambridge.
Skovgaard Ølykke G, Møllgaard P (2016) What is a Service of General Economic Interest? European Journal of Law and Economics 41:205–241.
Szyszczak E (2009) Modernising Healthcare: Pilgrimage for the Holy Grail? In: Krajewski M et al. (eds) The Changing Legal Framework for Services of General Interest in Europe – Between Competition and Solidarity. T.M.C. Asser Press, The Hague, pp 191–214.
Van de Gronden JW (2004) Purchasing care: economic activity or service of general (economic) interest? European Competition Law Review 25(2):87–94.
Van de Gronden JW (2011) The Treaty Provisions on Competition and Health Care'. In: Van de Gronden JW et al. (eds) Health Care and EU Law. T.M.C. Asser Press, The Hague, pp 265–294.
Van de Gronden JW (2018) Services of General Interest and the concept of undertaking. Does EU competition law apply? World Competition 41(2):197–224.
Van de Gronden JW (2023) Een stille revolutie op de Kirchberg: leidt de zaak Casa Regina Apostolorum tot een terugtrekkende beweging van het mededingingsrecht in de zorg? ("A quiet revolution in Luxembourg: does the Casa Regina Apostolorum judgment mean a step back for competition law in healthcare?") SEW 9.
Van de Gronden JW, Guy M (2021) The role of EU competition law in health care and the 'undertaking' concept. Health Economics, Policy and Law 16(1):76–89.
Van de Gronden JW, Rusu CS (2013) The Altmark Update and Social Services: Towards a European Approach. In: Szyszczak E, Van de Gronden JW (eds) Financing Services of General Economic Interest – Reform and Modernization. T.M.C. Asser Press, The Hague, pp 185–216.

Van de Gronden JW, Rusu CS (2017) EU competition law and policy and health systems. In: Hervey TK et al. (eds) Research Handbook on EU Health Law and Policy. Edward Elgar, Cheltenham, pp 267–290.

Van de Gronden JW, Rusu CS (2024) Competition Law in the EU: Principles, Substance, Enforcement, 2nd edn. Edward Elgar, Cheltenham.

Van de Gronden JW, Szyszczak E (2011) Conclusions: Constructing a 'Solid' Multi-Layered Health Care Edifice. In: Van de Gronden JW et al. (eds) Health Care and EU Law. T.M.C. Asser Press, The Hague, pp 481–495.

Van de Gronden JW, Szyszczak E (2014) Introducing Competition Principles into Health Care Through EU Law and Policy: A Case Study of the Netherlands. Medical Law Review 22(2):238–354.

Von der Leyen U (2020) State of the Union Address by President von der Leyen at the European Parliament Plenary, 16 September 2020.

Wehlander C (2016) Services of General Economic Interest as a Constitutional Concept of EU Law. T.M.C. Asser Press, The Hague.

Other Documents

Conference on the Future of Europe (2022) Report on the Final Outcome. https://www.europarl.europa.eu/resources/library/media/20220509RES29121/20220509RES29121.pdf.

Mary Guy is Senior Lecturer in Public and EU Law at Liverpool John Moores University. She is also co-coordinator of the EU Health Governance Research Network.

Chapter 3
Healthcare (Hospital) Mergers in the Netherlands and Services in the General Economic Interest

Daniel James Arthur Clark

Contents

Abstract This chapter explores how the Netherlands Authority for Consumers and Markets (ACM) could better integrate public interest considerations—specifically the concept of Services of General Economic Interest (SGEI)—into the substantive assessment of hospital mergers. The chapter argues that the current Dutch merger control regime, which historically has shown inconsistency in considering public interest objectives such as accessibility, affordability, and quality of care, lacks a robust analytical framework for systematically incorporating these goals. The article contributes a practical and comparative perspective on how competition law can evolve to accommodate non-market values in the healthcare sector without compromising legal certainty or institutional integrity.

Keywords Healthcare mergers · Public interest · Services of General Economic Interest (SGEI) · Dutch competition law · Merger control · Comparative competition policy

D. J. A. Clark (✉)
Rotterdam, The Netherlands
e-mail: clarkdja@gmail.com

N. Ghazaryan et al. (eds.), *Services of General (Economic) Interest and EU Law*, Legal Issues of Services of General Interest, https://doi.org/10.1007/978-94-6265-723-6_3

3.1 Introduction

The regulation of the healthcare sector has always and will likely remain a complicated and politically charged question, given the profound impact of the sector on people's lives and the conscience of the broader community.[1] Due to this link to the core values of humanity, there is an inherent political importance attached to mergers in the healthcare sector, which often involve 'public interests that are not easily caught by the competition policy framework'.[2] Competition was introduced to the Dutch healthcare market in 2006. The healthcare market has a number of important sub-markets, particularly those for health insurance and healthcare provision. The focus of this contribution falls on the particular sub-market of healthcare provision, more specifically the hospital market. In particular, the substantive assessment of mergers by the ACM in this particular sector.

This is a particularly topical issue, as the previous healthcare specific merger regime expired at the end of 2022. There is a standing legislative proposal for the so called tightening of this assessment regime including the transfer of certain powers from the NZa to the ACM.[3] However, as of the date of writing, these proposals have yet to be adopted.[4] Accordingly, it is an opportune moment to critically reflect on the current and historical substantive assessment of mergers in this politically and socially relevant market and opine on whether there may be beneficial changes that could be made.

With this in mind, the central research question of this chapter is, which role could or should SGEI play in the assessment of hospital cases by the ACM. In order to answer this question, this chapter will explore (i) the ACM's decision making record in selected hospital mergers; (ii) the interpretation of Article 41(3) of the Mw (the SGEI provision) in light of the PostNL merger saga; (iii) take some lessons from the South African experience of including public interest considerations in the substantive assessment of mergers, and (iv) apply these to the Dutch approach to healthcare mergers including highlighting shortcomings in this approach with respect to political interference, a lack of explicit interests and clear framework for the weighing up of these interests against public interest considerations.

Public interest considerations have been explicitly incorporated in the substantive assessment of mergers undertaken by the South African competition authorities, since the Competition Act 1998 came into force. Accordingly, there is a relatively well-developed body of case law and scholarly writing interpreting and assessing the inclusion of public interest considerations in the substantive assessment of mergers in South Africa, when compared with most other jurisdictions.[5] Therefore, the

---

[1] Canoy and Sauter 2009, p. 5.

[2] Ibid.

[3] Ministry of Health, Welfare and Sport 2020.

[4] See https://www.tweedekamer.nl/kamerstukken/wetsvoorstellen/detail?qry=wetsvoorstel%3A34445&cfg=wetsvoorsteldetails. Accessed 16 April 2023.

[5] Clark 2022, para 1.1.

South African experience in this context offers the opportunity to develop some key takeaways and apply these to the Dutch experience with hospital mergers.

3.2 ACM Assessment of Hospital Mergers

3.2.1 Introduction

Firstly, it is helpful to provide some key context surrounding the nature of competition and merger activity in the hospital market, including briefly introducing the ACM's attitude to a greater role being afforded to the 'public interest'. Secondly, several key cases are identified and discussed to illustrate the different approaches adopted.

In an explanatory note published on 5 December 2017, the ACM stated that it:

> [recognises] the desire among lawmakers and the public for extra safeguards for the public interests of affordability, accessibility, and quality, which have been explicitly identified as such for health care, or for additional interests such as 'the human dimension.[6]

Roos charts the development of the hospital market in the Netherlands and finds that it 'has become increasingly concentrated over the past 40 years'.[7] Following a thorough analysis of mergers (and similar transactional activity) in the sector, Roos concludes that 'given the often irreversible nature and potentially adverse consequences of consolidation in healthcare markets, policy measures that enhance or facilitate consolidation should not be taken lightly and should be carefully investigated before they are implemented'.[8]

3.2.2 Healthcare Specific Merger Control Regime

Pursuant to the Minister's formal indication, the previous healthcare specific merger regime expired at the end of 2022.[9] The previous regime included several elements that were healthcare specific. First, the scope for merger control in this sector was broader than for other markets due to the lowering of notification thresholds by Ministerial decree, with regard to mergers involving at least two parties that provide healthcare.[10] Second, the Minister has made a binding rule regarding concentrations of healthcare providers and healthcare insurers. Pursuant to this rule, if the merger would result in a market share of 35% or more, the ACM was required to take into

[6] ACM 2017, p. 3.

[7] Roos 2018, p. 44.

[8] Ibid., p. 247.

[9] Ministry of Health, Welfare and Sport 2022.

[10] Besluit van 6 december 2007, houdende tijdelijke verruiming van het toepassingsbereik van het concentratietoezicht op ondernemingen die zorg verlenen.

account certain healthcare specific factors, including transparency of quality of care and patient travel behaviour.[11] Lastly, the ACM has published specific guidelines for the healthcare sector.[12] Pursuant to these guidelines the ACM (previously the NMa) will request the NZa's opinion regarding a proposed merger.[13] The NZa investigates the impact that the proposed merger will have on the public interest. The specific public interests listed are the affordability, quality, and accessibility (collectively, the 'healthcare objectives') of the relevant healthcare concerned.

There is an existing proposal to provide for further tightening of the supervision of healthcare mergers. This proposal includes the shifting of the NZa specific merger related powers to the ACM.[14] However, it remains unclear whether this proposal will be adopted.[15]

3.2.3 Key Cases

Very few proposed mergers in the hospital market have been prohibited to date. Van de Gronden helpfully identifies three distinct approaches by the ACM in its decision making, with regard to the taking into account of these health care objectives.[16] This analysis is illustrative of the different approaches taken by the ACM (and its predecessor, the NMa) to this issue. The approach of the ACM has been inconsistent and a clear approach has yet to be developed by the Dutch courts or the ACM. Accordingly, given the large number of notified mergers in this sector, it is appropriate to simply set out a few examples of the diverging approaches of the ACM over the years.

In a merger involving two hospitals in the Gooi region, first notified in 2004, the ACM raised competition concerns for the first time in a hospital merger. Initially, the ACM decided that in the circumstances, a licence would be required.[17] During this initial phase, the ACM defined the relevant geographic market rather narrowly using a static method focused on the 'actual travelling behaviour of patients'.[18] Following

[11] Beleidsregel van de Minister van Economische Zaken van 5 juli 2013, nr. WJZ/13118300, houdende bijzonder regels betreffende concentraties van zorgaanbieders en zorgverzekeraars, Article 2.

[12] Richtsnoeren voor de zorgsector [Guidelines for the health sector]. ACM, March 2010 These guidelines are available at: https://www.acm.nl/nl/publicaties/publicatie/7083/Richtsnoeren-voor-de-zorgsector.

[13] Ibid., para 143.

[14] Ministry of Health, Welfare and Sport 2020.

[15] Schrijvershof D et al. (2022) Healthcare mergers reviews in 2022: ACM remains critical. https://www.maverick-law.com/en/blogs/healthcare-mergers-reviews-in-2022-acm-remains-critical.html. Accessed 10 April 2023.

[16] Van de Gronden and Szyszczak 2014, p. 249 ff.

[17] Van de Gronden and Szyszczak 2014, p. 250.

[18] Decision of the ACM No. 3897/156 of 8 June 2005 in Case No. 3897/*Ziekenhuis Hilversum – Ziekenhuis Gooi-Noord*, paras 58 and 60.

extensive further research, the ACM did not finally decide on the relevant geographic market. However, it did find that the market was broader than merely the Gooi region, as defined in its initial decision. On the basis of this, a number of hospitals nearby to the Gooi region were included in the market definition, which 'exercise sufficient competitive pressure'.[19] Accordingly, the ACM ultimately approved the merger based on a different approach to the geographic market definition.[20] Van de Gronden characterised this as an approach where competition-based concerns take precedence and healthcare objectives are only considered 'incidentally'.[21]

A change of strategy is identified in the approach of the ACM to a proposed merger of two hospitals in Zealand.[22] The ACM had previously rejected the proposed merger in 2005, which would broadly speaking, have left only one hospital to serve the remote province.[23] An efficiency defence was raised by the merging parties including a positive impact on the healthcare objectives. The ACM rejected this claim on the basis of insufficient substantiation and the parties withdrew the notification.[24] However, faced with a very similar proposed merger in 2009, the ACM gave far more consideration to the efficiency defence raised by the parties.

The merging parties argued that the merger was necessary with reference to the healthcare objectives. The ACM took the view that the efficiency defence could be applied to the healthcare objectives.[25] It is debatable to what extent this accords with the Horizontal Guidelines, which focus on economic benefits.[26] However, on application of the efficiency defence criteria, the ACM found insufficient evidence to show that the requirement of verifiable benefits had been met.[27] Ultimately, the ACM granted conditional approval, addressing this shortcoming through imposing conditions.[28] In doing so, the ACM emphasised the importance of the report issued by the Dutch Healthcare Inspectorate, which found that the merger was required to realise the healthcare objectives.[29] In short, this approach can be characterised as the ACM attempting to incorporate the healthcare objectives within the efficiency defence.[30]

[19] Ibid., para 102.

[20] Ibid., para 114; Van de Gronden and Szyszczak 2014, p. 250.

[21] Van de Gronden and Szyszczak 2014, p. 250.

[22] Ibid.

[23] Decision of the ACM No. 6424/427 of 25 March 2009 in Case 6424/*Walcheren Hospital – Oosterschelde Hospitals*; Van de Gronden and Szyszczak 2014, p. 251.

[24] Van de Gronden and Szyszczak 2014, p. 251. https://www.acm.nl/nl/publicaties/publicatie/5609/Aanvraag-vergunning-Zeeuwse-ziekenhuizen-ingetrokken. Accessed 7 May 2023.

[25] Decision of the ACM No. 6424/427 of 25 March 2009 in Case 6424/*Walcheren Hospital – Oosterschelde Hospitals*, p. 14; Van de Gronden and Szyszczak 2014, p. 252.

[26] Guidelines on the assessment of horizontal mergers under the Council Regulation on the control of concentrations between undertakings (OJ C 31, pp. 5–18), paras 76, 77 and 88.

[27] Decision of the ACM No. 6424/427 of 25 March 2009 in Case 6424/*Walcheren Hospital – Oosterschelde Hospitals*, paras 147–150.

[28] Ibid., paras 175–178.

[29] Ibid., para 58; Van de Gronden and Szyszczak 2014, p. 252.

[30] Clark 2022, para 5.2.

Van de Gronden then identifies another change in approach by the ACM to a series of proposed mergers around 2012 that involved the accretion of high market shares in the relevant markets.[31] The ACM's approach to clearing these mergers focused on the countervailing buyer power that healthcare insurance companies would exert on these merged hospitals.[32] In this approach, the healthcare objectives are incorporated within the economic and competition law concept of countervailing buyer power.[33]

Van de Gronden concludes that the manner in which healthcare objectives will be considered within the substantive assessment of mergers, remains an open question. He calls for a 'clearer and more transparent approach to be developed at EU level'.[34] Reflecting on some of the approaches of the ACM to healthcare mergers where public interest goals are so obviously at stake, Sauter finds that 'regular merger control is unlikely to be sufficient to stop mergers that are not in the public interest'.[35] Roosenboom notes the lack of a proper 'analytical framework' in which competition authorities can include the healthcare objectives in their assessments.[36]

It is clear that the current framework is unsatisfactory and inadequate to properly reconcile the public interests at play in hospital mergers with competition concerns.

3.3 SGEIs in Dutch Merger Control

Pursuant to Article 41(3) of the Mw, if at least one of the merging parties is tasked with the provision of an SGEI, then the merger can only be prohibited if that decision would not hinder the provision of this SGEI. Pursuant to guidance issued by the ACM, the provision should be interpreted restrictively, as it amounts to an exception by which the competition-based focus of the Mw is limited.[37] SGEIs are inherently goods or services, which are public in nature and may in certain cases not be offered on the market without government intervention. Accordingly, by providing this specific regime for SGEIs, the public interest is considered within the overall substantive assessment of mergers.

In the *PostNL* merger, the ACM considered the application of this Article 41(3) for the first time.[38] The ACM held that in the absence of the merger, the provision of the

[31] Van de Gronden and Szyszczak 2014, p. 252.

[32] See, for example, Decision of the ACM No. 7236/659 of 2 November 2012 in Case 7236/*Orbis – Atrium*, para 25, Decision of the ACM No. 7295/402 of 2 November 2012 in Case 7295/*TweeSteden Ziekenhuis – St. Elisabeth Ziekenhuis*, para 24 and Decision of the ACM No. 7332/92 of 14 February 2012 in Case 7332/*Spaarne Ziekenhuis – Kennemer Gasthuis*, para 21; Van de Gronden and Szyszczak 2014, p. 252.

[33] Van de Gronden and Szyszczak 2014, p. 253.

[34] Ibid., p. 255.

[35] Canoy and Sauter 2009, p. 9.

[36] Rosenboom 2018.

[37] Richtsnoeren voor de zorgsector (Guidelines for the health sector) (ACM, March 2010), para 175.

[38] Van Damme 2019.

SGEI could still be guaranteed. Accordingly, it did not deem it necessary to approve the merger to safeguard the provision of the SGEI concerned. The Minister then proceeded to approve the merger using section 47(1), whilst advancing arguments that primarily related to the continuity of universal postal delivery, an SGEI.

The Minister's decision taken on appeal, was subsequently annulled by the Rotterdam District Court on 11 June 2020, following a successful appeal.[39] The court ruled that the Minister's decision was not sufficiently substantiated.[40] Subsequently, the Minister approached the CBb for relief. In the interim, on 9 April 2021 the Minister again decided to grant a license for the merger pursuant to Article 47(1) of the Mw, with retrospective effect. This replacement decision automatically becomes part of the appeal proceedings in accordance with Articles 6:19 and 6:24 of the General Administrative Law Act (Awb). The Minister explained to Parliament that this decision was reached following additional research, in a clear reaction to the annulment of her previous decision.[41] The CBb gave final judgment on the appeal of the decision of the Rotterdam District Court, on 2 June 2022.

The CBb is the highest court in the Netherlands for merger control cases and, more generally, the public enforcement of competition law. The CBb's focus in this instance fell on the allocation of tasks between the ACM and the Minister, rather than assessing whether the new decision was now sufficiently substantiated as required by the Rotterdam District Court. The CBb outlined the clear delineation between the tasks of the Minister and the ACM when applying Article 47 of the Mw.[42] Subsequently, the CBb found that when making a decision pursuant to Article 47, the Minister is bound not only by the ACM's decision regarding a significant impediment to competition, but also the entire competition law assessment which forms the basis of this finding.

Pursuant to the CBb's judgment in the *Post NL* merger, the Minister is bound by the ACM's opinion regarding the SGEI assessment. This includes its analysis and conclusions drawn. By nature, the SGEI and public interest considerations are closely related and may overlap to a certain extent. However, the CBb's approach means that in its reasoning for approving the merger on public interest grounds, the Minister cannot rely on those grounds already assessed by the ACM in its enquiry. This essentially prevents the duplication of public interest considerations, by the ACM under Article 41 and by the Minister under Article 47.

In light of the central research question, it is interesting to consider whether Article 41(3) could not have been applied in the line of hospital mergers discussed earlier.[43] Whilst there may be issues with its specific application in each case, conceptually, if the public interest such as access to healthcare is implicated by a merger, arguably

[39] District Court of Rotterdam (Netherlands), *PostNL/Sandd*, Judgment, 11 June 2020, ROT 19/5687 and ROT 19/5708 (ECLI:NL:RBROT:2020:5122), para 14.1.

[40] Ibid.

[41] Ministry of Economic Affairs and Climate 2022, p. 2.

[42] Trade and Industry Appeals Tribunal (CBb) (Netherlands), Judgment, 2 June 2022, 20/638, 20/639, 20/1068 and 20/1069 (ECLI:NL:CBB:2022:289), para 6.5.

[43] Van de Gronden 2017, p. 254.

it could be considered that at least one of the undertakings is entrusted with the provision of an SGEI. Accordingly, based on the current wording of Article 41(3) of the Mw the enquiry would then be whether a refusal to approve the merger in this context would obstruct the performance of these entrusted duties by the undertakings concerned.

In a merger where one or more of the parties is involved in the provision of an SGEI, the possible public interest considerations raised by the Minister are affected by the ACM's assessment of the impact of the merger on the provision of the SGEI.

The so-called 'carve out' offered by the SGEI provision in the Mw provides a possible alternative method to reconcile the public interest with the competition-focused substantive test. Naturally, this would only be applicable if the requirements for application of this provision are met, particularly, that at least one of the proposed merging parties is charged with the provision of an SGEI.

As previously mentioned, the SGEI concept is an established one in the context of European state aid and competition law. At a European level, Röling argues that the 'SGEI exception' under Article 106(2) on the Treaty on the Functioning of the European Union, 'may be a useful legal instrument to protect public interests by state intervention within the competitive healthcare market'.[44] Furthermore, Röling discusses how this exception might be applied in the Netherlands in the healthcare sector as an instrument to protect certain public interests.[45] Importantly, certain criteria as set out in the Altmark case must be met for a member state to make use of the exception.[46] Röling concludes that the development of this instrument remains in its infancy and it is yet to be seen how this instrument could be used within the context of the liberalised and deregulated Dutch healthcare market.[47]

Accordingly, rather than trying to shoe-horn public interest considerations (in the form of the healthcare objectives) into the existing competition-centric approach, the SGEI mechanism approach could be used to balance the public interest in not obstructing the performance of an SGEI. The key being that this would only be the case in limited cases involving the provision of certain public healthcare services where this is justified as an exception to the market-orientated approach.

3.4 South African Experience

The competition authorities in South Africa are explicitly required to assess specific public interest factors in the substantive assessment of mergers.[48] There is a long line of case law and decisions in which the authorities have interpreted and applied

---

[44] Röling 2012, p. 26.

[45] Ibid., p. 40.

[46] Ibid., p. 49; CJEU, *Altmark Trans*, Judgment, 24 July 2003, C-280/00.

[47] Röling 2012, p. 50.

[48] Competition Act No. 89 of 1998 (South Africa), published on 30 November 1998, SA Act, s 12A.

the Competition Act (South Africa). An increasing politicisation of the substantive assessment of mergers together with an increasing focus on certain public interest considerations is clear from this experience.[49] This goes together with associated negative trends of uncertainty and a lack of transparency. However, several important lessons can be drawn from this experience.[50] In order to answer the sub-research questions, the focus in this part is on three major lessons, on the importance of: (i) managing political interference; (ii) explicit and sufficiently specified public interests; and (iii) a clear framework allowing for the reconciliation or weighing up competition and public interest considerations.

3.4.1 Managing Political Interference

Initially, decisions by the Competition Tribunal can be characterised as showing a circumspect approach by the decision-making bodies to the incorporation of public interest considerations in substantive merger assessment.[51] In the *Shell* case, the Tribunal emphasised the substantial importance of the public interest ground.[52] The Tribunal in this merger also warned against the dangers of being 'over-zealous' in its pursuit of its public interest mandate.[53]

Following from this initial period of circumspection, the merger of Walmart (the world's largest retailer) and Massmart and the manner in which the public interest concerns were assessed by the competition authorities, is seen by many as a significant moment in South African merger control.[54] A subsequent trend of increased ministerial involvement is identified by and attributed to this merger by many academics and practitioners alike.[55] The merger did not lead to any competition concerns as Walmart did not compete with Massmart and had a very limited procurement presence in South Africa.[56] However, several public interest concerns were potentially implicated by the merger, particularly regarding employment and the effect on the supplychain.[57] Faced with growing political pressure and several intervening parties, the Tribunal stuck to its previous non-interventionist stance regarding the public interest.[58]

[49] Clark 2022, para 2.5.

[50] Ibid.

[51] Angumuthoo et al. 2020, pp. 320 and 330.

[52] Competition Tribunal (South Africa), *Shell South Africa Proprietary Limited and Tepco Petroleum Proprietary Limited*, Decision, 22 February 2002, 66/LM/Oct01, para 38.

[53] Ibid., para 58.

[54] Griffiths and Gumbie 2015, p. 411; Davis 2019, p. 209.

[55] Angumuthoo et al. 2020, p. 323.

[56] Competition Tribunal (South Africa), *Walmart Stores Inc and Massmart Holdings Limited*, Decision, 29 June 2011, 73/LM/Dec10, para 26.

[57] Competition Tribunal (South Africa), *Walmart Stores Inc and Massmart Holdings Limited*, Decision, 29 June 2011, 73/LM/Dec10, para 22.

[58] Angumuthoo et al. 2020, p. 324.

In a particularly striking statement against the backdrop, the Tribunal noted that 'our job in merger control is not to make the world a better place, only to prevent it becoming worse as a result of a specific transaction'.[59] This decision was taken on appeal to the Competition Appeal Court of South Africa by the South African Commercial, Catering and Allied Workers Union (SACCAWU), based on 'criticism of the normative approach adopted by the Tribunal to the application of the Act'.[60] The CAC noted that the 'public interest concerns set out in s 12A demands that this court give tangible effect to the legislative ambition'.[61] This shows a further departure from the previous cautious or deferential approach followed by the Tribunal. The court emphasised that negative effects on the public interest must be addressed. The court noted the limitations of competition regulators. However, it maintained that effect be given to their public interest mandate.[62]

Subsequent cases, such as *Coca-Cola*[63] and *AB InBev*[64] show increasing involvement by government Ministers and/or powerful trade unions in the merger control process.[65] This has tended to result in more and more conditions being attached to mergers, even in some cases despite the absence of competition concerns.[66]

The development of the decision-making record in South Africa, serves to highlight the potential for political interference in the merger control process. When public interest concerns surround a merger, it often becomes a relevant matter of interest to 'society at large' or the 'general public' as it were. Politicians, key government ministers and other stakeholders desire to become involved. Explicitly including the public interest grounds in the substantive assessment framework and providing for broader stakeholder involvement, makes the South African competition authorities arguably more inherently open to political influence. The influence accorded to these political considerations must be carefully managed to avoid prioritising the public interest over competition concerns.[67] A transparent and consistent process is required to avoid each merger assessment becoming a 'bespoke engagement', which commentators have pilloried as 'merger control by negotiation'.[68] However, as is pointed out later in this chapter with reference to the *PostNL* merger saga, the Dutch

---

[59] Competition Tribunal (South Africa), *Walmart Stores Inc and Massmart Holdings Limited*, Decision, 29 June 2011, 73/LM/Dec10, para 32.

[60] Competition Appeal Court (South Africa), *South African Commercial, Catering and Allied Workers Union (SACCAWU) v Walmart Stores Inc and Another*, Judgment, 9 March 2012, 110/CAC/Jul11 and 111/CAC/Jun11, para 91.

[61] Ibid., para 154.

[62] Clark 2022, para 2.3.

[63] Competition Tribunal (South Africa), *Coca-Cola Beverages Africa Limited and Various Coca-Cola and Related Bottling Operations*, Decision, 22 April 2016, LM242Mar15/DSC005Apr16.

[64] Competition Tribunal (South Africa), *Anheuser – Busch InBev SANN and SABMiller plc*, Decision, 4 August 2016, LM211Jan16.

[65] Clark 2022, para 2.3.3.

[66] Ibid., para 2.4.1.

[67] Ibid., para 5.3.1.

[68] Ibid., para 2.4.1.

system of providing a separate expressly political procedure is not the silver bullet that addresses all of these concerns.[69]

If a specialised competition assessment body is required to assess public interest concerns, procedural safeguards must be in place to ensure and protect the independence of this body. The procedure should be as open and transparent as possible. This includes the manner in which other stakeholders such as Ministers and trade unions are consulted and communicated with during the process.[70]

3.4.2 *Specification of Public Interests*

In South African merger control, a list of specific public interest grounds is explicitly included in the substantive assessment to be undertaken by the competition authorities. The competition authorities are required to weigh up the competition and public interest concerns regarding a specific merger, which may not always point in the same direction.[71]

The more precisely the public interest grounds are defined by the legislator, the easier it is for the competition authorities to implement the public interest component of its assessment. It is important to reserve some level of flexibility given the broader nature of the interests concerned. However, a list of more concrete categories of public interest concerns or some examples of what should be considered, is helpful in providing a level of predictability and certainty for decision-makers and stakeholders. This list should provide an indication of what should be considered, without being exhaustive or overly restrictive.[72]

3.4.3 *Assessment Framework*

A critical analysis of the South African experience arguably shows that an inclusive approach can be a workable method to incorporate the public interest in substantive merger assessment.[73] In this context, workable means an approach that delivers relatively predictable and transparent results that accord sufficient priority to competition concerns, whilst still giving due consideration to the public interest. An inclusive approach means that the competition authorities are responsible for assessing both competition and public interest concerns regarding a merger and then weighing up these interests.[74]

---

[69] Ibid., para 5.3.1.

[70] Ibid., para 5.3.3 (g).

[71] Ibid., para 5.2.

[72] Ibid., para 5.3.3 (d).

[73] Ibid., para 5.3.2.

[74] Ibid., para 2.4.3.

Importantly, in addition to specifying which public interests should be considered, the manner or structural design and procedural method of this assessment should be clear. This becomes particularly important where competition interests and other public interests may point in opposite directions. For example, it could be stipulated that competition concerns take primacy and that other public interest concerns would only override these competition concerns in exceptional situations where there would be no other manner in which to address these concerns other than for example, approving an anti-competitive merger to ensure the accessibility of healthcare in a remote region.

3.5 Application of Lessons

The key lessons from South Africa set out above can be applied to both the substantive assessment of hospital mergers and SGEIs in the PostNL saga.

3.5.1 *Independence of the ACM*

Where the ACM is required to assess public interest considerations such as the healthcare objectives in hospital mergers or SGEIs in the PostNL case, the ACM must be empowered to make the assessment. Whilst the executive (in the form of a Minister) may be permitted to make certain general policy rules, the ultimate assessment of a particular case should remain with the ACM. Accordingly, a provision such as Article 47(1) of the Mw, which essentially allows the Minister to override a decision by the ACM, exposes the overarching substantive assessment process to undue political interference and subsequent uncertainty.

3.5.2 *Specification of Interests and Manner of Incorporation*

The specific public interests that the ACM is required to assess should be specified with sufficient clarity and particularity either in the Mw itself or a binding instrument. The greater detail with which these interests can be defined, for example how accessibility or affordability should be measured, the greater certainty and clarity there is in the ACM's decision-making. Furthermore, it is important that within the assessment framework, guidance is provided to the ACM on how to balance competing interests. For example, if an anti-competitive merger would benefit the public interest, it should be clear how the ACM would approach such an issue to reconcile these conflicting interests.

It is interesting to note that this conclusion aligns well with the ACM's view of what would be required, should the legislature decide to impose a healthcare specific merger assessment.[75] The ACM argues that it would be important to 'make these interests explicit and to incorporate them in the healthcare-specific merger assessment'.[76] Furthermore, the ACM notes that the 'substantive design of this assessment should be based on clear standards, for example, with regard to quality and healthcare accessibility'.[77]

3.6 Conclusions

The hospital market has become increasingly concentrated.[78] Accordingly, appropriate caution should be exercised when designing and implementing any mechanism or healthcare-specific regime that could lead to the approval of further mergers in the healthcare sector. Conversely, there is an acknowledgement by stakeholders such as the ACM itself of the importance of safeguarding certain public interests in this sector.

Two possible solutions were considered, both of which if implemented correctly, would allow for a workable method of incorporating important healthcare objectives in the substantive merger assessment framework. First, more use could be made of Article 41(3) of the Mw to ensure that the prohibition of a merger does not hinder the performance of an SGEI (i.e. the provision of healthcare). Alternatively, applying the lessons from South Africa, a clear and explicit amendment to the current substantive merger assessment framework could be made, to mandate the assessment of certain clearly defined healthcare objectives by the ACM and set a clear approach as to how the ACM will balance interests, should they be competing.

References

ACM (2017) Explanatory Notes – Intensified attention for anticompetitive risks of hospital mergers. https://www.acm.nl/sites/default/files/documents/2018-01/explanatory-notes-merger-control-hospitals_1.pdf. Accessed 7 May 2023.

Angumuthoo M et al. (2020) Public Interest in Mergers: South Africa. The Antitrust Bulletin 65(2):312–332.

Canoy M, Sauter W (2009) Hospital mergers and the public interest: recent developments in the Netherlands. TILEC Discussion Paper DP 2009-035. https://pure.uvt.nl/ws/portalfiles/portal/1112247/Sauter_hospital_mergers_SSRN_090910.pdf. Accessed 16 July 2022.

Clark D (2022) Public Interest in Merger Control: Lessons from the end of the world. LLM thesis, Radboud University, Nijmegen.

Davis D (2019) Public Interest, Industrial Policy and Competition Law Remedies: The South African Experience. In: Da Silveira PB, Kovacic WE (eds) Global Competition Enforcement: New

[75] ACM 2017.

[76] Ibid., p. 3.

[77] Ibid.

[78] Roos 2018, p. 44.

Players, New Challenges (International Competition Law Series, Volume 79). Wolters Kluwer, Alphen aan den Rijn, pp 1421–1476.
Griffiths M, Gumbie W (2015) The public interest test in the South African merger control regime. Journal of Antitrust Enforcement 3(2):408–424.
Ministry of Economic Affairs and Climate (2022) Kamerbrief over nieuw vergunningsbesluit voor concentratie PostNL – Sandd. https://www.rijksoverheid.nl/documenten/kamerstukken/2021/04/09/nieuw-vergunningsbesluit-voor-concentratie-postnl---sandd. Accessed 17 July 2022.
Ministry of Health, Welfare and Sport (2020) Kamerbrief over aanscherping fusietoezicht in de zorg. https://www.rijksoverheid.nl/documenten/kamerstukken/2020/02/18/kamerbrief-over-aanscherping-fusietoezicht-in-de-zorg.
Ministry of Health, Welfare and Sport (2022) Kamerbrief over Besluit verlaagde omzetdrempels zorg. https://www.rijksoverheid.nl/documenten/kamerstukken/2022/07/15/kamerbrief-over-besluit-verlaagde-omzetdrempels-zorg.
Röling IMC (2012) Services of General Economic Interest within the Dutch healthcare system. LLM thesis, Tilburg University.
Roos A-F (2018) Mergers and Competition in the Dutch Healthcare Sector. PHD thesis, Erasmus University Rotterdam.
Rosenboom N (2018) Hospital Mergers and the Incorporation of Non-Competition Concerns. European Competition and Regulatory Law Review 2:271–279.
Van Damme E (2019) De overname van Sandd door PostNL. Markt & Mededinging 22(5):160–174.
Van de Gronden JW (2017) Mededingingsrecht in de EU en Nederland. Uitgeverij Paris, Zutphen.
Van de Gronden JW, Szyszczak E (2014) Introducing Competition Principles into Health Care through EU Law and Policy: A Case Study of the Netherlands. Medical Law Review 22(2):238–254.

Daniel James Arthur Clark is currently employed as a Senior Legal Counsel (In-house) in the Netherlands and holds a BCom LLB from Stellenbosch University and an LLM in International and European Law from Radboud University; the author is also an admitted attorney of the High Court of South Africa.

Chapter 4
Facilitating Access to Services of General Economic Interest Through EU Internal Market Legislation: The Case of Healthcare

Heidi Suorsa

Contents

Abstract Healthcare services are subject to free movement across the EU internal market, allowing providers and users the freedom to receive and provide these services throughout the EU territory. However, owing to the significant role that healthcare enjoys in the welfare systems of states and the corresponding competences in the area which are primarily retained with the Member States, the legal framework of cross-border healthcare is far more complex. The complete freedom of movement of healthcare services could pose a threat to the budgeting and planning power of the Member States. As a result, the responsibility for the organization of healthcare systems lies with the Member States, and they have the authority to

---

H. Suorsa (✉)
Government and Law Research Group, University of Antwerp, Antwerp, Belgium
e-mail: heidi.suorsa@uantwerpen.be

N. Ghazaryan et al. (eds.), *Services of General (Economic) Interest and EU Law*, Legal Issues of Services of General Interest, https://doi.org/10.1007/978-94-6265-723-6_4

determine whether and/or which healthcare services constitute services of general economic interest (SGEI). Furthermore, it is essential to note that healthcare services are excluded from the scope of the Services Directive. Even if they were to be recognized as SGEIs, healthcare services are treated differently from most other SGEIs. This discrepancy in treatment arises due to the unnecessarily complex nature of the legal framework for EU patient mobility. Consequently, the freedom to access healthcare services, which could be recognized as SGEIs, is less accessible than for other SGEIs falling within the scope of the Services Directive.

Keywords Cross-border healthcare · Patient mobility · Free movement of services · Right to health care · EU competences · Internal market

4.1 Introduction

Directive 2006/123/EC on services in the internal market was adopted with the objective of facilitating the proper functioning of the internal market for services.[1] This means that, for the service providers, the procedures for cross-border service provision and establishment are simplified, while consumers benefit from transparency, better service quality, and increased consumer rights. The Services Directive achieves these objectives by introducing measures such as a single point of contact for procedures and formalities,[2] and the option to complete relevant processes electronically.[3] It also prescribes the information that should be easily accessible to both service providers and recipients, along with the conditions for authorization schemes related to cross-border services.[4] Perhaps most importantly, the Services Directive codifies the free movement of services, as given expression in Article 56 of the TFEU.[5] To that end, it lists the grounds of justifiable derogations from that freedom.[6]

While the Services Directive applies to '*services supplied by providers established in a Member State*',[7] it does not encompass healthcare services.[8] The Directive explicitly excludes '*healthcare services whether or not they are provided via healthcare facilities, and regardless of the way in which they are organized and*

[1] Directive 2006/123/EC of the European Parliament and of the Council of 12 December 2006 on services in the internal market, adopted 12 December 2006, published 27 December 2006, Services Directive.

[2] Services Directive, above n. 1, Articles 6–7.

[3] Services Directive, above n. 1, Article 8.

[4] Services Directive, above n. 1, Article 7.

[5] Services Directive, above n. 1, Article 16; Consolidated version of the Treaty on the Functioning of the European Union, signed on 13 December 2007, published 26 October 2012, TFEU, Article 56.

[6] Services Directive, above n. 1, Articles 16–18.

[7] Services Directive, above n. 1, Article 2(1).

[8] Services Directive, above n. 1, Article 2(2)(f).

financed at national level or whether they are public or private' from its scope.[9] Consequently, providers and users of cross-border healthcare services do not benefit from the facilitated access offered by the Services Directive. However, the EU has addressed cross-border healthcare through other legislation: Directive 2011/24/EU on the application of patients' rights in cross-border healthcare,[10] and Regulation No 883/2004 on the coordination of social security systems which is supplemented by Implementing Regulation No 987/2009.[11] This raises the question of whether the EU legislation on cross-border healthcare adequately facilitates access to foreign healthcare services classified as SGEIs.

To address this question, this contribution commences with an overview of the EU's capacity to influence the healthcare provision within the Member States, with an emphasis on EU healthcare competences and the role of internal market competences in healthcare. Subsequently, the chapter evaluates whether healthcare services align with the definition of SGEIs, aiming to identify which healthcare services fall within the scope. The legal framework governing cross-border healthcare is then examined. Next, an analysis of potential obstacles to cross-border healthcare mobility resulting from the aforementioned legal framework is presented, which finally allows for a conclusion to be reached.

4.2 The EU and Healthcare

Contrary to what one might interpret from individual treaty provisions alone, the relationship between the provision of healthcare services and the EU is not readily apparent. This complexity can be attributed, in part, to the structured web of legislation that governs EU influence on healthcare.[12] This legislative framework is carefully crafted around the EU's limited, yet somewhat intricate, healthcare competences.[13] Additionally, the presence of a right to healthcare expressed in Article 35 of the Charter of Fundamental Rights of the EU (CFREU), without robust tools for its enforcement, further contributes to the ambiguous nature of the matter. In this section, a concise overview of this legal landscape is provided.[14]

---

[9] Services Directive, above n. 1, Article 2(2)(f).

[10] Directive 2011/24/EU of the European Parliament and of the Council of 9 March 2011 on the application of patients' rights in cross border healthcare, adopted 9 March 2011, published 4 April 2011, PMD.

[11] Regulation (EC) No 883/2004 of the European Parliament and of the Council of 29 April 2004 on the coordination of social security systems, adopted 29 April 2004, published 20 April 2004, SSCR; Regulation (EC) No 987/2009 of the European Parliament and of the Council of 16 September 2009 laying down the procedure for implementing Regulation (EC) No 883/2004 on the coordination of social security, adopted 16 September 2009, published 30 October 2009, ISSCR.

[12] Purnhagen et al. 2020, pp. 297–306.

[13] Purnhagen et al. 2020, pp. 297–306.

[14] Frantziou 2014, pp. 332–348; Beetz 2018, p. 475.

4.2.1 Healthcare Competences

EU law is founded on the principle of conferral, which according to Article 5(2) TFEU, entails that the ability of the EU to act is limited to the competences that the Member States have vested it with in the Treaties. The competences of the EU can be exclusive, where only the EU can act;[15] shared, where both the EU and the Member States can act, but with the EU acting only if it can do so more efficiently than the Member States;[16] coordinating, where the EU can coordinate Member States' actions;[17] or supplementary, where the EU can support, coordinate, or supplement Member States' actions.[18] The protection and the improvement of human health falls in the latter category, meaning that the EU enjoys a supplementary competence.[19] Furthermore, the EU has the competence to coordinate Member States' social policies.[20]

Any legislation adopted by the EU must be based on a legal basis in the treaties which gives concrete expression to the aforementioned competences. In the area of healthcare, this competence can be found in Article 168 TFEU. This provision outlines the scope and limitations of the EU's competences in healthcare. Some important features include the healthcare mainstreaming obligation, i.e. the obligation of the EU to ensure a high level of human health protection in the definition and implementation of its activities and policies,[21] as well as the responsibility of the EU to complement domestic health policies,[22] to facilitate cooperation between the Member States on issues such as cross-border healthcare,[23] and the joint-responsibility of the EU and the Member States to foster cooperation with third countries in the area of public health.[24] Furthermore, the Council may adopt non-binding recommendations on the objectives of Article 168 TFEU.[25]

The EU may also adopt incentive measures based on the ordinary legislative procedure after consulting the Economic and Social Committee. Such measures can address cross-border health threats,[26] and other issues, like quality and safety standards for organs, blood (and its derivatives),[27] and medicinal products.[28] However,

[15] TFEU, above n. 5, Article 3.
[16] TFEU, above n. 5, Article 4.
[17] TFEU, above n. 5, Article 5.
[18] TFEU, above n. 5, Article 6.
[19] TFEU, above n. 5, Article 6(a).
[20] TFEU, above n. 5, Article 5(3).
[21] TFEU, above n. 5, Article 168(1).
[22] TFEU, above n. 5, Article 168(1).
[23] TFEU, above n. 5, Article 168(2).
[24] TFEU, above n. 5, Article 168(3).
[25] TFEU, above n. 5, Article 168(6).
[26] TFEU, above n. 5, Article 168(5).
[27] TFEU, above n. 5, Article 168(4)(a).
[28] TFEU, above n. 5, Article 168(4)(c).

this competence is subject to a crucial limitation—such measures cannot harmonize the Member States legislation.[29] Importantly, Article 168(7) TFEU explicitly states that the definition, organization, and delivery of health policy, health services, and medical care remain the responsibility of the Member States, which the EU must respect in its actions.[30] This national responsibility encompasses the allocation of resources to health and medical care service, and the management thereof.[31] Therefore, the organization, management, provision, financing, and other aspects of health and medical care remain the undoubted responsibility and competence of each individual Member State.

Furthermore, the EU has explicitly codified a right to healthcare in Article 35 of the CFREU.[32] Similarly to Article 168(1) TFEU, this provision includes a health mainstreaming obligation.[33] It notably encompasses the '*right of access to preventive health care and the right to benefit from medical treatment under the conditions established by national laws and practices*'.[34] The latter disclaimer, subjecting the substantive content of the provision to national measures, raises questions about the enforceability of the right to healthcare. This is due to the fact that Article 51(1) CFREU states that some provisions express rights, whereas others express principles, and the distinction lies in the fact that the former must be respected while the latter need only be observed.[35] However, the CFREU is silent on which provisions fall in which category.[36] It has been observed that when evaluating whether a provision of the CFREU (in social law) constitutes a right, the CJEU takes into account whether the provision in question is mandatory, unconditional, and an essential principle of social law.[37] This evaluation renders for instance, Article 21 on non-discrimination and Article 31(2) on paid annual leave, as rights rather than principles.[38] However, the right to healthcare within the meaning of Article 35 CFREU is subject to national laws and practices and therefore does not appear to meet the requirement of unconditionality. For this reason, it is unlikely that the CJEU would decide that it constitutes a right, or it would have to deviate from its previous line of case law. This is significant because principles do not give rise to direct effect, meaning that private parties

[29] TFEU, above n. 5, Article 168(5).

[30] TFEU, above n. 5, Article 168(7).

[31] TFEU, above n. 5, Article 168(7).

[32] Charter of Fundamental Rights of the European Union, published 26 October 2012, CFREU, Article 35.

[33] Ibid., Article 35.

[34] CFREU, above n. 32, Article 35.

[35] CFREU, above n. 32, Article 51(1).

[36] The Explanation to Article 52(5) CFREU provides a list of examples of provisions that constitute principles. Those are the rights of the elderly in Article 25, integration of persons with disabilities in Article 26, and environmental protection in Article 37. However, since the principles "include" these provisions, it appears that this list is not exhaustive. See Explanations relating to the Charter of Fundamental Rights, published 14 December 2007 (OJ C 303, pp. 17–35), Explanation on Article 52—Scope and interpretation of rights and principles.

[37] Barnard 2020, pp. 351–363.

[38] Barnard 2020, p. 363.

cannot invoke them before courts.[39] Finally, the provisions of the CFREU cannot extend the competences of the EU beyond what is stated in the treaties.[40]

The aforementioned limitations on Union competence echo Article 2(5) TFEU, which states that when the EU adopts measures in an area of supplementary competences, as in the case of healthcare, such measures cannot harmonize national laws and regulations.[41] Consequently, the planning, organization, and financing of the healthcare system remain the competence and responsibility of the Member States. However, as will be demonstrated next, EU internal market rules can influence these systems, particularly concerning EU cross-border healthcare legislation and access to it.

4.2.2 *The Role of Internal Market Competences for Healthcare*

The previous section might suggest that the EU's involvement in healthcare is marginal. However, internal market provisions, in particular, have considerable influence on matters including cross-border healthcare, as will be shown in the present section.

The introduction of the free movement of workers in Article 42 of the Treaty of the Economic Community (TEC) in 1957 (now Article 45 TFEU) has granted Europeans the ability, in principle, to access foreign EU healthcare systems by freely moving from one EU Member State to another.[42] Furthermore, the freedom to provide services, as enshrined in Article 49 TEC (now Article 56 TFEU), allows for providers and recipients of services, including healthcare services, to cross internal EU borders without hindrances. The fact that healthcare constitutes a service within the meaning of internal market legislation has been confirmed in the case law of the CJEU. Already in *Luisi and Carbone* in 1984, the CJEU established that the cross-border movement for the purpose of medical treatment falls under the free movement of services and not capital, even if an exchange of capital takes place in that transaction.[43]

The CJEU further solidified an EU-wide market of healthcare in the *Kohll* and *Decker* judgments, ruling that the request for prior authorization for healthcare cannot be rejected, even if the care is non-urgent, as that rejection would infringe upon the

[39] Explanations relating to the Charter of Fundamental Rights, above n. 36, Explanation on Article 52—Scope and interpretation of rights and principles.

[40] CFREU, above n. 32, Article 51(2).

[41] TFEU, above n. 5, Article 2(5).

[42] Treaty establishing the European Community, signed 25 March 1957, published 24 December 2002, Article 42.

[43] CJEU, *Graziana Luisi and Giuseppe Carbone v Ministero del Tesoro*, Judgment, 31 October 1984, 286/82 and 26/83, para 37.

free movement of services.[44] In short, CJEU case law introduced an EU-wide market of healthcare. However, this development either puts pressure on healthcare systems to accommodate foreign patients or finance foreign care for their nationals/residents. In the *Smits and Peerbooms* case, the CJEU was asked to decide whether hospital care should also be exempt from a prior authorization.[45] While prior authorization would violate the freedom to provide services,[46] its absence could pose significant planning problems for Member States in financing foreign hospital treatment.[47] Ultimately, the CJEU decided that prior authorization of hospital care was justified, enabling Member States to better control their healthcare costs.[48] However, the authorization cannot be refused if the treatment in question is '*tried and tested by international medical science*' and if equally effective treatment is not accessible without undue delay in the patient's home state.[49] This arrangement strikes a balance between the free movement of services and the protection of national healthcare systems.

Ultimately, the case law of the CJEU has established a pathway to foreign healthcare systems, allowing individuals to receive medical treatment with the same priority and cost as residents of the treatment state if they bear the upfront cost themselves. Afterward, the state of affiliation is responsible for reimbursing the costs of foreign treatment.[50] This route provides access without prior authorization from the state of affiliation if the situation is urgent, the treatment does not require hospital care, or if no major medical equipment is required.[51] Furthermore, if the state of affiliation covers costs such as accommodation outside the hospital or transportation costs related to the care, it must also cover these expenses for foreign care.[52]

To effectively implement this system of cross-border healthcare, it was incorporated into EU secondary legislation, specifically Directive 2011/24/EU on the application of patients' rights in cross-border health care (PMD).[53] The CJEU has confirmed that the PMD codifies the jurisprudence on the free movement of

---

[44] CJEU, *Raymond Kohll v Union des Caisses de Maladie*, Judgment, 28 April 1998, C-158/96, paras 20–21 and 29; CJEU, *Nicolas Decker v Caisse de Maladie des Employés Privés*, Judgment, 28 April 1998, C-120/95, para 46.

[45] CJEU, *B.S.M. Geraets-Smits v Stichting Ziekenfonds VGZ and H.T.M. Peerbooms v Stichting CZ Groep Zorgverzekeringen*, Judgment, 12 July 2001, C-157/99, para 40.

[46] Ibid., para 69.

[47] Ibid., paras 76–80.

[48] Ibid., para 82.

[49] Ibid., para 108.

[50] CJEU, *Raymond Kohll v Union des Caisses de Maladie*, Judgment, 28 April 1998, C-158/96, para 27.

[51] CJEU, *V.G. Müller-Fauré v Onderlinge Waarborgmaatschappij OZ Zorgverzekeringen UA* and *E.E.M, van Riet v Onderlinge Waarborgmaatschappij ZAO Zorgverzekeringen*, Judgment, 13 May 2003, C-385/99, paras 81–95; CJEU, *Georgi Ivanov Elchinov v Natsionalna zdravnoosiguritelna kasa*, Judgment, 5 October 2010, C-173/09, paras 43–51; CJEU, *European Commission v French Republic*, Judgment, 5 October 2010, C-512/08, paras 27, 42; Greer and Sokol 2013, p. 75.

[52] CJEU, *Manuel Acereda Herrera v Servicio Cantabro de Salud*, Judgment, 15 June 2006, C-466/04, para 38.

[53] PMD, above n. 10.

services,[54] which, according to the *Tedeschi* judgment, implies that the system adopted under Article 56 TFEU no longer applies alongside the PMD.[55] Additionally, the coordination of social security among EU Member States is regulated by Regulation (EC) No 883/2004 on the coordination of social security systems (SSCR) and the Implementing Regulation (EC) No 987/2009 (ISSCR), which provides an alternative route to foreign care.[56] In essence, these instruments create two different avenues for scheduled foreign care, each subject to different criteria.

In conclusion, healthcare services, as services within the meaning of EU law, are subject to the rules of the EU internal market. Therefore, the EU has the authority to enact legislation to facilitate access to these services, which it has done. Thus, it is crucial to analyze the extent to which EU internal market legislation grants access to these SGEIs, which necessitates an understanding of whether healthcare services indeed can constitute SGEIs.

4.3 Healthcare: A Service of General Economic Interest?

Services of general economic interest (SGEIs) are a legally recognized concept, with references found in the EU Treaties. Article 14 TFEU establishes a legal basis for the EU to adopt regulations, within the limits of its competences, to ensure that SGEIs '*operate on the basis of principles and conditions, particularly economic and financial conditions, which enable them to fulfil their missions*'.[57] Protocol (No 26) on services of general interest almost exclusively addresses SGEIs.[58] It outlines the values to be preserved in providing SGEIs, which include organizing them to meet user needs closely, acknowledging diversity among SGEIs to account for various geographical, social and cultural situations, and upholding values such as high level of quality, safety, affordability, equal treatment, universal access, and user rights.[59] Furthermore, Article 36 CFREU on access to services of general economic interest state that '*The Union recognizes and respects access to services of general economic interest*' which is subject to national laws and practices.[60] However, none of these instruments provide a precise definition of SGEIs, which necessitates exploring further interpretations of the concept.

[54] CJEU, *A v Veselības ministrija*, Judgment, 29 October 2020, C-243/19, para 66.

[55] CJEU, *Carlo Tedeschi v Denkavit Commerciale s.r.l.*, Judgment, 5 October 1977, 5/77, as cited in Van de Gronden 2021, p. 151.

[56] PMD, above n. 10; SSCR, above n. 11; ISSCR, above n. 11.

[57] TFEU, above n. 5, Article 14.

[58] TFEU, above n. 5, Protocol No. 26 on services of general interest, Article 1.

[59] Ibid.

[60] CFREU, above n. 32, Article 36.

4.3.1 *Defining Services of General Economic Interest*

The Quality Framework for Services of General Interest in Europe has provided a general definition of SGEIs.[61] Firstly, the concept comprises economic activities, which may appear conceptually curious, since it refers to economic interests rather than economic services explicitly.[62] SGEIs are expected to '*deliver outcomes in the overall public good*',[63] indicating their positive impact on the general public, not just a limited group of users of the service. The distinguishing factor between SGEIs and other services of general interest (SGI) lies primarily in the fact that SGEIs are provided by an entrusted operator that is bound by public service obligations.[64] Lastly, public intervention is deemed necessary for the delivery of such services, as they would not be provided at all or not in line with principles like '*quality, safety, affordability, equal treatment, or universal access*' without public intervention.[65] To gain a deeper understanding, it is necessary to examine the nature of market services, economic services, and entrusted operators.

4.3.1.1 Market Services v the Exercise of Public Authority

Access to healthcare is recognized as a fundamental right,[66] however, the healthcare market is characterized by a significant risk of market failure, which is why the free market alone cannot satisfy the public health demands.[67] It is therefore up to the public bodies to supply healthcare when the market does not create a sufficient incentive for private bodies to do so, or to create the necessary incentives.[68] Hence, the provision of SGIs is subject to specific public service obligations which seek to safeguard principles such as '*quality, safety and affordability, equal treatment, universal access, and users rights*'.[69]

However, the SGIs and the obligations of their providers are not uniform, leading to the classification of three sub-categories of SGI.[70] All SGIs fall somewhere on a sliding scale between "market services" and "the exercise of public authority",[71]

[61] Communication from the Commission of 20 December 2011 to the European Parliament, the Council, the European Economic and Social Committee and the Committee of the Regions: A Quality Framework for Services of General Interest in Europe, COM (2011) 900 final, p. 3.

[62] Ibid.

[63] Ibid.

[64] Ibid.

[65] Ibid.

[66] CFREU, above n. 32, Article 35; Baeten and Palm 2013, p. 388.

[67] Baeten and Palm 2013, pp. 388–389.

[68] Baeten and Palm 2013, p. 389.

[69] A Quality Framework for Services of General Interest in Europe, above n. 65, pp. 2–3.

[70] A Quality Framework for Services of General Interest in Europe, above n. 65, pp. 3–4.

[71] Neergaard 2009, p. 19.

with further categorization depending on their position on this scale.[72] In other words, SGIs encompass three types: services of general interest, non-economic services of general interest, and social services of general interest. Among these, SGEIs are the closest to market services.[73] These are services that must remain available even if market conditions do not allow for their profitable provision.[74]

4.3.1.2 Economic v Non-economic Services

In principle, EU internal market rules do not apply to non-economic activities.[75] This raises the question of whether the converse is true: are services subject to internal market rules considered economic by definition? If that is the case, then healthcare services cannot constitute non-economic services of general interest, insofar as they do fall within the scope of the freedom to provide services. Furthermore, the CJEU has held that certain services which fulfil an exclusively social function, such as state-imposed social security schemes based on solidarity and non-profit making, do not constitute economic activities.[76] In such cases, the benefits received by the users are not proportionate to the compulsory contributions made.[77]

Another pertinent question is whether healthcare services are provided for economic consideration. The recitals of the Services Directive maintain that SGEIs are performed for economic considerations.[78] However, fees paid by the users towards part of the costs for services carried out under the auspices of the social duties of the state, do not constitute economic consideration seeing as those services are still primarily publicly funded.[79] The extent to which the consideration covers the real cost of the service is, therefore, central to the determination of whether a service can constitute an SGEI.

4.3.1.3 Entrustment to a Specific Operator

SGEIs must be entrusted to a specific operator.[80] The recitals of Commission Decision of 20 December 2011 on the application of Article 106(2) of the Treaty on the Functioning of the European Union to State aid in the form of public service compensation granted to certain undertakings entrusted with the operation of services of general

[72] Neergaard 2009, p. 20.

[73] Neergaard 2009, p. 20.

[74] Communication from the Commission of 19 January 2001 on Services of general interest in Europe (OJ C 17, pp. 4–23), p. 7.

[75] Ibid., p. 9.

[76] Ibid.

[77] Ibid.

[78] Services Directive, above n. 1, recital 17.

[79] Services Directive, above n. 1, recital 34.

[80] A Quality Framework for Services of General Interest in Europe, above n. 61, p. 3.

economic interest, emphasize the need to distinguish whether the provision of an SGEI is entrusted to a public or private undertaking.[81] This implies that both public and private undertakings can be entrusted with the operation and provision of SGEIs. The rules on SGEIs are based on the principle of neutrality, meaning that they apply uniformly to both types of undertakings.[82]

The Commission Decision further specifies the circumstances under which public service compensations granted to undertakings entrusted with the operation of an SGEI are compatible with internal market rules.[83] In Article 2, the Decision defines the scope of public service compensation by listing specific services and the context in which they are provided. This includes '*compensation for the provisions of services of general economic interest by hospitals providing medical care, including, where applicable, emergency service*'.[84] The inclusion of such a provision would be redundant if medical care services provided by hospitals, in particular emergency care, could not constitute SGEIs. It must therefore be concluded that services provided by hospitals can indeed constitute SGEIs within the meaning of EU law. Furthermore, the decision also applies to '*compensation for the provision of services of general economic interest meeting social needs as regards health and long-term care,*'[85] which further implies that services that address health needs, i.e., healthcare, can also constitute SGEIs under EU law.

4.3.2 Positioning Healthcare in the Framework of Services of General Economic Interest

The relationship between economic and non-economic services is dynamic rather than static.[86] This means that a particular type of service is not fixed within one

---

[81] Commission Decision of 20 December 2011 on the application of Article 106(2) of the Treaty on the Functioning of the European Union to State aid in the form of public service compensation granted to certain undertaking entrusted with the operation of services of general economic interest (OJ L 7, pp. 3–10), recital 2.

[82] Communication from the Commission Services of general interest in Europe, above n. 74, p. 8.

[83] Commission Decision of 20 December 2011 on the application of Article 106(2) of the Treaty on the Functioning of the European Union to State aid in the form of public service compensation granted to certain undertaking entrusted with the operation of services of general economic interest, above n. 81, Article 1.

[84] Commission Decision of 20 December 2011 on the application of Article 106(2) of the Treaty on the Functioning of the European Union to State aid in the form of public service compensation granted to certain undertaking entrusted with the operation of services of general economic interest, above n. 81, Article 2(1)(b).

[85] Commission Decision of 20 December 2011 on the application of Article 106(2) of the Treaty on the Functioning of the European Union to State aid in the form of public service compensation granted to certain undertaking entrusted with the operation of services of general economic interest, above n. 81, Article 2(1)(c).

[86] Neergaard 2009, p. 35.

category, and diverse services within a category can fall under different SGEI classifications and may change over time. This dynamic nature of categorization also opens the possibility that some healthcare services may be considered SGEIs while others may not. What follows is that due to the diversity of healthcare systems, there can be no homogenous application of SGEI rules on healthcare services across all the EU Member States. In some states, private undertakings play a more significant role in healthcare service provision, while others rely primarily on public, tax-funded healthcare, with limited involvement of private actors.[87] Moreover, it is the prerogative of each Member State to decide how to organize their SGEIs, including which services constitute SGEIs, designating them as such through appropriate acts.[88]

To qualify as SGEIs, healthcare services must be provided in exchange for economic consideration.[89] The extent to which the users contribute towards the cost of healthcare, at the point of delivery, before, or after, largely depends on the state's healthcare system, the specific service in question, and the recipient. In view of the previously discussed definition, healthcare services are less likely to constitute SGEIs in healthcare systems where relevant services are offered free of charge on a universal and often tax-funded basis. Similarly, a symbolic fee charged to the patient, for instance, for gatekeeping purposes to prevent abuse of healthcare services, does not qualify as economic consideration. Hence, to fall within the scope of an SGEI, the patient or their insurer would need to cover the actual cost of the service. And finally, as previously mentioned, for healthcare services to be considered SGEIs, they must be provided by an entrusted undertaking, whether public or private.[90]

The conclusion can be drawn that healthcare services can be considered SGEIs, as determined by the Member States, insofar as they are provided by a public or private undertaking which has been specifically entrusted with the provision of such services, and as long as the service is provided in exchange for economic consideration, meaning that the service in question cannot be publicly funded. There are occasions where these criteria are met in the healthcare service context, most notably in the private healthcare sector. In some circumstances, the shortcomings of the publicly provided healthcare services drive users to seek alternative healthcare services.[91] Factors such as long waiting times or inadequate quality of care may lead users to opt for private healthcare services. Users may also opt for the private sector based on personal preference. Furthermore, certain healthcare services may not be covered by insurance packages, requiring patients to bear the entire cost through out-of-pocket payments or for instance by taking out a private health insurance. The role of private health insurance varies considerably among EU Member States.[92] These types of healthcare services can, in that case, constitute SGEIs within the meaning of EU law, yet they may fall outside the scope of the Service Directive. The next section

[87] See Wendt et al. 2009, pp. 70–90.

[88] Communication from the Commission Services of general interest in Europe, above n. 74, p. 8.

[89] Services Directive, above n. 1, recital 17.

[90] A Quality Framework for Services of General Interest in Europe, above n. 61, p. 3.

[91] Kanavos et al. 1999, p. 1157.

[92] Brooks and Stiernstedt 2022, p. 127.

seeks to analyze whether the legal framework on cross-border healthcare provides adequate access to foreign healthcare services, commencing with an overview of said framework.

4.4 The EU Legal Framework of Planned Cross-Border Healthcare

4.4.1 Prior Authorization

Article 8 of the PMD lists the grounds and limitations of prior authorization. According to para. 2 thereof, prior authorization may be required for treatments that involve planning and over-night hospitalization, the use of high-specialized or cost-intensive equipment or medical infrastructure, treatments that pose a risk to the patient or population, and treatments that raise concerns about the quality and safety of care.[93] It is evident from case law discussed in previous sections that healthcare system planning and budgeting are the primary reasons for implementing a system of prior authorization. The Member States are obliged to report to the Commission a list of treatments subject to such extensive planning.[94]

Article 8(6) of the PMD specifies circumstances under which prior authorization may be refused. These include instances where there is a reasonable certainty that the patient will be exposed to a safety risk, the general public with reasonable certainty will be exposed to a safety hazard, there are serious and specific concerns about the quality of the care and patient safety, and when the treatment in question can be provided in the home state within a medically justifiable time limit.[95] For the latter, the current state of health and the probable course of illness of the patient are used to determine what constitutes medically justifiable.[96] Finally, under Article 8(5) of the PMD, prior authorization cannot be refused when the care cannot be provided on the territory of the home state within a time limit which is medically justifiable. To this end, an objective medical assessment is based on the medical condition, the history and probable course of the illness, the degree of the patient's pain, or the degree of their disability.[97]

Article 20(1) of the SSCR maintains that individuals seeking to travel to another EU Member State for the purpose of receiving a benefit, in this case health or medical care, must seek prior authorization from the competent state.[98] Article 20(2) of the SSCR introduces two conditions that, when met together, preclude a state from

[93] PMD, above n. 10, Article 8(2).

[94] PMD, above n. 10, Article 8(2).

[95] PMD, above n. 10, Article 8(6).

[96] PMD, above n. 10, Article 8(6)(d).

[97] PMD, above n. 10, Article 8(5).

[98] SSCR, above n. 11, Article 20(1).

rejecting prior authorization. These conditions are that the foreign care falls within the scope of care that the patient would be entitled to in the home state, and the treatment cannot be given in the home state within a time limit which is medically justifiable.[99] Based on this, it can be concluded that the PMD provides more grounds for refusal of prior authorization compared to the SSCR. The significant difference is that prior authorization is the exception rather than the rule under the PMD, whereas the SSCR specifically facilitates scheduled foreign care with prior authorization. This means that the PMD might be more convenient for patients who do not need a prior-authorization under Article 8(2) PMD, while the SSCR might be more convenient for patients who would need a prior-authorization under Article 8(2) PMD, since there are more grounds which justify refusing the prior-authorization under the PMD than the SSCR.

4.4.2 Reimbursement of Costs

In cases where prior authorization is not required or has been granted, the home state is responsible for reimbursing the cost of healthcare in another EU Member State.[100] Under the PMD, the reimbursement amount must be at least equivalent to the costs that would have been incurred if the treatment had been provided in the state of affiliation.[101] However, Member States are free to offer a higher reimbursement.[102] Article 7(1) PMD maintains that the state of affiliation is responsible for reimbursing the costs incurred by the patient.[103] In practice this means that the patient must upfront the costs to the state of treatment, which are then reimbursed by the state of affiliation *ex post facto*. Whereas compensation for adjacent services such as transportation and accommodation has been facilitated under Article 56 TFEU, it remains unclear whether this is covered by the PMD, since it merely mentions that states may decide to reimburse such related costs.[104] Finally, states may limit reimbursement for overriding reasons in the general interest.[105] Such reasons include '*ensuring sufficient and permanent access to a balanced range of high-quality treatment in the Member State concerned*'.[106] However, such limitations must be necessary and proportionate.[107]

Under the SSCR, the competent state must reimburse an amount equivalent to the tariff of the care in the state of treatment.[108] As a result, if the costs of the care

[99] SSCR, above n. 11, Article 20(2).
[100] PMD, above n. 10, Articles 5(a) and 7; SSCR, above n. 11, Article 35.
[101] PMD, above n. 10, Article 7(4).
[102] PMD, above n. 10, Article 7(4).
[103] PMD, above n. 10, Article 7(1).
[104] PMD, above n. 10, Article 7(4); Greer and Sokol 2013, p. 77.
[105] PMD, above n. 10, Article 7(9).
[106] PMD, above n. 10, Article 7(9).
[107] PMD, above n. 10, Article 7(11).
[108] SSCR, above n. 11, Article 35.

are considerably higher in the state of treatment, it may generally be more favorable for the patient to seek foreign care under the SSCR rather than the PMD, unless the state of affiliation offers a reimbursement rate higher than the minimum required. Furthermore, the patient benefits under the SSCR from the coordinated manner of settling the costs that the instrument creates. The SSCR maintains that the patient shall receive benefits in kind in the host state, as if they were insured there,[109] which implies that the patient receives the care (i.e., the benefit in kind) and the costs are covered directly by the state of affiliation or other insuring party.

4.4.3 Application and Scope

4.4.3.1 Priority and Relationship

One of the most challenging aspects of EU secondary legislation on cross-border healthcare mobility is the relationship between the different instruments, and, in particular, their application. Firstly, the PMD applies without prejudice to the SSCR and the ISSCR.[110] However, the patient can nonetheless request to apply for cross-border healthcare under the PMD even if the SSCR is applicable.[111] The conclusion is therefore that the PMD cannot interfere with the rights under the SSCR from being realized, however, the patient may choose which framework they wish to be applied if both are applicable.

4.4.3.2 Personal Scope

Both instruments share similar criteria regarding their personal scope, i.e., the individuals for whom foreign healthcare is accessible under the different frameworks. Article 20 of the SSCR maintains that prior authorization should be sought by insured persons seeking treatment in another Member State.[112] According to Article 1(c) of the SSCR, an insured person means someone entitled to benefit from relevant care in the competent state.[113] This implies that, for instance, under a national healthcare system, the person seeking prior authorization would have to be a beneficiary of that system, or under a compulsory health insurance system, they should be a holder of a qualifying health insurance. These provisions further apply to family members of an insured person.[114] Here the definition of a family member is subject to the definition

---

[109] SSCR, above n. 11, Article 20(2).

[110] PMD, above n. 10, Articles 2(m) and 7(1); Greer and Sokol 2013, p. 77.

[111] Van de Gronden 2021, p. 153.

[112] SSCR, above n. 11, Article 20(1).

[113] SSCR, above n. 11, Article 1(c).

[114] SSCR, above n. 11, Article 20(3).

of members of a household under the national legislation of the competent state.[115] In the absence of such a definition, the family members shall comprise the spouse, minor children, dependent children, and dependents of the insured person if they live in the same household.[116] Furthermore, the SSCR only applies to nationals of EU Member States, stateless persons and refugees who are or have been subject to the legislation of an EU Member State, and their survivors and family members as well as survivors and family members of persons who have been subject to the legislation of an EU Member State if the survivor and family members live in or are subject to the legislation of an EU Member States.[117]

Access to reimbursement of costs of foreign healthcare is also facilitated for insured persons under the PMD.[118] The PMD borrows the definition of an insured person from the SSCR, including the scope of family members.[119] It further adds that insured persons include third-country nationals if they are covered by Regulation (EC) No 859/2003 or Regulation (EU) No 1231/2010, or they are entitled to the benefit in question in the Member States of affiliation.[120]

4.4.3.3 Material Scope

Another point of convergence between the instruments can be found in determining the sending state, i.e., the state from which the patient departs and where prior authorization is issued, and where applicable, costs are reimbursed. The primary objective of the SSCR is to determine which state is responsible for the social security of an individual, which is referred to as the competent state. The criteria are the state of employment, the state that the administration that a civil servant is working for is subject to, the state paying an unemployment benefit, the state where one carries out a military or civil service, or if none of the above are applicable, the state of residence.[121] Furthermore, special rules apply in cases where a person is economically active in multiple Member States or is a posted worker, etc.[122] It is for the competent state to issue a prior authorization and to reimburse the costs if applicable.

Here again, the PMD borrows its scope of application from the SSCR. For insured persons and their family members and survivors, the Member State of affiliation is the competent state within the meaning of the SSCR.[123] For the survivors and family members of persons who have been subject to the legislation of an EU Member

[115] SSCR, above n. 11, Article 1(i)(1)(i).

[116] SSCR, above n. 11, Articles 1(2) and 1(3).

[117] SSCR, above n. 11, Article 2.

[118] PMD, above n. 10, Article 7(1).

[119] PMD, above n. 10, Article 3(b)(i).

[120] PMD, above n. 10, Article 3(ii).

[121] SSCR, above n. 11, Article 11(2).

[122] SSCR, above n. 11, Articles 12 and 13.

[123] PMD, above n. 10, Article 3(c)(i).

State, the Member State of affiliation is determined by Regulation (EC) No 859/2003 or Regulation (EU) No 1231/2010.[124] In conclusion, the main difference is the semantic discrepancy between the state of affiliation and the competent state, which in practice most often constitutes the same state.

4.4.3.4 Legal Nature of Regulations and Directives

The legal nature of a directive requires that it be implemented individually by each Member State in their national legislation.[125] A private person seeking to invoke their patient mobility rights under the PMD must therefore do so under national legislation. Consequently, the rules on prior authorization of foreign care under the PMD constitute minimum standards, but the Member States are free to adopt less restrictive measures than those presented next. Unlike the Directive, the Regulation is directly applicable in all EU Member States from the moment of entry into force.[126]

4.4.4 Patients' Access to Information

Under Article 6 of the PMD, all EU Member States are required to introduce and maintain at least one national contact point (NCP).[127] The Member States must inform the contact details of these NCPs to the Commission, which then makes this information publicly available.[128] The primary objective of the NPCs is to provide patients with information about '*healthcare providers, including, on request, information on a specific provider's right to provide services or any restrictions on its practice, […] as well as information on patients' rights, complaints procedures and mechanisms for seeking remedies, according to the legislation of the Member State, as well as the legal and administrative available to settle disputes, including in the event of harm arising from cross-border health care.*'[129]

The NCPs must, upon the request of the patient, provide information about the standards and guidelines regarding quality and safety which are applicable in the state of treatment.[130] Furthermore, healthcare providers in the state of treatment must inform the patient about treatment options, their pricing and an itemized

[124] PMD, above n. 10, Article 3(c)(ii).

[125] TFEU, above n. 5, Article 288.

[126] TFEU, above n. 5, Article 288.

[127] PMD, above n. 10, Article 6(1); Den Exter et al. 2015, p. 284.

[128] PMD, above n. 10, Article 6(1).

[129] PMD, above n. 10, Article 6(3).

[130] PMD, above n. 10, Articles 4(2)(a) and 6(3).

invoice.[131] They must also be informed about the availability, quality, and safety of these treatment options.[132]

The NPCs must cooperate with the Commission and each other, ensuring patients have access to contact details of relevant NPCs.[133] They must also provide the healthcare professionals in the state of treatment with the information they are under an obligation to disclose to their patients.[134] All aforementioned information must be made available in an accessible manner, electronically, and in a manner which makes it accessible for persons with disabilities.[135]

4.5 Access to Healthcare Services of General Economic Interest Through EU Cross-Border Mechanisms

4.5.1 Challenges for Cross-Border Healthcare

4.5.1.1 Normative Clarity and Legal Certainty

The two avenues to cross-border healthcare provided by EU secondary legislation present significant challenges in terms of understanding their relation and application. The PMD offers provisions for both planned and non-planned care, with the former requiring a prior authorization whereas that is not necessary for the latter. The SSCR, however, enforces a blanket requirement for prior authorization, which must be granted under certain circumstances. Furthermore, the PMD lists more grounds which can justify the refusal of prior authorization. There are also differences in the amounts of reimbursements of costs incurred from foreign care, with the SSCR being more advantageous if the costs of care abroad are higher than they would be at home, without requiring the patient to cover the costs upfront. Another complication arises from the fact that directives, such as the PMD, need to be transposed into national legislation, leading to variations in practices concerning prior authorization and reimbursement levels among the Member States, as they can adopt more favorable measures.

When both instruments are applicable to a patient, they may decide which one they find more beneficial. However, given the complexity of these systems, it can be challenging for patients to make such a distinction. The intricate web of rights and obligations may discourage individuals from accessing foreign care, even when it is available. Hence, there is an argument to be made that the complexity of these

[131] PMD, above n. 10, Article 2(b).

[132] PMD, above n. 10, Article 2(b).

[133] PMD, above n. 10, Article 6(2).

[134] PMD, above n. 10, Article 6(4).

[135] PMD, above n. 10, Article 6(5).

instruments and their relationship with each other may hinder the accessibility of cross-border healthcare services.

4.5.1.2 Personal Financial Burden

The PMD and the SSCR differ not only in their levels of reimbursement, but also in terms of how the costs are covered by the state of affiliation/competent state. The PMD operates based on a *post facto* reimbursement by the competent state. This means that private individuals are responsible for financing their foreign care until they receive said reimbursement. Under the SSCR, the debt is settled directly between the states.[136] Furthermore, the level of reimbursement depends on whether the PMD or the SSCR is applicable.[137] Under the SSCR, the patient must be treated as if they were insured in the host state, resulting in that the level of reimbursement is equal to the total cost.[138] However, under the PMD, access to foreign care cannot interfere with the financing of the healthcare system of the state of affiliation, leading to reimbursement equivalent to the costs of comparable care in that state, unless more favorable national provisions apply.[139] Consequently, the patient may be liable to cover a substantial amount themselves if the costs of foreign care exceed those of comparable care at home.[140] This can deter patients from seeking foreign care under the PMD.

Consequently, foreign care becomes more accessible for individuals with greater personal financial resources, unless they can rely on the SSCR for their foreign care. However, this aspect sets healthcare services apart from other SGEIs, as these services are rarely fully paid for directly by the recipients, necessitating a mechanism for the coordination of costs. Hence, the unequal financial accessibility cannot be compared with other SGEIs, since healthcare services which fall within the scope of a solidary social security scheme can themselves not constitute SGEIs. It is nonetheless an interesting observation that the implementation of this mechanism has resulted in cross-border healthcare services not being equally financially accessible for all.

4.5.1.3 Language Skills and Bureaucratic Literacy

Navigating a foreign healthcare system can be extremely difficult, especially if the information is only available in languages that the patient does not understand.[141] Furthermore, with the diversity of healthcare systems which co-exist within the EU, it is understandable if patients find it overwhelming to navigate the bureaucracy of

---

[136] Berki 2019, p. 70.

[137] Ibid.

[138] SSCR, above n. 11, Article 35(1).

[139] PMD, above n. 10, Article 7(4).

[140] Berki 2019, p. 70.

[141] Ibid., p. 69.

unfamiliar healthcare systems.[142] In addition, patients considering seeking foreign care are likely to experience emotional and physical stress already due to the reasons that lead them to seek such care. This is an entirely non-legal issue, however, as it is a natural ramification of how healthcare mobility within the EU is currently organized.

The present system primarily facilitates foreign care for those who have the expertise or familiarity with the relevant foreign healthcare system and/or the language in which it operates.[143] Alternatively, it facilitates access to foreign care for those who have the resources or contacts that allow them to outsource research into the foreign healthcare system. However, individuals with the skills or resources to navigate the foreign system are also likely to belong to the demographic that is not financially overburdened by pre-financing foreign care.[144] This further reinforces the potential inequality in accessing cross-border healthcare services.

4.5.2 Improving Cross-Border Healthcare Opportunities

The current legal framework of cross-border healthcare mobility poses challenges to the equal accessibility of cross-border healthcare, owing in particular to the lack of normative clarity that the introduction of two separate avenues results in, the potential excessive costs initially borne by the patients before reimbursement, and the administrative complexities of navigating foreign healthcare systems. Therefore, the question arises: how can accessibility, affordability, and equality of access to scheduled foreign healthcare be improved under EU law, while respecting the responsibilities of the Member States to organize their healthcare system?

To enhance normative clarity, adopting a single framework for cross-border healthcare would be beneficial instead of maintaining multiple avenues. This would promote equality among patients by preventing the well-informed from seeking foreign care under more favorable conditions. By evaluating the best practices from the existing frameworks, we can establish a comprehensive approach. A potential solution could involve integrating the reimbursement system of the SSCR and the NCPs from the PMD. Moreover, consolidating prior authorization rules into a single set of criteria would lead to greater clarity. The rules regarding prior authorization should be subject to what the political consensus among the EU Member States and the EU institutions produces.

Secondly, personal pre-financing of foreign care should be eliminated. The *rationale* behind patient fees or pre-financing part of the care is usually to discourage individuals from abusing the healthcare system by seeking unnecessary medical attention.[145] However, in the EU cross-border healthcare context, this approach becomes redundant as the circumstances under which individuals may seek foreign care are

[142] Ibid., p. 67.

[143] Mossialos et al. 2010, p. 462.

[144] Berki 2019, p. 70.

[145] Ahmadi 2023, p. 596.

already limited, and in many cases, the patient must seek prior authorization from the home state. The necessary gatekeeping measures to prevent abuse are therefore already in place.

The system under the SSCR, where costs are settled directly between Member States, is preferable even for services which are not subject to prior authorization under the PMD since the home state would be responsible for covering (at least part) of those costs as well. This further reduces the bureaucratic burden for both the states as well as the patient. However, the question then arises regarding the ideal level of reimbursement.

A compromise could involve distinguishing between services that do not require prior authorization, and the ones that do. For the former, the minimum level of reimbursement could amount the costs that would be incurred if the care were provided in the home state. For the latter, the level of reimbursement would amount to the total costs. These costs would be settled between the states themselves directly, and the patient would be liable to cover their share afterwards to the home state, if applicable. This mechanism would allow for the facilitation of patient mobility while maintaining planning power with the Member States.

4.6 Conclusions

This chapter has demonstrated that the cross-border healthcare framework does provide access to healthcare services that could be recognized as SGEIs by the Member States. However, it falls short of providing the same level of convenience and seamlessness as the Service Directive would offer. It is not within the scope of this contribution to assess whether this outcome is justified considering the protection of domestic solidarity mechanisms and healthcare systems. Nonetheless, it is important to acknowledge the discrepancy in the cross-border access to healthcare services compared to other services that can be considered SGEIs.

Especially in the private sector, and in circumstances where certain healthcare services fall outside of the insurance coverage, the EU Member States could deem healthcare services to constitute SGEIs. However, in circumstances where patients would find themselves in need of access to those services abroad, they are faced with a complex scheme for cross-border patient mobility which can prove to be a significant obstacle. The functionality of the internal market for healthcare is therefore undermined by the coexistence of two legal avenues for foreign care with an unclear relationship.

This chapter has illustrated how healthcare services could benefit from a well-functioning internal market, by adopting a single cross-border health care mechanism that ensures equal access through the abolition of pre-financing by patients. To maintain the freedom of the Member States to plan their own healthcare systems, this unified framework would require a clear distinction between services subject to prior authorization and those that are not, with varying levels of reimbursement. Finally, patients ought to be guided through these processes with the assistance of NCPs, not much unlike what is currently prescribed by the PMD. Such reforms would enhance the accessibility, affordability, and equality of cross-border healthcare services while respecting the responsibilities of Member States.

References

Ahmadi A (2023) Fees for primary care: passion and emotion are integral to the conversation. British Medical Journal 380:596.

Baeten R, Palm W (2013) Preserving General Interest in Healthcare Through Secondary and Soft EU Law: The Case of the Patients' Rights Directive. In: Neergaard U et al. (eds) Social Services of General Interest in the EU. T.M.C. Asser Press, The Hague, pp 385–412.

Barnard C (2020) Are social 'Rights' rights? European Labour Law Journal 11(4):351–363.

Beetz J (2018) A two-tier conception of European Union peoplehood: A realist study of European citizens' bonds of collectivity. European Law Journal 23(6):467–481.

Berki G (2019) Patient Mobility in the EU: A Playground for All of Us? La Revue belge de sécurité sociale 1:65–80.

Brooks G, Stiernstedt P (2022) The Private Healthcare Insurance sector: A victim of fraud. Journal of Criminology 55(1):125–139.

den Exter A et al. (2015) One Year after the EU patient Mobility Directive: A Three-Country Analysis. European Law Review 40:278–292.

Frantziou E (2014) Case C-176/12 Association de Médiation Sociale: Some Reflections on the Horizontal Effect of the Charter and the Reach of Fundamental Employment Rights in the European Union. European Constitutional Law Review 10(2):332–348.

Greer SL, Sokol T (2013) Rules for Rights: European Law, Health Care and Social Citizenship. European Law Journal 20(1):66–87.

Kanavos P et al. (1999) Cross border health care in Europe. British Medical Journal 318(7192):1157–1158.

Mossialos E et al. (2010) Health Systems Governance in Europe: the role of European Union law and policy. Cambridge University Press, Cambridge.

Neergaard U (2009) Services of General Economic Interest: The Nature of the Beast. In: Krajewski M et al. (eds) The Changing Legal Framework for Services of General Interest in Europe: Between Competition and Solidarity. T.M.C. Asser Press, The Hague, pp 17–50.

Purnhagen K et al. (2020) More Competences than You Knew? The Web of Health Competence for European Union Action in Response to the COVID-19 Outbreak. European Journal of Risk Regulation 11:297–306.

Van de Gronden JW (2021) Grensoverschrijdende zorg: vrij verkeer van patienten in een oerwoud van regels. In: de Graaf KJ et al. (eds) Grensoverstijgende rechtsbeofening Liber amicorum Jan Jans. Uitgeverij Paris, Zutphen, pp 149–156.

Wendt C et al. (2009) Healthcare System Types: A Conceptual Framework for Comparison. Social Policy & Administration 43(1):70–90.

Heidi Suorsa, FWO Postdoctoral researcher at the University of Antwerp, Government and Law Research Group.

Part II
Digital Services and SGEIs

Chapter 5
Big Technology Platforms and Digital Services of General (Economic) Interest

Anna Gerbrandy

Contents

Abstract This contribution provides an overview of the interaction between Big Tech business-led developments and services of general (economic) interest. It notes three ways of a thickening relationship between Big Techs and the public domain: some services of Big Tech companies might be seen as public-service-like market services; Big Tech companies are entering 'classical' public services; and government services are (becoming) dependent on services provided by Big Tech companies. This takes place in a rapidly changing technological context of an increasingly digitally-mediated society. A normative idea is proposed that in this context, a public service is a service to which access is deemed necessary to live a full life as a citizen. The above leads to questioning whether the existing EU legal framework needs updating, to fit these technological and societal developments and to protect the EU's notion of protection of public services.

Keywords Digital transition · Public services · Big Tech · Economic services · Government services

A. Gerbrandy (✉)
Utrecht University School of Law, Utrecht, The Netherlands
e-mail: a.gerbrandy@uu.nl

N. Ghazaryan et al. (eds.), *Services of General (Economic) Interest and EU Law*, Legal Issues of Services of General Interest, https://doi.org/10.1007/978-94-6265-723-6_5

5.1 Introduction

As the digital transition is progressing and impacting increasingly larger swaths of society, this seems a good moment for a competition law scholar to also refocus attention on the interplay between the European Union's notion of services of general (economic) interest and this digital transition. In this contribution, I am taking a starting point that is focused on the powerful platform companies (the 'Big Techs') and their role in a digital society.[1] This contribution, which reflects a key-note presentation I held at the Radboud University Nijmegen conference in October 2022, provides a high-level overview of the interaction between Big Tech business-led developments in providing (public) services, and classical and novel services of general (economic) interest. It is set up as follows: Sect. 5.2 focuses on the notion of public services. Section 5.3 sketches the current context and the direction of development of digitalization and the digital society—here I throw in some references to relevant sci-fi novels. Section 5.4 notes three developments in how the relationship between Big Tech platforms' activities and the public domain intersect and is thickening, briefly discussing how some services of Big Tech companies might be seen as public-service-like market services, how Big Tech companies are entering 'classical' public services, and where government services (economic and non-economic) are (becoming) dependent on services provided by Big Tech companies. Section 5.5 will conclude that the relationship between Big Tech companies and public services has evolved, leading to questions about the possible reaction of the legal system.

It is important to stress that the intention of the key-note—and this contribution—is to, based on what is happening in the 'tech-space', sketch a possible future direction of developments, which might be relevant for the notion of services of general economic interest/public services within the European legal system. These tentative words are chosen deliberately and fit the aim of this contribution. The aim is not to provide an in-depth discussion of case-law or doctrine into some of these foundational legal concepts, and I also do not really answer my own questions (as my conclusion is that further interdisciplinary research is necessary). The aim is to show that what is happening in the world of technological development also may have deep ramifications for the fairly staid and placid EU competition law notions related to public services.

[1] As part of the ERC-funded project on 'Modern Bigness', which questions the concept of 'power' in relation to big technology platforms and focuses on possible regulatory responses to negative effects of this power. See for an overview of the project https://www.uu.nl/en/research/modern-bigness. Accessed 28 July 2025.

5.2 Public Services

From an EU competition law perspective, the starting point for any application of its rules is the notion of 'economic activity'. That this is the starting point is, in turn, based on a general dividing line between the market and the state: the market realm is that of economic activities, and the state is not, where the market is the instrument for furthering the private interest of companies and consumers, and the state is focused on furthering the public interest, for the common good. Competition law applies fully to the market-realm; its function is to support markets, to make competition (on the merits) happen.

However clear the lines seem to be drawn, already in the Treaty this clear-cut division is bisected by the recognition that straddling the market-realm and the state-realm are 'services of general economic interest' (in Article 106 TFEU).[2] In the European Union setting these services generally encompass the services that the European Commission mentions in its communications on this topic, but also encompass those services that the Member States decide to label as such.[3] Legally, these categories do not necessarily overlap, though in practice, of course, they do. For example, in most EU countries the provision of energy and water, the organization of healthcare and public transport, communication and education would be considered such services of general (economic) interest. Though not really the focus of this contribution, such a labeling, in turn, leads to charging companies that are charged—explicitly, by the state—with providing these (economic) services with some form of universal service obligations and, from a competition law perspective, to a possible carve out of the application of the abuse of dominance prohibition (and the state aid regime).

There is quite a bit of very specific legal language involved here: the Commission has tried to clarify that the services of general economic interest-concept is part of the broader notion of 'services of general interest', which might either be economic in nature (in which case they are services of general economic interest),

---

[2] See Lalikova's contribution, in Chap. 6 of this volume, for a more in-depth discussion of the related concepts of SGEI and public services.

[3] There is no 'ultimate' EU-approved list as—indeed—Member States define their own services of general economic interests (under the European Union Court's scrutiny); but see several examples mentioned in Communication from the Commission of 20 December 2011 to the European Parliament, the Council, the European Economic and Social Committee and the Committee of the Regions: A Quality Framework for Services of General Interest in Europe, COM(2011) 900 final; Commission Staff Working Document of 6 December 2013 accompanying the document Report from the Commission to the Council and the European Parliament on the application of Directive 2006/54/EC of the European Parliament and of the Council of 5 July 2006 on the implementation of the principle of equal opportunities and equal treatment of men and women in matters of employment and occupation; SWD(2013) 512 final and Commission Staff Working Document of 29 April 2013 Guide to the application of the European Union rules on state aid, public procurement and the internal market to services of general economic interest, and in particular to social services of general interest, SWD(2013) 53 final/2. As to the Member States having leeway in deciding what constitutes a service of general economic interest, see, as an example, CJEU (GC), *Stichting Woonlinie and Others v European Commission*, Judgment, 15 November 2018, T-202/10 RENV II and T-203/10 RENV II.

or non-economic in nature (non-economic services of general interest, often social services (of non-economic interest)). The clear-cut division is even further muddled by the rules and regulations related to 'regulated sectors'. All of these distinctions are ultimately fairly logical, though there are obvious difficulties in the categorization at the boundaries of these concepts, including at the boundaries of the concept of 'undertaking' itself. But that is inherent in any legal categorization.

At any rate, for what I am trying to do in this contribution—for which it is useful to temporarily go beyond these specific categorizations and the specific requirements for the carve-out of European competition law to be applicable—it makes sense to think of *all* these services of general interest (including the 'economic' ones) as based on notions that can be encapsulated by the term 'public services', so that the analysis below—in which I will sketch three developments that seem to thicken the interplay between Big Tech corporations and public services—is not immediately bogged down in these distinctions. Ultimately, I will conclude that what is happening in this space might not fit these categorizations but still might merit a (legal) response. So, public services' is the term I will use for now; its blurry delineations suit my purpose.

This is a vague concept which feeds into the more legally defined concepts of services of general (economic) interest, but, importantly, it is necessary to recall that what is termed a 'public service' (and service of general (economic) interest) is both context and time specific. Part of this context is provided by the shift in the previous century towards liberalization and the introduction of the market mechanism into (some of the) services that had previously been mostly state-provided. Important also is the current context of an apparent pushback against marketization and privatization having gone too far. Another relevant part of the context is the current state of technological development, its possible future direction, and the social embeddedness of digital and other technologies in everyday lives. These contexts are relevant when considering how Big Tech companies' businesses intersect with public services.

However, to understand, and possibly to react to, the phenomenon of the thickening interplay between Big Tech companies' services and the notion of public services, a more '*substantive definition*' of public services is useful. Such a substantive notion gives a normative underpinning for *why* we label services as 'public service' or regulate them as 'services of general economic interest' and goes beyond the institutional approach in which it is the state that decides that it is so.

Building upon notions inherent in the EU's constitutional set-up, a quick but sensible definition seems to be that a public service is a service which (a society deems) it is necessary that all citizens have access to, to be able to live a full life as a citizen. This shifts the definition to what such 'a full life' means, for which I would suggest that (in the EU) this would connote a life that is lived with both dignity and with (the possibility of) full participation in society. Such a small sentence carries a large meaning, where human dignity ties into autonomy and agency, the inherent worth of an individual, and theories of justice; and where 'the citizen' would tie into the idea of EU-citizenship status, to EU-ideas and values of meeting social, cultural and economic needs, but also to the exercise of citizen-political rights of participation. All this is part of a *political* identity too, of living in a democratic society based on the rule of law, in which—in the specific societal context of time and place—what is, and what is not, necessary to live a full life as a citizen is defined. However, some elements contradict, because this short definition would (in part) exclude non-citizens, while human dignity and autonomy are, by their very nature, never tied to a granted status of citizenship. That limitation can of course be addressed by using a different starting perspective which, however, would go beyond what is present in the EU constitutional set-up today: e.g., by using the capability approach. This might lead to defining those services as public services where access is necessary for *all* to be able to *flourish* as a human being. For my purposes in this contribution, however, the substantive notion of 'a full life of a citizen' suffices.

To label services as public services is thus a societal, often political, context-dependent decision. Both the notion of public services and such a decision are underpinned by the idea of solidarity and infused by the 'social contract' between citizen and state.[4] But such a decision is also based on shifting public values and changing views on what a society values and what citizens (thus) need to live a full life. Relevant here is that both of what is valued as necessary to live a full life as a citizen and thus might be considered a public service, but also—coming back to the start of this section –the delineation between what is market and what is non-market, are impacted by the digital transition. I turn to some elements of that digital transition next.

5.3 The (Future of) the Digital Transition

In this section, I will briefly lay out five elements of the relevant context of the digital transition, to be able to understand the interplay between public services and Big Tech platforms corporations (in Sect. 5.4).

First, though an obvious point, Big Tech corporations' services and activities both shape and are shaped by the digital transition. Here the 'digital transition' is understood as meaning that both in the economy, but also in society in the wider sense, including within the government and when it comes to the relationship between state and citizen, a growing number of interactions are intermediated by using digital technologies, including by algorithms and other forms of artificial intelligence. These interactions generate data and are themselves shaped by datafication. In contrast to the sustainability transition, which is as fundamental as the digital transition for the shape of future economies and societies and, at least at the start, was led by government actions, the digital transition is currently mostly business-led: the incentives for innovation lie with businesses and their mostly data-based business-models, and much of the transition is driven by companies (though of course some central innovations, such as the internet itself, are based upon state-led or state-funded research). The state (including the EU), in its regulatory capacity is secondary, even though a regulatory catching up is currently underway in the EU.

[4] See, again, on solidarity also Lalikova, in Chap. 6 of this volume.

That the digital transition is mostly business-led is fairly obvious, but it is also of fundamental importance: the market and business-driven logics that are at play are different from the logic of the state, which in most liberal, rule of law-based democratic societies is expected to be focused on providing for the public good and public values. The institutional logic of the market, driving innovation and the direction of the digital transition, may conflict with the institutional logic of the state. This is nothing new—and is putting the bisection mentioned above of what is economic (and thus subject to competition law) and what is not (and thus not subject to competition law), in the terminology of institutional logics. (The viewpoint of institutional logics is to focus on how norms and beliefs shape understanding and behavior of actors, including on how time and space is organized (in institutions)). It reiterates the point that is also underlying much market regulation, including regulation relating to digitalization, from the GDPR to the DSA and the DMA:[5] the underlying logics of these regulatory instruments, and therefore the driving values, but also the perceived desirability of futures, often do not align with the business-driven direction. Clearly this conflict of institutional logics becomes visible in the interplay between Big Tech and public services as well.

Second, in the context of this article it seems useful to be a bit more precise about the technicality of the digital economy. There are many ways to go about this, but for people like me—lawyer by training, exposed to the technicality of the digital transition for reasons of understanding the shape of a fitting legal system—a sensible way is to use the term 'cyberspace', the virtual space of communication and interactions. Cyberspace is generally held to consist of three layers, and this understanding of layers is useful when thinking of the 'space' or 'location' of a (digital) public service in the digital domain. The first layer is a physical layer of hardware and infrastructure, such as fiber optic cables, the servers and computers, with a geographical location: we can pinpoint to these components and generally note their physicality.[6] The second layer is the logical layer or network layer, the layer that covers the protocols and technologies that make it possible to actually communicate (by sending data between networks and nodes); these are infrastructures as well, but of a different kind. The third layer is the content layer, which connotes all the information itself: the websites and databases, the emails, streaming videos, the social media-content more generally and the applications that make it possible to make and share this information. And again, the notion of 'infrastructure' is also used to connote

[5] Regulation (EU) 2016/679 of the European Parliament and of the Council of 27 April 2016 on the protection of natural persons with regard to the processing of personal data and on the free movement of such data, and repealing Directive 95/46/EC, published on 4 May 2016, General Data Protection Regulation; Regulation (EU) 2022/1925 of the European Parliament and of the Council of 14 September 2022 on contestable and fair markets in the digital sector and amending Directives (EU) 2019/1937 and (EU) 2020/1828, published on 12 October 2022, Digital Markets Act; Regulation (EU) 2022/2065 of the European Parliament and of the Council of 19 October 2022 on a Single Market For Digital Services and amending Directive 2000/31/EC, published on 27 October 2022, Digital Services Act.

[6] The 'geography' has shifted over time: from local (decentralized) capacity in devices itself (such as pcs), to more centralized computing and storage facilities, and now moving to 'edge' computing to reduce latency.

this content layer. In each of these layers, services that make interactions possible are offered by a myriad of companies; it is especially (but not exclusively) in the logical and content layers, however, that the Big Tech companies operate.

Thirdly, it makes sense at this point to at least try to delineate 'Big Tech' a bit better. Generally, the notion covers the large technology-based platforms Amazon, Meta/Facebook, Alphabet/Google, Apple and Microsoft. Platforms, of course, indicate a multi-sidedness of interactions, but the Big Tech corporations have expanded their platforms beyond multi-sidedness and across activities and services, each developing their own technology-stacks to build and run their products and services. Importantly, it is also these Big Tech platform companies that are leading in the development of new digital technologies. Innovation by smaller startups is, of course, possible, but either restricted or ultimately encapsulated into the platforms of the Big Tech companies.

Big Tech companies are powerful, at the very least in a more colloquial sense, but that does not necessarily mean that they have a 'dominant economic position' in the sense of European competition law, for each of their activities. These companies are also gatekeepers, which has a similar sense of essentiality that belies the notion of public services (but is not necessarily the same). Elsewhere we have discussed how the corporate power of these big technology platforms, cannot really be captured by the competition law concept of 'market power' (to establish a dominant position), and have developed a theory to grasp this power more fully. We introduced the notion of 'Modern Bigness', to distinguish between three power-dimensions (instrumental, structural and discursive) and the impact on different domains (the economic, the political, the social and the personal domain).[7] If the interplay between Big Tech companies and public services is thickening—as I suggest it is, in the next section—this richer conceptualization of dimensions of power may be useful for a deeper understanding of the context in which this thickening takes place.

Fourthly, it is relevant to—in as far as possible—focus on the future direction of the development in this digital space. Something new seems to happen every couple of years, but two developments have surfaced at this moment in time (that is, November 2022): the metaverse and generative AI. Generative AI is potentially a very impactful development (think: Chat GPT, but then a couple of iterations in the future), which might have huge ramifications for all kinds of activities, including work. It might also, if the development of something like a 'metaverse' continues in the direction that Meta at least aimed it at, become an integrated development.[8] If so, a *layered* reality with in-built apparent intelligence based on generative AI will

---

[7] See Gerbrandy and Phoa 2022.

[8] Though the text of this contribution is based on a keynote of November 2022, later edits were made. In Spring 2023 the state of play with regards to generative AI, is, in comparison to just six months previously, that it has gone through a tremendously quick further development phase, while at the same time the focus on the/a metaverse has waned (at least in the public discourse). However, I have not substantively changed the text of this contribution as the *direction* of the development on an overarching level is still the same: digital technologies are becoming more ubiquitous, more encompassing and more integrated into more activities.

become, well, real. This might mean that our 'real life'-reality, the physical in-the-real-world reality humans have lived in for millennia, will be able to have an *overlay* of augmented reality functions. Think: the augmented reality game Pokémon Go, but then not just for fun games, but for all kinds of everyday activities, such as shopping, working, finding extensive travel information while looking at the timetable for our daily commute, and reading the personalized label of prescribed medicines. Our 'real life'-reality might also be supplanted by a digitally rendered reality—a virtual reality—in which we move seamlessly from one space, in the metaverse, to another. Though I say that 'we move' in this virtual reality, of course our bodies will stay in the same physical location, but our mind-experience will be one of moving from space to space; we might be sensorily totally immersed in this virtual reality too. Perhaps we will be assisted (or herded) by AI-systems to work, play, relax and interact. Think: Stephenson's *Snow Crash* (of course) or Gibson's *The Peripheral*.[9] Such a metaverse also includes the interaction of a citizen with public services, public services-providers, and government-entities, as one could 'move' from playing an online multiplayer game (think: Fortnite) to the virtual desk of the municipality to get a new passport.

All this can be linked. One might play a sophisticated Pokémon Go game in the park, move about in an AR-layered gym, and talk to a virtual assistant, rendered in the physical space in the municipality headquarters to renew a passport. In a virtual reality it does not really matter where the physical body is located, as long as there is access to high-speed internet. Such a virtual reality might *feel* disconnected from the physical world, though of course, for now at least, human cognition is tethered to the physical (but think: Anne Leckie).[10] Ultimately no one has a solid idea of what this might look like, but maybe—and this is purely based on the information that is now available and my own vivid mindscapes—it will start with having pockets that are as boring as an immersive zoom-type meeting (as portrayed by the early Meta depictions of the Metaverse, but with legs and more seamless human interactions). But it might grow to encompass cozy pockets of Chambers-like relations between AI and humans; it will most probably, at least in some spaces, have the raucous teenage energy of massive online games; and will probably struggle to contain the radical, the rebellious and the revolutionary. It might end up a fantastically rich, both rosy- and grim-textured mixture of all of the above, reminiscent of Stephenson's *Diamond Age*, mixed with Reynolds' depiction of the planet Yellowstone's Glitter Band.[11]

---

[9] Stephenson 1992; Gibson 2014. Now also an Amazon series with the same name. Stephenson's *Snow Crash* introduced the notion of the metaverse. Gibson (though not in *The Peripheral*, but in *Neuromancer* (Gibson 1984)), introduced the term cyberspace. In *The Peripheral*, though when plugged into a gaming machine the body stays in one place, human consciousness is present in a future time-space (a virtual but also alternate reality).

[10] Leckie 2013. The main character in this book embodies technological posthumanism.

[11] Our future reality will inevitably be very different from what my mind conjures up when reading and thinking about the referenced books: Chambers 2014, 2016, 2018, 2021. The series features—usually peaceful—close interpersonal interactions between AI and humans and other intelligent species. Stephenson 1995 focuses on a 'post-cyberpunk' world, in which nanotechnology is omnipresent, with widely differing (sometimes deliberately chosen) impacts on different

Fifth and finally, though much more mundane, political-legislative developments are terribly relevant too. Above I have stated that when it comes to the digital transition, the direction is led by business logics; the regulatory framework in which this takes place is important. Here, the focus of the past decades in the EU (and the Netherlands) on the market as the most suitable mechanism for providing goods and services, has shifted. While many previously state-provisioned services were moved towards the market, and wherever possible, liberalization and privatization were used as instruments for the public good of having a leaner state, a bigger market, and more efficient and cost-effective provision of services, it seems now that, while there is not so much a going back to state-provided (public) services (because trust in the state, or in politics at least, seems to have weakened too), certainly the belief that a mostly unfettered market delivers greatest benefits for society when it comes to public services has tumbled. In this current ideological space, there are calls for a return to greater state involvement, for an end to the current extractive economic system for reasons of planetary boundaries, and, in the realm of technology and digitalization, calls for further regulatory intervention.

A slightly separate, but crucial element of this political-legislative development is that, though the Big Tech corporations mostly provide their services across the globe, the differences in current and future regulatory interventions will almost inevitably mean a differentiation in the provision of their services. This geopolitical aspect is clearly visible when it comes to China but may increasingly be true also for diverging trajectories between large (democratic) markets/jurisdictions, such as the USA, the EU, and India. The value that is given to public services, the value of free markets, and interpretations of what freedom means in the digital space, already differ between them. Whether the 'Brussels-effect' will hold up in this pressure cooker remains to be seen;[12] it might also lead to a further diverging of regulatory frameworks and a differentiated digital development path, if it is deemed necessary to react to the thickening of the interplay between Big Tech companies and public services in, for example, the EU.

The five developments I laid out in this section—the digital transition, the dominance of business-logics in this transition, the role of Big Tech companies within this transition, the possible development towards a layered, integrated, and AI-supported

swaths of society. Reynolds 2000 has as its backdrop the planet Yellowstone, which at the point of its main storyline is in decline of its so-called *Belle Epoque*. During the *Belle Epoque* a system of 10,000 habitats called The Glitter Band encircled Yellowstone; this is what I am referring to here. It is still fully functioning in Reynolds 2007, and is governed not by democracy but by *Demarchy*, in which everyone has the right to vote, fairly constantly and directly via implants, but including to subject themselves to experimentation in social systems, such as submission to tyrannies. There is a series of books set in the *Revelation Space* universe, which encompasses an extremely rich diversity when it comes to imaginings of the future.

[12] The 'Brussels effect' is the effect that the strictest regulation, in this case: from the EU, ends up the *de facto* standard, so that the international conglomerates do not have to differentiate in how they offer services in different jurisdictions. Bradford 2019. The GDPR is said to have had such an effect. However, in social media content moderation practices there are diverging practices, as the legislative bottom-line standard of what is illegal speech differs between countries, including between the EU and the USA.

reality, and the regulatory environment in which all these elements are embedded—are interrelated. All kinds of services, including public services such as healthcare provision, education, and public transport, but also government activities such as decisions on welfare or allocation of subsidies, can, or will, be part of these developments. The state, however, may not necessarily have the know-how and capacity to shape or control these developments fully, operating at national, or regional levels; while, of course, the Big Tech companies not only have the know-how and capacity, but also operate on a global level, have a ferocious data-appetite and might be able to move into providing public services seamlessly. In the next section, I will try to show how the interplay between Big Tech and public services is already thickening.

5.4 The Interplay Between Big Tech and Public Services

In this section, I will zoom in a bit more on three developments relating to the interplay between Big Tech corporations and public services.

5.4.1 Big Tech Companies Are Providing Public-Service-Like Market Services

The first development I would like to highlight is that Big Tech companies already seem to provide market-based services that are becoming (or perhaps: have become) like public services, in the sense of services to which access is necessary to live a full life as a citizen. To grasp this development, I return first to the question of what someone needs, today, to live the full life of a citizen. As mentioned above, this is an answer that is decided upon by society and is context and place dependent. So on the one hand, my answer—as a citizen of The Netherlands (and thus: the EU), as a professor of competition law, as a white woman of—let's say—a certain age, with my individual story of how I came to be in the position where I am, in other words: from my individual positionality—is not necessarily the answer of someone else. On the other hand, it will almost certainly have elements of shared commonality with people that are part of same societal context of which I am part. More academically relevant, it is, furthermore, grounded in both European Union and national policies related to public services, and more generally on the values and principles enshrined in European constitutionalism, including in its foundational treaties.

Thus, my (not necessarily, full) answer would be something like this: to live a full life of a citizen people need education and the means to access education; they need access to health care, including access related to reproductive health; this means (also for more general reasons) they need to be able to travel, so that they can access these services, which probably means access to (public) transport; they need to be able to communicate, to be able to stay informed and be able to be involved in public discourse, which means access to for example postal services (physical post; but also digital post), (public) broadcast services, and news; they need access to energy and water; they need a socially accepted minimal income, also in old-age and through sickness; they need to be able to vote, to be informed on what they are voting for, and to be able to run for office; they need access to child-care facilities, to libraries, to financial services and many, many other services.

In the digitalized society other services might be added: can we live the full life of a citizen, with dignity and participation in society without access to high-speed internet (which is also increasingly used by the state to provide its services), access to a search engine, to e-identity services, to cybersecurity protection, to digital storage? Can we live the full life of a citizen without having (access to) a device from which to access those services? Can we live such a life without the digital skills to be able to access online-provided government or financial services? Can all have such a life in a democratic rule of law-based society in which a widening digital divide makes for growing inequality?

Even when focusing on the *economic* or *market* (digital) services (access to voting, for example, is not in the economic realm) it should be clear that to label any of these or other services as 'public services' does not necessarily mean an intervention by or provision through the state. Where access to these services, including the digital services mentioned, is either 'free', or widely provided through the market-mechanism, there is, in an economic sense, no clear market failure and thus no immediate economic theory based rationale for regulatory intervention by, in legal terms, labeling these as services of general economic interest, and charging a company with a universal service type obligation or having the state provide these services directly. Most of the mentioned economic digital services to which access might be deemed necessary to live a full life are, indeed, offered by market-based companies.

However, there can be reasons beyond direct market failures to regulate a service, which is a public service for access reasons. For part of these essential services, access is only possible through one of the large technology platforms, owned by one of the Big Tech companies. These corporations have, in general, powerful positions (see above, Sect. 5.3). They certainly have power over the shape, costs and access to their services. While access to, say, Google search, cloud-computing or—at the moment of writing—AI-generated creative support seems to be almost unrestricted and, in a monetary sense at least, often free, this is not to say that this will remain so in the future. And, certainly, that the services are 'free' in the monetary sense, does not mean that the provision by these powerful corporations does not come with costs to its users or societal costs: misinformation and disinformation; doxing or other nefarious online practices; a possibly spiraling effect on (some groups of) users, such as increased body-dysmorphia or radicalization; a generally shrinking private space; increased surveillance; increased vulnerability to cyberattacks. Thus, there might be reasons beyond increased positive externalities (economical and societal) that lie in pure solidarity and equality-infused public value rationales, not just to label such services as 'public services', but also to pose some restraints or positive obligations. At the same time, at this moment, it is not entirely clear to me which of the market-services might, or should, be seen as public services. Or, even, if we do know which services are public services, what that would mean concretely for a regulatory framework.[13]

The contextual elements (mentioned in Sect. 5.3) are relevant here too. First, it seems clear that in a context of geo-political implications for and of digital regulation—for example the differentiation of access to 'the internet' between the USA, the EU, China and other jurisdictions—and in the context of protecting the fabric of a democratic rule of law-based liberal society, it does make sense to consider this question of whether some of the services, and on which level of the infrastructure of cyberspace, that are now provided by Big Tech companies are 'public-service-like' and what that might mean for a regulatory response. Second and more specifically, when it comes to access to information and access to (public) discourse, the intermediation of this access through the social media, search, and generative AI functions offered by Big Tech platforms necessitates a deeper understanding of the '*discursive*' power dimension affecting the political domain of democracy and society. Thirdly, and this is a conclusion for the two next subsections too, a more thorough understanding of both (digital and infrastructural) technology, the shape and nature of the activities of the Big Tech corporations (and other companies) and a normatively laden reconsideration of what ought to be a 'public service' in a digital society is necessary.

5.4.2 Big Tech Companies Entering 'Classical' Public Services

The second development mirrors the development of Big Tech companies providing services that are public-service-like: Big Tech companies are also entering what in the European Union would be recognized as the domain of 'classical' public services. Though not all of these activities (already) extend to the EU, important examples relate to education, in which Google (Google Classroom) and Microsoft (such as Teams) are active, and in health care, in which services from Amazon Care (and Amazon Clinics and Amazon Pharmacy) and Google Health have entered the field. Some Big Tech corporations are also becoming involved in energy-provision and transition to sustainable energy, including by offering 'smart home' technology to limit energy usage, but also by greening their own production of energy. Big Tech companies are also involved in the financial sector: Apple Pay, Amazon Pay, and Google Pay offer payment services; Facebook had cryptocurrency plans (its Libra-plans, which ended up a failure). There is also involvement of the Big Tech corporations in the digitalization of agriculture, which might play a role in the further platformization of this sector: Amazon has the 'Farm to Table' initiative, Google has taken over the Climate Corporation, Microsoft is partnering with 'Granular', and Apple has a program on 'developing sustainable agriculture'. Clearly, in the EU,

[13] Lalikova provides, in Chap. 6 of this volume, an example in considering Google Search as a public service.

agricultural policies have a specific significance, also when it comes to precision farming in the move to greening agricultural production. Furthermore, there are links between these companies and the development of human spaceflight-capabilities: Amazon's CEO Jeff Bezos' Blue Origin project, Google's investment in SpaceX, which has Elon Musk as its CEO/CTO. Some of these companies are also involved in developing technologies that support (future) space-missions, such as Microsoft and Apple.

The above is a very brief overview and provides hardly any information on the exact scope and direction of activities and services. But even so, it raises questions when it comes to the theme of this contribution. While it would be necessary to understand better the intricate corporate structures within, and the rivalry and networks between, these corporations in all these domains, and gain a deeper sense of the technology stacks involved, the fundamental questions relate, again, both to the notion of public services and how these corporate activities are both a possible threat and a possible boon to these services. For example, when it comes to education and health, the services offered by these companies seem to mostly *support* existing education and health services, which might lead to cost savings and improvement of (access to) these services. This is important, as the services offered do not reach the core of education or healthcare, but might help keep services available, also in light of a shortage of education and healthcare workers. It is also important to note that especially in these sectors there is much attention paid to privacy protection and the need for limiting data-collection of pupils or students, and patients. However, there seems less attention for the possible future direction and expansion of these activities and what this means for the model (or notion of providing for) public services overall: is the incursion into the edges of existing public services a precursor to further expansion and would that threaten their solidarity basis? What happens to dependencies and lock-in effects in the long run (see also the third development, below)?

Quite different—at least for the everyday life of most people—is the issue when focusing on spaceflight; however, a development similar to that occurring in education and health care is visible here too (though, admittedly, on a different time-horizon). The development of human spaceflight capabilities has historically not been squarely in the corporate realm. In its core spaceflight itself—up till very recently at least—was not possible for corporations, and thus it was neither seen as an economic activity, nor as a public service. It has been a state activity, and *access* to spaceflight certainly is not (yet) a public service, nor has, as far as I am aware, the development of spaceflight capacity and capability been framed as such. However, developing spaceflight capabilities, also in part based on the deep pockets of some wealthy individuals, is now also done by private companies. Yet, what does that mean for commons such as space, for the moon, or for the future of asteroid-mining?[14] What does this mean in the long-term? It is not unthinkable that in the future, access to spaceflight will

[14] Yes, yes, there is relevant sci-fi here too: see e.g. the novels on moon exploration, exploitation and colonization, starting with McDonald 2015. Its story is centered on private exploitation of (habitation on) the Moon. Oxygen is a scarce resource, provided mostly by the few large corporations which vie for dominance over the Moon.

be necessary to be able to live a full life (for example, to escape a dying Earth; or more mundane, as part of intra-solar-system public transport); or that access to sufficient oxygen, when living on the moon, is necessary to live such a life. It is also not an impossibility that the resources from asteroid-mining are necessary resources to be able to live a full life elsewhere.[15] Obviously, I am aware that in comparison to education and healthcare, which are currently understood (in the EU) as public services, spaceflight services are so far-fetched that it can seem irrelevant to bring them into the discussion. However, this is an example of a future possibility, which is being shaped today. Thus, for both education and healthcare, and for spaceflight, a better understanding in relation to what we term public services seems necessary.

5.4.3 Governments' Dependency on Big Tech Services

The third development when it comes to the relationship between public services and Big Tech companies relates to the growing dependency of governments and government services on the services of Big Tech companies. This development partly overlaps with the second development, described above, as also public or (partly) public-funded educational institutes and health service providers, and other public service providers, are using the services offered by Big Tech companies to function. Governments rely on the proprietary software, cloud services and infrastructures of Big Tech companies for their own *internal* processes and their *interactions* with citizens, including for decision-making relating to individual citizens. For example, in decisions on (state and local) taxes to be paid, decisions relating to welfare payments or other support, or decisions on policing, including possible fraud in using public funds. Leaving the algorithmic government decision-making issues aside here (which can be problematic quite apart from relying on Big Tech companies), examples are the provision of cloud computing and web development services, offering cybersecurity services, support and services in shaping smart city technologies, and, of course, the offering of very day-to-day productivity and communication tools that many people working in government use.

This is nothing new. Governments use services offered by companies, including by very large corporations, constantly (and this is also why there are public procurement rules on how to procure those services). That the use of (Big Techs') services by the government might lead to lock-in effects is not new either; in that sense, the government is not different from other buyers. However, it is again in the context in which this development is set that questions arise. For example, the dependence on Big Tech corporations for the continuation of everyday functioning, but also for the continuation of critical public services and including protection against cyber-attacks on the provision of these services, seems qualitatively different in this context. In a possible

[15] For example, parallel to having access to energy for heating/cooling is necessary to live a full life. In that parallel, this does not necessarily mean that the procurement of resources, such as rare metals or ice, from asteroids is also a public service, but it does show the connection.

metaverse, this context also includes a consideration of government presence within (or link to) virtual reality or realities, including the necessity of interconnectivity, and safety and identification issues. In this third development, the focus is not so much on whether the services and infrastructures provided by technology corporations to the government (and to public service providers in, e.g. healthcare and education) should themselves be considered a public service in the substantive sense I identified above. The focus here is that the provision of existing and novel public services may become (more) dependent on the services of Big Tech corporations, to the point that this dependence might become problematic in light of the necessity of those public services for citizens. But again, a more thorough understanding of technology and the provision of services for both day-to-day running of governments, and the impact of dependencies for provisions of government and public services in a digital society seems necessary.

5.5 Conclusions

This is a contribution to a volume on services of general economic interest. It may seem that I have moved away quite a bit from that topic. I sketched three developments in the thickening relationship between Big Tech companies and public services, and I stressed the point—several times—that these developments take place in a continuing (and rapidly) changing technological context of an increasingly digitally-mediated society and economy. Indeed, I hardly focused on the notion of services of general economic interest or their intersection with regulated markets or general competition law. I purposefully used the term 'public service' instead, because I wanted to first move *away* from the discussion on sub-categorizations and fitting developments immediately into existing pigeonholes, where they might not immediately fit. To make matters more complex, if we must use the conceptualizations existing around the services of general economic interest concept, the thickening relationship between Big Techs and public services is perhaps best understood by considering these services as *digital public services* or *digital services of general economic interest* (the latter is useful so as to distinguish governments providing their non-economic public services digitally). But since we are moving towards (almost) all services becoming more or less digitalized, at least for some components, I am uncertain whether such labels are helpful or just add to existing complexities.

At any rate, the underlying theme of my contribution fits this volume. It is the same theme that underlies the interplay between European competition law (and regulated markets) and the exception for undertakings entrusted with a service of general economic interest. It focuses on the relationship between what is, or ought to be, provided through the market mechanism, and what lies outside (or is only partly within) the realm of this market logic, or ought to be. (I have left out the consideration of the in-between sphere: an option of organizing counter-power or shaping alternatives in the in-between.) Though I have proposed a normative idea of why we would consider a service a public service—proposing it could be services to which access is deemed necessary to live a full life as a citizen—I have also stressed that society, in a specific context and time, decides on what that means.

But, as is often the case, societal questions are also, or become also, ultimately questions for the law, including for European competition and regulatory law: whether—if the developments mentioned above become further entrenched in a digitalized society in which some Big Tech companies hold positions of a complex and multilayered power—the thickening of the interplay with public services is potentially a threat to continued provision of specific public services or the more general notion of a society that is explicitly built upon the idea that public services and services of general economic interest are foundational for its solidarity-based fabric. Regulation, protection of access, the exception enshrined in European competition law, would then come into play; existing pigeonholes may have to be stretched, or new ones invented, to fit these technological and societal developments to protect the EU's notion of protection of public services. In the rapid technological changes in the near (and slightly less near) future, many developments that I mentioned in this contribution might not happen (or happen very differently). However, as stressed in the introduction, the aim of this contribution was not to show the precise direction of technological developments, but that these also have relevance for the corner of the legal discourse that focuses on the interplay of services of general (economic) interest, sectoral regulation and European competition law.

References

Bradford A (2019) The Brussels Effect: How the European Union Rules the World. Oxford University Press, Oxford.

Chambers B (2014) The Long Way to a Small, Angry Planet. Wayfarer Series. CreateSpace Independent Publishing Platform.

Chambers B (2016) A Closed and Common Orbit. Wayfarer Series. CreateSpace Independent Publishing Platform.

Chambers B (2018) Record of a Spaceborn Few. Wayfarer Series. CreateSpace Independent Publishing Platform.

Chambers B (2021) The Galaxy and the Ground Within. Wayfarer Series. CreateSpace Independent Publishing Platform.

Gerbrandy A, Phoa P (2022) The Power of Big Tech Corporations as Modern Bigness and a Vocabulary for Shaping Competition Law as Counter-power. In: Bennett M et al. (eds) Wealth and Power. Routledge, New York City/Abingdon (Oxon), pp 166–185.

Gibson W (1984) Neuromancer. Ace Books.

Gibson W (2014) The Peripheral. G.P. Putnam's Sons, New York City.

Leckie A (2013) Ancillary Justice. Orbit Books, London.

McDonald I (2015) Luna: New Moon. Gollancz (UK).

Reynolds A (2000) Revelation Space. Gollancz S.F.

Reynolds A (2007) The Prefect. Gollancz S.F.

Stephenson N (1992) Snow Crash. Bantam Books, New York City.

Stephenson N (1995) The Diamond Age: or, A Young Lady's Illustrated Primer. Bantam Spectra.

Anna Gerbrandy is a professor of Competition Law at Utrecht University School of Law. This research is funded by ERC StG No. 853005. Anna is also a Crown Appointed member of the Social and Economic Council of the Netherlands.

Chapter 6
Google Search as a Public Service

Laura Frederika Lalikova

Contents

Abstract Digital services increasingly exhibit characteristics akin to public services. While policy discussions have begun to reflect this reality, there remains a notable absence of explicit legislative recognition within the European Union (EU). This chapter explores the extent to which EU can regulate such digital services—namely search engine services—as a public service. It does so by examining the relevant concepts and provisions under EU law, assessing existing regulatory practices, and evaluating their potential applicability to search engine services, taking Google Search as an example. The chapter concludes that introducing universal service obligations could help safeguard access to search engine services and affirm users' rights as citizens, thereby rectifying the initial consumerfication of big tech platforms users.

Keywords Public services · SGI · EU digital policy · Digital platforms · Big Tech · Search engines

L. F. Lalikova (✉)
Faculty of Law, Economics, and Governance, Utrecht University, Utrecht, The Netherlands
e-mail: l.f.lalikova@uu.nl

N. Ghazaryan et al. (eds.), *Services of General (Economic) Interest and EU Law*, Legal Issues of Services of General Interest, https://doi.org/10.1007/978-94-6265-723-6_6

6.1 Introduction

Now more than ever, big tech companies challenge and bridge the public-private divide. They are private entities without explicit public tasks delivering services of public importance. They attend to our daily needs as customers and citizens by providing entertainment, markets, or backbone infrastructures of our daily communications and information intake. Search engines stand out as a prime example of such an essential role.

While the conduct of the big tech companies was initially primarily corrected through competition law enforcement, stronger regulatory efforts have been witnessed recently. The European legislator has been attempting to respond to the challenges posed by the nature of big tech platform services through a range of regulatory instruments. Perhaps the most noticeable being the Digital Markets Acts and Digital Services Act.[1] Both instruments form part of the European Commission's strategy on *A Europe fit for the digital age*, which maintains that "[…] additional rules may be needed to ensure contestability, fairness and innovation and the possibility of market entry, as well as public interests that go *beyond* [emphasis added] competition or economic considerations".[2] This implies that there are compelling reasons to treat platforms of big tech companies beyond their economic impact, and a necessity to enforce their societal significance legislatively. This chapter therefore examines the proposition that the concept of public services, accompanied by universal service obligations and public service objectives, could offer a viable approach to address the aforementioned need for rules ensuring the public interests beyond competition and economic considerations in the realm of digital markets.

This chapter will first discuss the concept of public services at the EU level. Subsequently, the characteristics intrinsic to public services will be discussed and simultaneously applied to the operation of Google Search as case study in the market of search engines, illustrating compelling grounds for recognising Google Search as a public service. The following section will discuss the imposition of universal service obligations or broader public interest objectives (as falling within the remit of the concept of public services at the EU level). The conclusion of the evaluation suggests that regulating search engines in this manner could promote the public interest value that goes beyond their competition and economic value, and may further enhance the rights of users as citizens.

---

[1] Regulation (EU) 2022/1925 of the European Parliament and of the Council of 14 September 2022 on contestable and fair markets in the digital sector and amending Directives (EU) 2019/1937 and (EU) 2020/1828, published on 12 October 2022, Digital Markets Act; Regulation (EU) 2022/2065 of the European Parliament and of the Council of 19 October 2022 on a Single Market For Digital Services and amending Directive 2000/31/EC, published on 27 October 2022, Digital Services Act.

[2] European Commission 2020, p. 5.

6.2 The Concept of Public Services at the EU Level

To begin, it is necessary to first discuss the concept of public services, the related concepts and provisions at the EU level. In principle, public services are the competence of Member States, and historically, each Member State has cultivated its distinctive public service tradition.[3] Despite the array of traditions and definitions present, there is at minimum a common understanding and fundamental unity about the *raison d'être* of the concept of public services. That is, that some activities, owing to the societal value they offer, cannot be regulated by markets and competition alone, and must therefore adhere to another form of regulatory intervention. Such intervention aims to guarantee certain rights (e.g. access), or to build and enforce solidarity and cohesion.[4] In this context, the EU assumes primarily a 'regulatory state' function, as it merely possesses the competence to coordinate national policies or to set standards.[5] Conversely, the EU has an exclusive competence over competition rules necessary for the functioning of the internal market, and thus, its main involvement in terms of public services derives from ensuring that the provision of public services does not distort the competitive process.[6] Moreover, the EU's other focus rests on access rights witnessed through universal service obligations, or Article 36 EU Charter of Fundamental Rights on access to services of general economic interest, as well as on public service objectives (e.g. environmental protection) belonging to the remit of the universal service field.[7]

The EU generally avoids the use of the term 'public service' (apart from Article 93 TFEU in relation to transport) and instead utilises the label of 'services of general interest'. The latter is not to be considered an equivalent of any Member State's tradition of public services, as the concept has its standalone history and context. Instead, services of general interest are defined as: "[...] services that public authorities of the EU member countries classify as being of general interest and, therefore, subject to specific public service obligations."[8] The definition entails both economic and non-economic activities. The economic activities come under the label of "services of general economic interest", and are defined as activities which deliver outcomes in the overall public good that would not be supplied or would be supplied under less ideal conditions if supplied by the market alone.[9] They are conducted in exchange for remuneration, such as postal services, and fall under the purview of European

[3] Bauby and Similie 2012, p. 4.

[4] Ibid.

[5] Consolidated version of the Treaty on the Functioning of the European Union, signed on 13 December 2007, published 26 October 2012, TFEU, Article 5(3). See also Sauter 2014, p. 3.

[6] Ibid., Articles 3(1) and 106.

[7] Finger and Finon 2011, p. 60.

[8] https://commission.europa.eu/topics/single-market/services-general-interest_en. Accessed 14 November 2023.

[9] Communication from the Commission of 20 December 2011 to the European Parliament, the Council, the European Economic and Social Committee and the Committee of the Regions: A Quality Framework for Services of General Interest in Europe, COM(2011) 900 final, p. 3.

internal market and competition rules, albeit with derogations to those rules to safeguard citizen's access to them. Non-economic activities, on the other hand, are not subject to competition and internal market rules, and encompass services such as police or justice. Finally, there are 'social services of general interest', which can be either economic or non-economic in nature, and pertain to services that respond to the needs of vulnerable citizens such as social security scheme or employment services. See footnote 8 above.

The position of services of general interest within the legal framework rests on a triad of provisions:

i. Article 36 CFREU on access to services of general economic interest;
ii. A legal basis for legislating on services of general economic interest: a positive provision, found in Article 14 TFEU, together with the Lisbon Protocol No. 26 on services of general (economic) interest;
iii. A derogation from competition rules under Article 106(2) TFEU: a negative provision.[10]

These provisions emphasise the significance of the services of general interest, and lay out the guiding principles for the EU's approach in this sphere. While Member States have the general competence to define, provide, and organise the services of general interest, Article 14 TFEU provides an opening for the EU to legislate on principles and conditions such as economic and financial, which enable the services of general economic interest to carry out their task. And Protocol No. 26 (discussed in more detail in the next section) puts forward fundamental principles which are applicable to all services of general interest, for the first time at the level of primary law.

However, despite the presence of Article 14 TFEU, the Commission has historically favoured a sector-specific approach over an EU framework regulation on services of general economic interest as envisaged by Article 14 TFEU given that, a sector-specific approach arguably allowed for a more tailor-made approach to each sector.[11] Thus, the EU's direct and positive involvement in public services took and takes the clearest manifestation through universal services obligations and public service objectives, which formed part of several pieces of sectoral legislation during and in the aftermath of the process of liberalisation. In addition, Protocol No. 26 should be mentioned, through which the EU mandates six shared values applicable to all services of general economic interest in the EU; unequivocally signalling the ongoing commitment to promoting public services in the EU.

---

[10] Charter of Fundamental Rights of the European Union [2012] OJ C326/391 (CRFEU); the Treaty on the Functioning of the European Union [2012] OJ C326/47 (TFEU); Protocol (No 26) on services of general interest [2008] OJ C115/308.

[11] Ibid., p. 5.

6.2.1 Protocol No. 26

Indeed, Protocol No. 26 markedly highlights and strengthens the institutional place of services of general interest, by enshrining, in primary legislation, the six shared values that not only shape the EU activities in the sphere of public services, but also guarantee and secure the fulfilment of the tasks of services of general interest in the EU. The values listed include a high level of quality, safety, affordability, equal treatment, the promotion of universal access, and of user rights.[12]

When zooming in on the value of quality, key factors such as reliability, continuity of the service, or the promotion of environmental protection and sustainability are commonly noted.[13] By way of example, in Directive 97/67/EC on postal services and the improvement of quality of service, the entirety of Chapter 6 is dedicated to quality of services, with a focus on routing times, regularity and reliability, or access to complaints mechanisms.[14] In 2011, the Commission also introduced the "Quality framework for services of general interest", outlining its approach for establishing a quality framework on ensuring access to essential services for all citizens, and on ensuring that specific needs are addressed.[15] With regards to the second value, safety, it is the Member States that primarily define the level of safety for services of general economic interest, whilst the EU steps in predominantly when global issues emerge, or when the situation concerns a cross-border safety.[16] This is exemplified by the existence of a number of European safety agencies in sectors with cross-border safety concerns such as the European Union Aviation Safety Agency (EASA) or the European Union Railway Agency (ERA). The third value, affordability, is closely linked to the goal of cohesion pursued by the EU and has been emphasised in the liberalisation policies. Two approaches can be discerned. One with a universal dimension, and one with a focus on the vulnerable or disadvantaged.[17] The value of affordability generally falls under the scope of universal service obligations as pursued by the EU in sectors like telecommunications or postal services. The fourth value, equal treatment is, unlike the previous three values which aim for "a high level of [...]", an absolute.[18] It is considered a general principle of EU law, which warrants equal, albeit not identical, treatment. It justifies positive discrimination in order to prevent social exclusion related to various factors like race, gender, or sexual orientation. It is recognised through a number of provisions of the EU Charter of Fundamental Rights, such as those regarding the rights of children or the integration

---

[12] Protocol (No 26) on services of general interest [2008] OJ C115/308.

[13] Bauby and Similie 2012, p. 6.

[14] Directive 97/67/EC of the European Parliament and of the Council of 15 December 1997 on common rules for the development of the internal market of Community postal services and the improvement of quality of service, published on 21 January 1998, Directive 97/67/EC.

[15] A Quality Framework for Services of General Interest in Europe, above n. 9.

[16] Bauby and Similie 2012, p. 7.

[17] Ibid.

[18] Bauby and Similie 2012, p 8.

of people with disabilities.[19] The fifth value is the promotion of universal access. The call for universal access is the recognition of the right to access to services of general economic interest under Article 36 CFREU, and forms part of the universal service obligations imposed on the service providers in, for instance, telecom or energy sectors as a recognition that markets alone cannot always provide universal access or sufficient geographical coverage. However, universality does not necessarily imply that the needs of the entire population are met. Rather, limited territorial or material coverage can still maintain a universal quality.[20] The sixth and the last value is the promotion of user rights, which, since the Treaty of Maastricht, is a shared competence with Member States having the primary competence to define user and consumer rights in the absence of EU-level regulation.[21] Promotion of user rights is part of the recognition that pursuing the internal market goals and enforcing competition objectives markets alone might not provide users, who are also citizens, with a sufficient promotion and protection of their rights.

Overall, Protocol No. 26 ensures uniform provision of services of general economic interest across the Member States in line with the EU's endorsed values, all the while establishing a framework of values for EU's policy and regulatory activities in this sphere.

6.2.2 Universal Service Obligations and Public Service Objectives

Having discussed Protocol No. 26, the next aspect of EU's involvement in the public service realm that warrants attention regards the concepts of universal service obligations and public service objectives. While the former is based on universality of access, the latter may have additional broader goals, such as ensuring environmental protection.

Following the earlier process of EU liberalisation strategies within the traditional network industries sectors, the Commission began to pursue harmonised regulatory frameworks (generally under Article 114 TFEU), with the aim of securing the delivery of diverse public service guarantees. And thus, the concept of universal service obligations was put forth. The Commission has in the past noted that the concept "[…] is the expression in Europe of the requirements and special features of the European model of society in a policy which combines a dynamic market, cohesion and solidarity".[22] It is considered a changing and a responsive concept that must be regularly revisited to reflect the social, economic and technological

[19] Charter of Fundamental Rights of the European Union, published 26 October 2012, Articles 22–26.

[20] See CJEU (GC), *BUPA*, Judgment, 12 February 2009, T-289/03.

[21] Bauby and Similie 2012, p. 9.

[22] Communication from the Commission of 11 September 1996 on Services of General Interest in Europe, COM(96) 443 final, para 32.

advances across the EU.[23] Formally, the concept is employed to identify a specific group of services within which the universal service obligations have been defined, at least to some extent, at the EU level, thus 'curbing' the discretion of Member States in this area of public services. The concept presents a series of principles and obligations applicable across all Member States, underscoring the necessity for a basic service accessible to all across various sectors. It includes a geographical aspect, catering to cohesion across regions, and a social aspect, which safeguards affordability. The Commission defines universal service obligations as "[...] a type of [public service obligation] which sets the requirements designed to ensure that certain services are made available to all consumers and users in a Member State, regardless of their geographical location, at a specified quality and, taking account of specific national circumstances, at an affordable price".[24] And, emphasises the concept's role in addressing challenges arising from the simultaneous presence of public services and market forces.[25]

At the EU level, universal service obligations have thus far been defined in the traditional network industries (such as postal sector, electronic communications, or electricity) but also in newer industries (basic banking services). Within those, a specialised regulatory framework has emerged, utilising the safeguards of universal service obligations to justify and thereby advance the process of liberalisation. However, in some pieces of sectoral legislation, broader public service objectives can also be seen, enforcing the argument that the EU legislator recognises and incorporates the broader concept of public service (broader than the concept universal service obligations) within its frameworks. Public service objectives concerning social or environmental protection take centre stage in a directive, such as Directive 2019/944 on rules for the internal market for electricity, and are recognised as a crucial aspect of the broader general economic interest.[26]

Universal service obligations offer very clear and enforceable rights and results.[27] For instance, in the postal sector, Directive 97/67/EC defines minimum requirements of the universal service to be guaranteed by each Member State. It mandates (with exceptions) that a high quality postal service (delivery of letters and parcels to home and businesses) must be provided at minimum five days a week throughout the whole of a Member State's territory, and at an affordable cost.[28] In the telecom sector, now electronic communications, Directive 2018/1972 prescribes universal service

---

[23] Communication from the Commission to the European Parliament, the Council, the European Economic and Social Committee and the Committee of the Regions – White Paper on services of general interest, COM(2004) 374 final, p. 8; Directive (EU) 2018/1972 of the European Parliament and of the Council of 11 December 2018 establishing the European Electronic Communications Code (Recast), published on 17 December 2018, Directive 2018/1972, recital 210.

[24] A Quality Framework for Services of General Interest in Europe, above n. 9, p. 4.

[25] Ibid.

[26] Directive (EU) 2019/944 of the European Parliament and of the Council of 5 June 2019 on common rules for the internal market for electricity, published on 14 June 2019, Directive 2019/944, Article 9.

[27] Sauter 2008, p. 177.

[28] Directive 97/67/EC, above n. 12, Article 3.

obligations as a safety net to ensure that at least the minimum service of adequate broadband internet access and voice communications services are available to all end-users and at an affordable price to prevent a risk of exclusion from full social and economic participation in society.[29] It is envisaged in the Directive that an affordable and adequate service is available to citizens regardless of their location, income or disability, and, for instance, that the broadband internet has sufficient bandwidth for supporting at least the minimum set of service set out, which include email, search engines, instant messaging or internet banking.[30] In the banking services sector, we observe an access obligation at the retail level that is not referred to as a universal service obligation but does materially resemble one.[31] Directive 2014/92/EU materialised the findings of the impact assessment which found that access to basic payment services is essential for financial and social inclusion and allows consumers to benefit wholly from the EU's single market.[32] The Directive calls for the Member States to ensure that consumers have access to payment accounts with basic features irrespective of their financial circumstances, including their employment status or credit history.[33] Accordingly, payment accounts with basic features include the ability to place or withdraw funds, the ability to undertake payment transactions such as receiving income or paying bills, or the ability to purchase goods and services online, and are not to be restricted to online services, so as not to exclude those without access to internet.[34]

Taking into account the regular sectoral revisions, there is no doubt that the process of revisions in the realm of universal service obligations and of public service objectives (and overarchingly in the context of public services) is current and ongoing. It is therefore suggested that some services of digital platforms may now be ripe for similar access safeguards, considering their evolving role in society, which increasingly resembles that of a public service. This prompts the question of what parameters should be considered to determine whether a service provided by a digital platform qualifies as a service of essential value, in line with the concept of public service. The following section will discuss this very question, using Google Search (search engine as a service) as an illustration.

---

[29] Directive 2018/1972, above n. 20, Article 84.

[30] Ibid., recital 219 and Article 84.

[31] Sauter 2014, p. 17.

[32] Directive 2014/92/EU of the European Parliament and of the Council of 23 July 2014 on the comparability of fees related to payment accounts, payment account switching and access to payment accounts with basic features, published on 28 August 2014, Directive 2014/92, recital 6. See also Commission, 'Proposal for a Directive of the European Parliament and of the Council on the comparability of fees related to payment accounts, payment account switching and access to payment accounts with basic features' COM (2013) 266 final, section 2.

[33] Ibid., recital 35.

[34] Directive 2014/92/EU recital 44.

6.3 Public Service Characteristics of Google Search

General and often vague terminologies such as "there is a general political consensus", "services of indispensable nature" or "essential", do not clarify what makes public service different from other services, and what underscores their significance to the public. This is further perplexed by the fact that any service can have a public interest dimension, and that what is valued as public at a certain period of time may not be at another point in time. Indeed, there is a general understanding of the importance of big tech services beyond their economic value, however, even within the platform ecosystems not all services are equally essential. How then is essentiality defined within the concept of public services? There is not one common definition of what constitutes a public service; instead, existing literature provides a myriad of criteria, measures, characteristics, or conditions that define the notion. From these, a number of overlapping characteristics, entailing broader, societal values, as well as market related values can be discerned:[35]

i. the scope of the service recipients;
ii. its societal role;
iii. its economic role;
iv. abiding by public service standards, or performing a quasi-regulatory function;
v. being imperative to social, political or civil citizenship.

The next few sections will see the application of these five characteristics to Google Search as an illustration of how the characteristics defining the traditional notion of public services hold up in the realm of big tech platform services.

6.3.1 The Scope of Service Recipients

The first characteristic is the scope of service recipients, i.e. the greater the number of service recipients (of those seeking the service) incorporating a broad range of interest groups, the greater its essentiality.[36] The scope of Google Search's service recipients alone is undeniably immense, and likely to continue to increase, given the existence of positive network effects, which allow Google Search to continuously improve the experience of each user from the search queries and behaviours of other users.[37] At the time of writing, Google Search processes approximately (on average) 100,000 search queries every second.[38] This translates to close to nine billion search queries a day, and to more than three trillion search queries a year.[39] To add to the magnitude of search engines' scope of recipients, it was found that 68% of all trackable website

[35] Cremer et al. 2001, p. 7; Haque 2001; Helberger et al. 2021, p. 203; Marshall 1950.

[36] Haque 2001, p. 68.

[37] Gregory et al. 2021, p. 543.

[38] https://www.internetlivestats.com/google-search-statistics/. Accessed 14 November 2023.

[39] Ibid.

traffic was sourced from search engines, which vastly exceeded other channels of display or social character.[40] Search engines, and in particular Google Search are gatekeepers to digital realms for the most. As Haider and Sundin point out, "[the] search-ification of everyday life has turned a once complex professional practice into something seemingly simple and made it available for everyone".[41]

6.3.2 *Societal Role*

The second characteristic lies in the magnitude and intensity of the service's societal role.[42] It implies that the service plays an active role and is capable of accommodating to a societal demand, public interests or needs, and is considered reliable. Knowledge, information, and communication play a pivotal role in globalised contemporary society.[43] And search engines, such as Google Search, are seen as its information infrastructures.[44] Search engines are responsible for habitualising a form of economy of information seeking and knowing not present before.[45] Google Search's role, in particular, is embedded in the structure of our societies with a magnitude that it becomes omnipresent to a point of being institutionalised.[46] Search engines have the ability and potential to increase association, giving voice to information sources that would normally not be encountered, or conveying an inclusive discourse between normally disconnected channels. This is highlighted also in the Digital Service Act which zooms in explicitly on the societal importance of search engines. In Recital 75, it notes that very large online search engines facilitate public debate, economic transactions and the dissemination of information, opinions and ideas, and influence how recipients obtain and communicate information online.[47] In the same recital, the Act acknowledges the critical role of such platforms in locating and making information retrievable, and the need for additional obligations to address public policy concerns (influence over public opinion and discourse). The societal role of Google Search was vividly demonstrated during the Covid-19 pandemic when it served as the platform for accessing reliable information related to public health from sources such as the WHO or national health authorities.[48] Facing constraints in accessing and

---

[40] Brightedge Research 2019, p. 3.

[41] Haider and Sundin 2019, p. 81.

[42] Haque 2001, p. 69.

[43] Schirato and Webb 2003.

[44] Sundin and Carlsson 2016.

[45] Andersen 2018, p. 1141.

[46] See ibid.; Haider and Sundin 2019.

[47] Regulation (EU) 2022/2065 of the European Parliament and of the Council of 19 October 2022 on a Single Market For Digital Services and amending Directive 2000/31/EC, published on 27 October 2022, Digital Services Act.

[48] Pichai 2020.

utilising search engines can thus lead to de facto exclusion from essential information and discourse.

Finally, the definition of a socially valuable service also incorporates the aspect of reliability. Multiple empirical studies and surveys indicate users' confidence in the search engine's ability to provide accurate and credible information. Laboratory studies have shown that Google's ranking trumps users' individual assessment or other influencing factors.[49] Similar expressions of trust were found in a survey of a representative sample commissioned by the European Commission and presented in *Special Eurobarometer 447 on Online Platforms*.[50] The survey concluded that attitudes towards search engines are generally positive and are perceived as effective and enjoy a high level of trust with 78% of European internet and online platforms users agreeing that they trust the search results provided are the most relevant.[51] This again signals the necessity for an in increased scrutiny regarding access safeguards, and conditions under which users are given access.

6.3.3 Economic Role

Network and information systems, which includes search engines, are positioned as objects of strategic importance with a profound economic role and consequences.[52] There is an implicit understanding of the indispensability of accessing information in achieving stable functioning of the internal market. In Recital 1 of the Digital Markets Act, digital services are described as playing an increasingly important role in the economy, particularly in the internal market.[53] They are viewed as enabling businesses to reach users throughout the EU, by facilitating cross-border trade and by opening entirely new business opportunities to the benefit of companies and consumers. Similarly, in Regulation 1150/2019 (P2B Regulation) online search engines are viewed as capable of significantly affecting commercial success in the internal market.[54] Accordingly, search engines are capable of accomplishing such impact through a degree of integration within other networks, vertical integration and cross-sectorisation.[55] For instance, Google Search is vertically integrated within the advertising market through Google's operation of the search engine and its advertising platform Google Ads. Another example of its vertical integration is

[49] See Pan et al. 2007, p. 816; Schultheiß et al. 2018; Unkel and Haas 2017.

[50] European Commission 2016.

[51] Ibid., p. 16.

[52] Haider and Sundin 2019, p. 52.

[53] Regulation (EU) 2022/1925 of the European Parliament and of the Council of 14 September 2022 on contestable and fair markets in the digital sector and amending Directives (EU) 2019/1937 and (EU) 2020/1828, published on 12 October 2022, Digital Markets Act.

[54] Regulation (EU) 2019/1150 of the European Parliament and of the Council of 20 June 2019 on promoting fairness and transparency for business users of online intermediation services, published on 11 July 2019, P2B Regulation, recital 4.

[55] See Cremer et al. 2001, p. 7; Helberger et al. 2021, p. 203.

through its software and hardware products such as Google's smartphone or voice assistant. An example of cross-sectorisation is Google's role in advertising markets, healthcare or education. Google has partnered with various educational institutions to offer digital learning tools, or to allow Google Career Certificates to be translated into college credit.[56] In terms of healthcare, Google has partnered with various healthcare providers and research institutes to develop new technologies and tools.[57] Overall, Google Search's integration and cross-sectorisation offers a more comprehensive and thus a more essential service to users.

6.3.4 Public Service Standards or a Quasi-Regulatory Function

The fourth characteristic indicates that the public service abides by public service standards or has a quasi-regulatory function. Public service standards are in the context of public services more prescriptive than descriptive. This implies that a service does not need to adhere to public service standards as a condition for it being considered a public service, but such standards may be imposed onto the provision of the service once the service is recognised as having a public service character. Equally, if a service already embodies public service standards, such presence can be seen as a reflection of users' expectations and requirements for the service. The most prominent public service standards are impartiality, equality and representation, and responsiveness.[58] The standard of impartiality implies an assessment of information, to achieve accuracy and fairness, understood in terms of detachment from ideas, opinions or interests.[59] Impartiality standard is often coupled with the standard of objectivity, and thus, while impartiality relates to absence of bias, objectivity is concerned with identifying facts.[60] The standard of equality on the other hand is envisaged in terms of access, while the standard of representation is envisaged in terms of representation in the process of decision making. The final standard is responsiveness, which foresees that the public service is responsive to the demands of its service recipients.

In order to assess the degree to which search engines adhere to the standards noted above, it is important to discuss the underlying process. Google Search, to illustrate, works in three stages. These three stages include "crawling", "indexing",

---

[56] Porat 2021.

[57] "Google Cloud will secure and store Mayo Clinic's data, while working with Mayo Clinic to apply AI and other cloud computing technologies to solve complex health care problems". Anastasijevic D (2019) Mayo Clinic selects Google as strategic partner for health care innovation, cloud computing. Newsnetwork Mayo Clinic. https://newsnetwork.mayoclinic.org/discussion/mayo-clinic-selects-google-as-strategic-partner-for-health-care-innovation-cloud-computing/. Accessed 14 November 2023.

[58] Haque 2001, p. 67.

[59] Sambrook 2012, p. 5.

[60] Ibid., p. 3.

and "serving" search results. During the first stage—crawling—Google continuously downloads texts, images, and videos from web pages it finds using programs called "crawlers".[61] It then stores these webpages in its "index" (a register of the crawled webpages). During the second stage—indexing—Google processes and analyses the text, key content tags, and attributes of a page. Google then determines if that page is "the canonical", meaning that the page that is most representative of the content and may thus be shown on the result page.[62] During the final stage—serving search results—Google's machines search the index for matching pages and return the results which it determines to be of the highest quality and most relevant to user's query. Although the exact details of the algorithm determining the relevancy are not public, it is reportedly (also) determined by factors such as the words of the query, location, language, device, usability of pages, authoritativeness, trustworthiness, or expertise of sources, and the weight given to each factor is dependent on the nature of the query entered.[63] Thus, during the first two stages of its workings, Google Search is set up to search for tags and attributes, which are applied in a factual manner to all webpages crawled (thus being objective as described above), while the last stage of serving search results can be considered absent of bias (thus impartial) as it presents a search results that is of highest quality and most relevant to user's query. Impartiality in this sense ensures consistent assessment of information, to achieve accuracy and fairness. Despite Google's episodic deviation from the impartiality standard, evident in the General Court's judgment in *Google Shopping* on Google's abusive behaviour in the form of self-preferencing; from a user's perspective and its underlying business model, Google Search operates impartially as it merely reacts to quantifiable signals to assess relevance.[64] The second set of standards listed above were equality and representation. As noted above, equality here is envisaged in terms of equal access. *Stricto sensu*, with the exception of those that are firewalled, Google Search service is accessible to all.[65] Google Search can thus be considered to abide by the standard of equality in terms of access (however, more on equality later). Naturally, not every user receives equal output (taking into consideration personalisation offered by Google), however, each user is treated as an equal. Next, the standard of representation in the process of decision making is arguably adhered to through the representation of each user as data processed through algorithms. Its technical capabilities enable Google to continuously improve the experience of each user from the search queries and behaviours of other users. Thus, each user's behaviour is adapting the service, albeit without any control over the exact decision making. Finally, the standard of responsiveness. Generally, responsiveness entails a responsive public service which

---

[61] https://developers.google.com/search/docs/fundamentals/how-search-works#:~:text=Crawling%3A%20Google%20downloads%20text%2C%20images,which%20is%20a%20large%20database. Accessed 14 November 2023.

[62] Ibid.

[63] Ibid.

[64] See CJEU (GC), *Google Shopping*, Judgment, 10 November 2021, T-612/17.

[65] The Economist (2018) China's great firewall is rising. https://www.economist.com/china/2018/01/04/chinas-great-firewall-is-rising. Accessed 14 November 2023.

recognises and adapts to the heterogeneity of recipient's needs.[66] Accordingly, a responsive public service deploys an approach that is inclusive of the diversity of service recipients' needs, and proactively seeks and incorporates recipients' feedback. This also includes an element of reasonable timeliness. Google Search excels at recognising and adapting to the heterogeneity of recipients' needs. Its ability to personalise its service to each individual user, in real-time, has introduced a level of responsiveness that is unprecedented.

An alternative to the public service standards that can indicate a public service character of a service is the fact that the service performs a quasi-regulatory function. In essence, a search engine's design (back and front) can function as a method of regulating the behaviour of those utilising it.[67] For instance, content moderation practices have a direct impact on citizen's freedom of expression and information. The extent to which we can exercise our fundamental rights is determined by these quasi-regulatory mechanisms.[68]

6.3.5 *Imperative to Citizenship*

The final characteristic concerns an enrichment of citizenship. Following T.H. Marshall's conceptualisation, there are three categories of citizenship: civil, political and social.[69] Civil rights include rights to, for example, speech or association, which make up individual freedom. Political rights form the basis of free and fair exercise of voting rights and participation in government. Whilst social citizenship entails the right to education, healthcare, or the right "[…]to live the life of a civilised being according to the standards prevailing in the society".[70] Marshall did not see the three categories as separate, rather he viewed each category as overlapping, and one generating the other, i.e. in order to exercise a meaningful vote (political right), the state must ensure the provision of education (social right).[71] Thus, education has a bearing on citizenship, and when state guarantees education, "[…] it has the requirements and the nature of citizenship definitely in mind".[72] Public services are seen as forming part of social rights, which ultimately stimulate the growth of a citizen. Social citizenship here is seen as a component of "democratic-welfare-capitalism", as a medium of balancing the tension between capitalism and democracy, and as a result of the mediation between civil and political rights.[73]

---

66 OECD 2013, p. 158.

67 Helberger et al. 2021, p. 190.

68 Ibid.

69 Marshall 1950.

70 Ibid., p. 11.

71 Revi 2014, p. 454.

72 Marshall 1950, p. 25.

73 Revi 2014, p. 454.

In contemporary times, this concept of citizenship includes the digital realm and with it the associated needs and rights. It can be argued that search engines have assumed a secure place in the civilised life and prevailing standards of the European society, capable of enriching citizenship in all three categories. First, in terms of civil rights, the availability of information can elevate civic engagement by enabling individuals to make informed decisions and providing the information needed to form their opinions and viewpoints. It facilitates access to information, thus enabling participation in local community, or enabling individuals to mobilise around common interests and needs. Second, the exercise of political rights is enhanced through access to government information. Search engines not only grant access to information regarding laws and governmental policies, but also foster political engagement by offering details on voting, including election dates and voter registration. Additionally, they provide information on public hearings and campaigns, thus enabling stronger political engagement. Finally, search engines play a role in bolstering social rights as they have the capacity to promote democracy by nurturing an informed and an engaged citizen.

Search engines, such as Google's, offer a critical channel for accessing information and assisting citizens in staying informed about public discourse, thereby contributing to the collective welfare of society. They specifically demonstrate comparable characteristics to institutions closely tied to social citizenship, with the capacity to foster a citizen's development towards a meaningful expression of their citizenship.

6.4 Regulating Google Search as a Public Service

The preceding section arguably illustrates compelling grounds for recognising search engines', such as Google Search's, critical role as understood by the notion of public services. Despite the existence and acknowledgments of their public interest, search engines have not been recognised as public services, nor had explicit universal service obligations or public service objectives been imposed on them. Most pertinent to search engines in the sphere of public services is Directive 2018/1972 on electronic communications code. This directive, as previously mentioned, requires access to adequate broadband internet service, and sufficient bandwidth to support at least the minimum set of services, including search engines.[74] Similarly, Regulation 2015/2120 concerning open internet access, which also forms part of the larger telecommunications regulatory framework, confirms the significance of dependable access to content and services online.[75] These legislative instruments acknowledge the necessity of safeguarding users' rights with respect to internet access and illustrate the

[74] Directive 2018/1972, above n. 20, Annex 5.

[75] Regulation (EU) 2015/2120 of the European Parliament and of the Council of 25 November 2015 laying down measures concerning open internet access and amending Directive 2002/22/EC on universal service and users' rights relating to electronic communications networks and services

need for a regulatory intervention to preserve them.[76] Regulating search engines in a similar fashion could preserve the rights of users to a similar, albeit downstream from internet access, essential service. Although, the importance of search engines has been acknowledged and emphasised in a number of EU legislative instruments, a more direct public service approach through universal service obligations and public service objectives may enhance and empower the position of users both as citizens and as consumers. This section will discuss the implementation of such an approach.

First, although the concepts of services of general (economic) interest, universal service obligations or public service objectives are found at the EU level in traditional network or utility sectors such as telecommunications or energy, which were previously provided by the Member States and were later liberalised, the concepts have been utilised in newer sectors too. A good example of this is the banking sector, where basic banking services, traditionally not overseen by Member States, have been confirmed to be classified as an essential service by the Commission in its *Communication on a Quality Framework.*[77] Second, the noted public service concepts are dynamic concepts. This means that services that have once been considered non-essential, may become of public interest as a result of technological, societal and market developments. A case in point is the broadband service, which, since the last reform in the telecom sector, is now considered a service of general interest, while the earlier reforms have disregarded it as such.[78] This points towards the fact that it is formally viable to identify new sectors (including those that have not been previously provided by the Member States) as falling within scope of the public service concepts, once public interest becomes sufficiently pronounced. Consequently, it becomes feasible to mandate universal service obligations and public service objectives.

6.4.1 *Setting the Obligations*

The synopsised constituents of universal service obligations that appear in the existing relevant pieces of legislation and that could be imposed are: quality, continuity, access, equality, and affordability.[79] In contrast, public service objectives appear to address broader general interests such as social or environmental protection.

and Regulation (EU) No 531/2012 on roaming on public mobile communications networks within the Union, published on 26 November 2015, Regulation 2015/2120, Article 3(1).

[76] See Helberger et al. 2021.

[77] A Quality Framework for Services of General Interest in Europe, above n. 9, p. 5.

[78] Helberger et al. 2021, p. 174.

[79] https://www.concurrences.com/en/dictionary/universal-service-118054. Accessed 14 November 2023.

6.4.1.1 Quality

Regarding the obligation of quality, the Commission mandates across its existing policy documents and applicable legislations "[...] essential services of high quality".[80] To meet this required standard, essential services must be provided at certain minimum quality standards, such as reliability or basic service features. While the traditional purpose of this obligation is to address disparities between rural and urban communities and to promote cohesion, there is now an added focus on preventing a digital divide amid the expanding digital society. Examples of obligations pertaining to quality can be taken from the postal or the basic payment service legislations. For instance in the postal sector, the minimum level of quality is achieved by mandating routing times, while the minimum level of quality in payment services is achieved by prescribing basic features such as the ability to purchase goods and services online.[81] In the context of search engines, it could equally be envisaged that, at minimum, search engines should universally provide certain basic features. At first glance, this might appear superfluous, considering that many search engines, including that of Google, currently offer one standardised service. However, it can be argued that an increase in subscription-based models for the services of digital platforms may soon be witnessed more frequently—with X (formerly Twitter) leading the way among the big tech companies by introducing a partly subscription-based service in 2022.[82] Even more recently, Meta launched a paid ad-free subscription to its Facebook and Instagram products.[83] It is thus conceivable that search engine providers, like Google Search, might consider implementing a subscription-based service. In this scenario, those able to afford the 'premium' subscription could avail themselves of exclusive features such as advanced search tools. Imposing a quality obligation could therefore ensure that basic features, considered to be the minimum quality standards for search engines, are provided irrespective of the opted subscription plan. Worth noting in this regard is the Digital Services Act, which introduces some quality obligations that could be construed as universal obligations for search engines. Namely, an obligation not to design interfaces in a way that deceives or manipulates the recipients of the service in a way that impairs the ability of the recipients to make free and informed decisions.[84] Or, an obligation to ensure a high level of privacy, safety, and security of minors.[85] Further, the Act merely recommends the development and implementation of voluntary standards and codes of conduct.[86]

---

[80] See A Quality Framework for Services of General Interest in Europe, above n. 9.

[81] Directive 97/67/EC, above n. 12, Article 16; Directive 2014/92, above n. 28, recital 44.

[82] Euronews et al. (2022) Elon Musk announces $8 monthly Twitter subscription for blue tick and other features. https://www.euronews.com/next/2022/11/01/elon-musk-announces-8-monthly-twitter-subscription-for-blue-tick-and-other-features.

[83] Kastrenakes J (2023) Facebook and Instagram launch a paid ad-free subscription. The Verge. https://www.theverge.com/2023/10/30/23938283/facebook-instagram-ad-free-subscription-eu. Accessed 14 November 2023.

[84] Digital Services Act, above n. 1, Article 25.

[85] Ibid., Article 28.

[86] Ibid., Articles 44–45.

6.4.1.2 Continuity

Continuity (in essence forming part of the quality element) prescribes that the service is provided without interruption.[87] Examples include Article 3 of Directive 97/67/EC on postal services, which mandates "[...] the right to a universal service involving the permanent provision of a postal service", or Directive 2018/1972 on electronic communications code which mandates that "[...] providers of voice communications services take all necessary measures to ensure uninterrupted access to emergency services and uninterrupted transmission of public warnings."[88] Just as voice communications services, search engines enable access to information of public importance. The Covid-19 pandemic has underscored the role of search engines, such as Google's, as an essential service for citizens in accessing credible public health information, simultaneously serving as a medium for national health authorities to disseminate local guidance and information.[89] Accordingly, there are strong justifications for introducing a comparable stipulation regarding continuity, aligning with practices seen in other sectors. This may involve enforcing measures to secure uninterrupted access. The Digital Services Act touches upon this obligation by recommending the drawing up of voluntary crisis protocols for addressing crisis situations.[90]

6.4.1.3 Access

In terms of access, the concept of universal service obligations delineates the access requirement from two angles. The first angle pertains to physical access through network/infrastructure connection (wholesale access), while the second angle outlines access in terms of requiring the service provider to enter into a contract (retail access). In the context of the latter obligation, users of search engines could enjoy enhanced safeguards in terms of access to the service. Again, while such obligation may appear superfluous at present, given that search engines, like Google, are generally fully accessible, this obligation could ensure that the basic access is guaranteed in the event of a switch to a subscription-based model, and that any termination of access follows the necessary procedural safeguards.

6.4.1.4 Equality

Obligation pertaining to the element of equality is perhaps the most self-explanatory. The obligation seeks to promote equal service in equal conditions. Supported by

---

[87] Green Paper of 21 May 2003 on Services of General Interest, COM(2003) 270 final, para 55.

[88] Directive 97/67/EC, above n. 12, Article 3(1); Regulation (EU) 2021/782 of the European Parliament and of the Council of 29 April 2021 on rail passengers' rights and obligations (recast), published on 17 May 2021, recital 40; Directive 2018/1972, above n. 20, Article 108.

[89] Pichai 2020.

[90] Digital Services Act, above n. 1, Article 48.

Article 21 CFREU, it is visible in a number of sector specific legislations even beyond universal service obligations. For instance, in Directive 2019/944 on rules for the internal market for electricity. Article 10 (6) on basic contractual rights prescribes that suppliers shall not unduly discriminate between customers based on a payment method opted for, and that any chargers related to payment methods shall be objective, non-discriminatory and proportionate.[91] Other provisions amongst the sector specific legislations cover grounds such as nationality, place of residence, disability, political, religious or even ideological considerations. In the context of search engines, it is not difficult to envision an obligation that would underscore the need for special attention to accessibility for persons with disabilities. In this regard, the Commission currently merely vows in Article 47(1) of the Digital Services Act to encourage and facilitate the drawing up of codes of conduct at the EU level with the involvement of providers of online platforms and others to promote access and particular needs of persons with disabilities.

6.4.1.5 Affordability

Last is the obligation of affordability, which generally stipulates that prices are set in a manner that all users are able to access the service. An example of this is Directive 97/67/EC on postal services.[92] Affordability can also mandate that the service is not tied to a subscription to facilities or services that are not deemed to be a part of the minimum service. Such stipulation is present in Directive 2014/92/EU on access to basic payment services, ensuring that access to a payment account with basic features is not tied to subscription of additional services.[93] Affordability currently does not raise any concerns in the realm of search engine services, given that they are commonly provided at no charge. Nevertheless, two points warrant consideration. First is the angle that data equals price.[94] In essence, even when a service is provided free of charge, users pay through their data. The question then becomes whether the quantity of data (that is ultimately monetised by the provider of the service) is not excessive and thus unaffordable in terms of data protection.[95] The second angle to the obligation on affordability that warrants consideration is that, while most search engines are currently free, in the scenario that subscription-based models become more prevalent, this obligation could safeguard affordable access.

[91] Directive 2019/944, above n. 22, Article 10(6).

[92] Directive 97/67/EC, above n. 12, Article 3(1).

[93] Directive 2014/92, above n. 28, Article 16(9).

[94] See, for instance, OECD 2016, para 56; Ocello et al. 2015, p. 6.

[95] Helberger et al. 2021, p. 198.

6.4.1.6 Public Service Objectives

Finally, public service objectives belonging to the remit of the universal service field concern broader general interest areas such as social or environmental protection. In terms of social protection, some of the existing legislative provisions ensure the protection of vulnerable customers, defining a vulnerable customer in terms of financial hardships, special social needs, or disability.[96] Regarding environmental protection, Directive (EU) 2019/944 on rules for the internal market for electricity serves as a great example, as it stipulates the general promotion of an "[…] environmentally sustainable internal market for electricity within the Union".[97] Such public service objectives could provide an additional path for addressing concerns over platform accessibility for persons with disabilities, or environmental concerns in the digital sector such as energy efficiency of data centres (also applicable to search engines).[98]

6.4.2 The Outcome

The preceding section examined how regulating search engines as a public service, through the imposition of universal service obligations or public service objectives, could contribute to safeguarding access to the service and preserving the rights of users as citizens. It is put forward that, imposing obligations that pursue a degree of universality in terms of access, conditions of access, and broader public service objectives, can rectify the initial consumerfication of big tech platforms users, thereby alleviating the vulnerable position of users with regards to a service that now arguably exhibits characteristics intrinsic to public services. The concept of public services is, as earlier noted, a changing and a responsive concept that must be regularly revisited to reflect the social, economic and technological advances across the EU.[99] Recognising and safeguarding the increasing public interest value of certain big tech platform services, such as search engines, can promote the rights of users as citizens—a perspective that can often be trumped by a more user-consumer oriented approach pursuing different goals.

On the whole, treating search engines as public services and imposing universal service obligations and promoting broader public interest objectives:

---

[96] Ibid., recital 46; Directive 2019/944, above n. 22, Articles 28–29; Directive 2009/73/EC of the European Parliament and of the Council of 13 July 2009 concerning common rules for the internal market in natural gas, published on 14 August 2009, Article 3(3). See also Directive 2018/1972, above n. 20, Articles 85(2) and 111; Directive 2019/944, above n. 22, Article 10(7).

[97] Directive 2019/944, above n. 22, Article 58(a).

[98] See European Commission 2022.

[99] Communication from the Commission to the European Parliament, the Council, the European Economic and Social Committee and the Committee of the Regions – White Paper on services of general interest, COM(2004) 374 final, para 21; Directive 2018/1972, above n. 20, recital 210.

a. allows for the public interest in such services to be defined in terms of clear tasks on behalf of the providers, and in terms of tangible rights of users;
b. can complement existing regulatory rules in terms of providing alternative routes to user protection or supplementing the existing market rules with additional obligations;
c. can increase future-proofness as obligations can focus on broader goals such as affordability, or vulnerable users;
d. re-enforces user's rights as citizens.

6.5 Conclusions

This chapter discussed the possibility of regulating search engines, with the example of Google Search, as a public service through the imposition of universal service obligations or broader public service objectives. Upon discussing the concept at the EU level, the attention shifted to examining the characteristics of a public service and determining if search engines would fit such a classification. The analysis presented compelling grounds for recognising search engines (such as Google's) as a public service, on the basis of its scope of users, its societal impact, or its market role. Moreover, it has been argued that the search engines fundamentally adhere to public service standards, reflecting users' needs and expectations. Or that they assume a quasi-regulatory function to the extent that the exercise of our fundamental rights may be restricted. Finally, it was argued that search engines can be regarded as imperative to citizenship (following T.H. Marshall's conceptualisation), as they demonstrate characteristics akin to institutions that bolster civil, political and social rights. Subsequently, the chapter discussed the imposition of universal service obligations and public service objectives. The analysis concluded that regulating search engines, such as Google's, as a public service (by imposing obligations of such a nature) could safeguard their public interest value that goes beyond the competition and economic considerations, and further enhance the rights of users (as citizens).

References

Andersen J (2018) Archiving, ordering, and searching: Search engines, algorithms, data- bases, and deep mediatization. Media, Culture & Society 40(8):1135–1150.

Bauby P, Similie MM (2012) Providing High-Quality Public Services in Europe Based on the Values of Protocol 26 of the Lisbon Treaty on Services of General Interest; Short Version. CESI Europe Academy, Brussels.

Brightedge Research (2019) Organic Search Improves Ability to Map to Consumer Intent: Organic Channel Share Expands to 53.3% of Traffic. https://videos.brightedge.com/research-report/BrightEdge_ChannelReport2019_FINAL.pdf.

Cremer H et al. (2001) Universal service: an economic perspective. Annals of Public and Cooperative Economics 72(1):5–43.

European Commission (2016) Special Eurobarometer 447 on Online platforms. Publications Office of the European Union, Luxembourg.
European Commission (2020) Shaping Europe's digital future. Publications Office of the European Union, Luxembourg.
European Commission (2022) Study on Greening Cloud Computing and Electronic Communications Services and Networks: Towards Climate Neutrality by 2050. Publications Office of the European Union, Luxembourg.
Finger M, Finon D (2011) From the "public service" model to the "universal service" obligation. In: Finger M, Kunneke RW (eds) International Handbook of Network Industries. Edward Elgar Publishing, Cheltenham, pp 54–69.
Gregory WR et al. (2021) The Role of Artificial Intelligence and Data Network Effects for Creating User Value. Academy of Management Review 46(3):534–551.
Haider J, Sundin O (2019) Invisible Search and Online Search Engines: The Ubiquity of Search in Everyday Life. Routledge, Abingdon (Oxon).
Haque SM (2001) The Diminishing Publicness of Public Service under the Current Mode of Governance. Public Administration Review 61(1):65–82.
Helberger N et al. (2021) EU Consumer Protection 2.0: Structural Asymmetries in Digital Consumer Markets. BEUC (The European Consumer Organisation), Brussels.
Marshall TH (1950) Citizenship and social class. Cambridge University Press, Cambridge.
Ocello E, Sjödin C, Subočs A (2015) What's Up with Merger Control in the Digital Sector? Lessons from the *Facebook/Whatsapp* EU merger case. Competition Merger Brief 2015(1):1–7.
OECD (2013) Government at a Glance 2013. OECD Publishing, Paris.
OECD (2016) Big Data: Bringing Competition Policy to the Digital Era. OECD Publishing, Paris.
Pan B et al. (2007) In Google We Trust: Users' Decisions on Rank, Position, and Relevance. Journal of Computer-Mediated Communication 12(3):801–823.
Pichai S (2020) Covid-19: How we're continuing to help. https://blog.google/inside-google/company-announcements/covid-19-how-were-continuing-to-help/. Accessed 14 November 2023.
Porat R (2021) Expanding pathways into higher education and the workforce. https://blog.google/outreach-initiatives/grow-with-google/higher-education-partnerships/. Accessed 14 November 2023.
Revi B (2014) T.H. Marshall and his critics: reappraising 'social citizenship' in the twenty-first century. Citizenship Studies 18(3–4):452–464.
Sambrook R (2012) Delivering Trust: Impartiality and Objectivity in the Digital Age. Reuters Institute for the Study of Journalism, Oxford.
Sauter W (2008) Services of general economic interest and universal service in EU law. European Law Review 33(2):167–193.
Sauter W (2014) Public Services in EU Law. Cambridge University Press, Cambridge.
Schirato T, Webb J (2003) Understanding globalization. Sage, London/Thousand Oaks, USA/New Delhi.
Schultheiß S et al. (2018) We still trust in Google, but less than 10 years ago: an eye-tracking study. Information Research 23(3).
Sundin O, Carlsson H (2016) Outsourcing trust to the information infrastructure in schools: How search engines order knowledge in education practices. Journal of Documentation 72(6):990–1007.
Unkel J, Haas A (2017) The effects of credibility cues on the selection of search engine results. Journal of the Association for Information Science and Technology 68(8):1850–1862.

Laura Frederika Lalikova is a PhD candidate in Competition Law and Digital Markets at Utrecht Law School. This research is part of the fulfilment of Modern Bigness ERC project, under the leadership of Prof. Mr Dr Anna Gerbrandy, which has received funding from the European Research Council (ERC) under the European Union's Horizon 2020 research and innovation programme (grant agreement No. 852005).

Part III
Sustainability and SGEIs

Chapter 7
Setting the Scene for Sustainability and Services of General Interest: From Wicked Problems to Understanding Sustainability and the Potential Role of Adaptive Law and Governance

Esther G. H. M. van Zimmeren

Contents

Abstract The objective of this chapter is to set the scene and to share some ideas as to how services of general interest (SGIs) can be addressed through the lens of sustainability. It provides an explanation of the relevance of the concept of wicked problems for services of general interest, briefly elaborates on the concept of sustainability and then explores to what extent law can be designed in such a way to create more resilience in addressing modern wicked problems. The chapter raises the question of to what extent in a situation of global polycrisis, societal uncertainty and anticipated societal transitions, ensuring legal certainty is still possible and whether a more adaptive legal system is what is needed. I conclude with some ideas on topics for further research on SGIs and propose that the literature on resilience and adaptive law and governance may offer an inspiring starting point for future research.

Keywords Services of General Interest · Sustainability · Wicked problems · Adaptive law and governance · Trust

E. G. H. M. van Zimmeren (✉)
Faculty of Law, Research Group Government & Law, University of Antwerp, Antwerp, Belgium
e-mail: esther.vanzimmeren@uantwerpen.be

N. Ghazaryan et al. (eds.), *Services of General (Economic) Interest and EU Law*, Legal Issues of Services of General Interest, https://doi.org/10.1007/978-94-6265-723-6_7

7.1 Introduction

The societal, economic, and financial situation resulting from what has been called a "global polycrisis" has highlighted more than ever the fundamental role of various services of general interest (SGIs). Although one may argue that polycrisis is a buzzword, the term clearly highlights that we are in a period where crises in various world systems are influencing, speeding up and strengthening each other, which is having a major impact on the world and its population.[1] The global polycrisis refers to the financial crisis, the climate crisis, the energy crisis, the health crisis, the food crisis, and migration crisis and the wars on several continents leading to high numbers of civilian casualties every day. Even though this edited volume focuses on the EU, an examination of services of general interest through the lens of the concept of sustainability requires a holistic, multilevel, global, and intergenerational perspective. As is explained in Sect. 7.3, the concept of sustainability is rather broad, and different interpretations and operationalizations have been developed, promoted and adopted. This contribution invites readers to seriously consider within the context of services of general interest the three dimensions of sustainability, the environmental, social and economic dimensions of sustainability, and the interface between these dimensions. Moreover, the global implications of national and European actions and measures related to services of general interest need to be addressed; also when we are focusing our (legal) analysis on the EU. In this respect, it is essential to recognize the "wicked" nature of societal challenges addressed by policies related to services of general interest. This is particularly important when we propose changes to the legal framework, case law, or legal innovations, as we are operating in a space and time characterized by significant uncertainty. As the solutions and transformations that we engage in today will have a major impact on future generations, also the intergenerational nature of sustainability is essential.

In fact, many of the earlier mentioned crises are related to "services of general interest" (SGIs).[2] SGIs are services that public authorities of the EU Member States classify as being of general interest and, therefore, subject to specific public service obligations. SGIs can be provided either by the state or by the private sector. Examples of SGIs include housing, water and energy supply, waste disposal, public transport,

[1] The term polycrisis was popularized at the occasion of the World Economic Forum and explained by economist Adam Tooze. Tooze explained the term as a concept which to captures a historical moment characterized by multiple global crises unfolding at the same time on an almost unprecedented scale. World Economic Forum (2023) This is why 'polycrisis' is a useful way of looking at the world right now. https://www.weforum.org/agenda/2023/03/polycrisis-adam-tooze-historian-explains/. Accessed 19 August 2023.

[2] In this context, a distinction is generally made between so-called "services of general *economic* interest", which are basic services that are carried out in return for payment, such as postal services. This group of services is subject to EU internal market and competition law. However, the case-law of the CJEU allows for some derogations to these rules if necessary to protect citizens' access to basic services. Social services of general interest are those that respond to the needs of vulnerable citizens, and are based on the principles of solidarity and equal access. They can be both of an economic or non-economic nature. Examples include social security schemes, employment services and social housing. In this chapter the broader term services of general interest is used.

health, social services, education, culture and critical information, and communication infrastructures. SGIs have the potential to ensure that everyone has the right to access essential goods and services, to safeguard social cohesion and integration and to contribute to the protection of fundamental rights. Therefore, they are a key component of economic, social and territorial cohesion, and sustainable development policies. In areas such as health care and social housing, these services provide an essential safety net for citizens. Nonetheless, at the same time budget constraints require that high-quality services are provided as efficiently and cost-effectively as possible and that trade-offs are made. The variety of subsequent and parallel crises have put additional pressure on SGIs globally and in the EU Member States.

Safeguarding access to a wide variety of affordable and high-quality SGIs is challenging and, in a way, a "wicked problem" in itself. Horst W.J. Rittel and Melvin M. Webber, professors of design and urban planning at the University of California at Berkeley, described the notion "wicked problem" already in a 1973 article.[3] According to Rittel and Webber, wicked problems have innumerable causes, they are tough to describe and no "right" answer or solution exists (for a more detailed description of the characteristics of wicked problems, see Sect. 7.2). Rittel and Webber distinguish the wicked problems from hard but ordinary problems, which people can solve in a finite time period by applying standard techniques. Conventional solutions are inappropriate for tackling wicked problems and may actually exacerbate the problems by generating undesirable consequences. Environmental degradation, poverty and the aging society are classic examples of wicked problems and key challenges that needs to be addressed within the context of SGIs.

I acknowledge that "wicked problem" is the second term used in this chapter, which has become a buzzword. However, terms like wicked problems and sustainability are not mere buzzwords. They are increasingly used in academic literature and in policy documents for a reason; they emphasize the complexity and the sense of urgency of critical societal challenges which have been flouted for too long. A reflection of the sense of urgency and the need for a systemic societal transformation to deal with the complexity and interdependent nature of wicked problems, was the adoption of the European Green Deal.[4] The Green Deal did not provide a simple policy framework; it is a complex web of policy initiatives proposed by the European Commission covering many policy areas, from transport to agriculture to construction to the energy industry, with the aim of transforming the EU's economy for a sustainable future. Ultimately, it should contribute to making Europe climate neutral, requiring very ambitious targets such as the reduction of net greenhouse gas emissions to zero by 2050. In short, the goals of the Green Deal are making the Union's economy sustainable, turning climate and environmental challenges into opportunities, and ensuring a fair, just and inclusive energy transition (see for a more detailed

[3] Rittel and Webber 1973.

[4] Communication from the Commission of 11 December 2019 to the European Parliament, the European Council, the Council, the European Economic Aid and Social Committee and the Committee of the Regions. The European Green Deal, COM(2019) 640 final. For more information, see: https://commission.europa.eu/strategy-and-policy/priorities-2019-2024/european-green-deal_en. Accessed 19 August 2023.

analysis of the goals Sect. 7.4). The goals of the EU Green Deal therefore illustrate the three dimensions of sustainability; environmental, social and economic (see Sect. 7.3). Nonetheless, the social dimension is traditionally weaker, and in practice socio-economic considerations increasingly result in stalemates regarding negotiations on vital parts of the Green Deal. Polarization between right-wing populists and centre-left groups in the European Parliament has led to an emerging shift in environmental and climate debates towards distributional concerns as a central theme of the transition towards climate neutrality. These divisions tend to emerge along ideological lines. This shows that opinions about equity and justice are increasingly dominating environmental and climate discussions and underscores their importance in shaping future EU sustainability debates.[5]

It is essential to tackle the systemic socio-economic injustices at the root of climate and environmental crises, such as inequalities based on income and wealth.[6] Such inequalities are actually exacerbated by climate change and environmental degradation's disproportionate impact on marginalized groups and people in vulnerable situations. This is especially also important to elaborate upon in operationalizing such policies for SGIs at the local and regional level.[7] Operationalizing global Sustainable Development Goals (SDGs) in the context of SGIs, thus, requires a multilevel perspective. Although many EU Green Deal policy initiatives have been translated through concrete actions, directives, regulations and investment schemes, their implementation and operationalization are increasingly encountering pushbacks at the local, national and European level from citizens, most notably farmers' protests and certain political parties.[8] Not all parts of the Green Deal have been equally affected. The opposition tended to focus on agriculture reforms and the conservation of nature.[9]

A growing body of policy reports and academic literature emphasizes the importance of innovation for realizing the desired transformations. Innovation is generally understood in a broad sense covering technological, business model, social,[10] and

---

[5] Pollex 2025, pp. 217–236 and Bocquillon 2025, pp. 124–134.

[6] E.g. Filipović et al. 2022, p. 112759.

[7] This is, for instance, recognized in the guidance provided under the heading of the European Committee for the regions in Implementing the European Green Deal: Handbook for Local and Regional Governments (2022). https://cor.europa.eu/en/our-work/political-priorities/green-deal-going-local/green-deal-going-local-handbook.

[8] Bocquillon 2025, pp. 130–131.

[9] Ibid., p. 131.

[10] The OECD provides a very helpful definition for social innovation: "Social innovation refers to the design and implementation of new solutions that imply conceptual, process, product, or organizational change, which ultimately aim to improve the welfare and wellbeing of individuals and communities. Many initiatives undertaken by the social economy and by the civil society have proven to be innovative in dealing with socio-economic and environmental problems, while contributing to economic development. To fully tap the potential of social innovation, an enabling policy framework is needed to support public, non-profit and private actors to co-construct and implement socially innovative solutions and thereby contribute to address socio-economic issues, build stronger territorial resilience and better respond to future shocks." https://www.oecd.org/regional/leed/social-innovation.htm. Accessed 11 April 2024.

public[11] innovation. As these innovations need to respond to wicked problems, interdisciplinary collaboration between different actors and at different governance levels is required. Moreover, investments in new technologies often also requires that they are embedded in new business models, public sector regulations and uptake by social actors. For instance, the implementation of more personalized medical treatments, involves research and development in medicines and medical treatments (technological) (including overcoming all complex challenges in the research and development and regulatory approval cycle), but also a paradigm shift in the business models in the pharmaceutical sector, the operations of health agencies and insurers (public/private) and the participation by patients and doctors (social). Interestingly, research regarding legal and regulatory pathways appears to be relatively conservative, emphasizing the need for legal certainty whereas also *legal* innovation to adapt to such paradigmatic would be desirable.[12] In my view, it is actually unrealistic to adopt a static approach towards legal certainty when addressing wicked problems and major societal transitions in an age of significant societal uncertainty.[13] A more flexible approach towards law may be more appropriate.

The objective of this chapter is to set the scene and to share some ideas as to how SGIs can be addressed through the lens of sustainability. It provides an explanation of the relevance of the concept of wicked problems for SGIs in Sect. 7.2, a non-exhaustive summary of the concept of sustainability in Sect. 7.3 and then explores to what extent law can be designed in such a way to create more resilience in addressing modern wicked problems. I raise the question to what extent in a situation of global polycrisis, societal uncertainty and anticipated societal transitions citizens can still expect legal certainty and whether a more adaptive legal system is what is needed (Sect. 7.4). Obviously, this is a very fundamental question of legal design and innovation. Providing a complete answer to this question is a research project in itself and goes beyond the scope of this short contribution. Therefore, I conclude this chapter with some ideas on topics for further research for researchers working on SGIs who want to contribute to legal innovation which may stimulate sustainable societal transformation. I argue that the literature on resilience and adaptive law and governance is an excellent and inspiring starting point for future research.

[11] Public innovation or public sector innovation refers to significant improvements to public administration and/or services. Such innovation happens often with respect to services of general interest through the implementation by a public sector organization of new or significantly improved processes, methods or services aimed at improving a particular unit's operations and outcomes.

[12] E.g. Hagan 2022; Ruhl et al. 2021; Cosens et al. 2020; Arnold and Gunderson 2013.

[13] Similarly to what is implied by the notion of a global polycrisis, Breakwell 2020 argues that the early 21st Century is an age of societal uncertainty, where previously established beliefs and values are severely challenged and change at many different levels is occurring rapidly and unpredictably.

7.2 What Is so "Wicked" About "Wicked Problems"?[14]

Although the term wicked problem is nowadays used for very diverse problems and issues, it was introduced in the 1970s by Horst Rittel and Melvin Webber in a very specific context. They introduced the term to draw attention to the complexities and challenges of addressing land use planning and social policy issues. Today it is used in the context of climate change, biodiversity loss, the large influx of refugees, poverty, access to public health, artificial intelligence, etc. Rittel and Webber distinguished between "tame" complex problems found in mathematics and chess and complex and "wicked" problems in spatial planning. They argued that in contrast to those "tame" complex problems, in spatial planning it is often extremely difficult to clarify the delineation of the problem, its goals and possible solutions. This is related to the specific features of those problems. Rittel and Webber described ten key characteristics of wicked problems that are also of great importance when thinking about sustainability and SGIs. These ten characteristics are obviously closely related, but it is still useful to discuss them separately. Indeed, those characteristics reflect very clearly the challenges currently faced by legislators and policymakers in designing legal solutions to wicked problems.

1. Wicked problems are problems that have no definitive formulation; they are subject to change, and identifying the actual problem is part of the problem.
2. Wicked problems have no "stopping rule"; in other words, these problems lack an inherent logic that indicates when they are solved.
3. Solutions to wicked problems are not true or false, only good or bad. Because there is not one right solution, political beliefs, personal values, preferences, and biases come into play in determining the solution.
4. Solutions to a wicked problem cannot be directly tested, because implementation takes time and is often linked to other strategies.
5. Wicked problems cannot be studied by "trial and error". Because the selected solutions are usually irreversible, every attempt to reach a solution counts. For many scientific problems, one can "try out" multiple solutions through lab experiments and simulations, but this is much more difficult for wicked problems because so many factors come into play. Moreover, each implemented solution leaves permanent traces.
6. As many different solutions and approaches to a wicked problem are possible, it is very difficult to make policy choices. Such policy choices are often fundamental in nature and touch on political preferences and visions.
7. All wicked problems are essentially unique; they heavily depend on the context and background.
8. Wicked problems are often closely related to other problems; they are the "symptom" of other problems.

[14] The description of the notion of wicked problems in this section is based on Rittel and Webber 1973 and on the text of an article written in Dutch for a series of articles on sustainability in the journal Tijdschrift voor Europees en economisch recht (SEW): Van Zimmeren 2023.

9. The way a particular wicked problem is described and delineated determines the possible solutions.
10. Those who propose the solutions are responsible for the consequences of the solutions, but they can have a major impact and affect many people's lives. The impact of random pilots, legal experiments and sandboxes, and new legislative proposals is substantial, and executive and legislative branches will be held accountable for the choices that are made. As a result, negotiations and decision-making processes are delayed and end up in stalemates.

Unequal access to health care, a key topic for SGIs, is pre-eminently a wicked problem. It is complicated to describe the problem succinctly and it is impossible to solve it in a way that is simple or definitive. Over time, there have been different views on how to organize and fund health care systems. Unique factors determine the local impact of lack or limited access to healthcare services. Moreover, the quality of and access to health care cannot be separated from the multilevel biopharmaceutical ecosystem. Therefore, addressing access to healthcare issues requires a holistic perspective considering long-term, future-proof solutions that consider access by vulnerable groups, the aging society, the impact of the environment on health, the development of the knowledge and innovation ecosystem, etc. In many countries, healthcare systems are confronted with rising prices for medicines and equipment, shortages in healthcare personnel and stressful working environments. Choices must be made out of a multitude of possible, often irreversible, solutions while large companies are lobbying to influence decision-making processes and while geopolitical tensions have an impact on access as well: two issues also drive the focus towards economic sustainability rather than environmental and social sustainability.

7.3 From Wicked Problems and SGIs to Sustainability

Whereas a simple keyword search related to competition law and sustainability immediately results in a large number of recent publications by academics and practitioners and several policy documents at the European and national level, a similar keyword search on the specific combination of SGIs and sustainability leads to only a few results. Honestly, as a researcher in innovation and intellectual property law and governance, this was quite surprising to me, as an obvious link seems to exist between wicked problems, SGIs and the need for sustainable solutions. However, before delving deeper into this, it is essential to position the notion of sustainability.

No global consensus exists on the definition of the concept of sustainability and sustainable development. The concept has evolved over time, but most publications related to sustainability refer to the notion of sustainable development as defined in the "*Our Common Future*" report.[15] According to the report, sustainable development is a form of socio-economic development "that meets the needs of the present without

[15] World Commission on Environment and Development 1987. Gro Harlem Brundtland, prime minister of Norway and chair of the Universal Commission on Environment and Development at

compromising the ability of future generations to meet their own needs".[16] The link between nature conservation and economic development was expressed as early as 1972 in the Declaration of the United Nations Conference on the Environment in Stockholm. Thanks to the Brundtland Report, the concept of sustainable development became more widespread amongst a large group of international policy makers. However, it is still relatively recent that the concept of sustainability became familiar to the general public. The concept of sustainable development is now generally understood to cover three "pillars" or "dimensions": an environmental, social and economic pillar. However, it is unclear and controversial how these dimensions need to be considered, weighed and integrated in practice.

The concept of sustainable development was "translated" into the non-legally binding Millennium Development Goals (MDGs) and the Sustainable Development Goals (SDGs). In 2000, the concept of sustainable development was further developed in the MDGs with the goal of reducing extreme poverty by 2015 (UN Millennium Declaration, 2000). The MDGs received a lot of criticism:[17] on the one hand, because no legal consequences were attached to whether or not they were met, and on the other hand, the goals were said to have been too ambitious, difficult to measure, and the indicators used unreliable. It was also claimed that the needs of developing countries and underlying factors, such as climate change and social inequality, were not sufficiently taken into account. In response to some of these criticisms the UN General Assembly in September 2015 adopted a global sustainable development agenda, the 2030 Agenda for Sustainable Development (Agenda 2030).[18] Agenda 2030 includes the 17 SDGs and 169 detailed sub-targets intended to drive the transition to a fairer and more peaceful future. Central to Agenda 2030 are five crucial dimensions: planet, peace, people, prosperity and partnership, also known as the 5 Ps. Agenda 2030 calls on each member state to implement the 17 SDGs and their sub-targets in their own countries and to support the implementation of the goals in all other parts of the world by 2030. In doing so, the international community aimed to bridge the still prevailing North-South divide in global environmental and development policy. Whereas the MDGs were focused on development goals and primarily aimed at developing countries, and the remaining countries were expected to provide the necessary financial and technological assistance, the SDGs are thematically broader in nature and directly applicable to all countries.[19] Each year, the UN Secretary-General presents an SDG progress report, which is developed from a

---

the time, presented this report to the United Nations General Assembly in August 1987. The report is, hence, often referred to as the "*Brundtland Report*".

[16] Ibid., para 27.

[17] For a literature review discussing several points of criticism, see Fehling et al. 2013.

[18] United Nations 2015, Transforming our world: the 2030 Agenda for Sustainable Development. https://sdgs.un.org/2030agenda.

[19] Sachs 2012; Sachs et al. 2019.

framework of indicators and data produced by national statistical systems and information collected at the regional level. The use of these indicators and the way this information is collected is, however, controversial.[20]

Agenda 2030 also recognized the wicked nature of issues such as poverty, health, education, gender inequality, housing, safety, environmental degradation, etc., and affirmed that they are very closely intertwined. More than the 8 MDGs, the 17 SDGs form an integrated system and are based on the idea that action in one area will influence outcomes in other areas and that sustainable development must take into account environmental, social and economic dimensions.[21] Agenda 2030 thus sought to draw lessons from the MDG process and the problems that arose from fragmented implementation.[22] Clarifying interconnections between different policy areas is thus essential and an opportunity to create positive synergies between the SDGs. However, progress achieved in certain areas should not come at the expense of progress in other areas. Attempts were made to create linkages into the SDG architecture, but those linkages are in practice not always easy to operationalize.[23] To achieve the SDGs, difficult political trade-offs are crucial, but also challenging.[24] This is, therefore, also especially relevant and challenging when considering sustainability and SGIs.

In addition, risks of "SDG washing" are identified. SDG washing is the phenomenon where an organization is embracing the SDGs by listing social and environmental initiatives with a link to the SDGs, without actively implementing them with a specific purpose and intent, and central to the organization model. It relates to the dissemination of inaccurate or incomplete information by an organization to create an environmentally friendly public image.[25] To counter SDG washing, some authors focus on the importance of transparency, good measurement mechanisms and indicators that are easily accessible and standardized.[26] Other authors have a more fundamental critique and argue that the SDGs threaten to further legitimize existing power structures. Focusing fully on the SDGs would leave insufficient time and energy to focus on essential structural reforms.[27]

An even more fundamental criticism regarding the SDGs relates to the fact that the SDGs are still very anthropocentric and based on a Western modernist worldview.[28] They pay little attention to the interrelationship between people, nature and

[20] Mair et al. 2018; Allen 2021.

[21] Nilsson et al. 2016.

[22] Vandemoortele 2011; Waage et al. 2015.

[23] Kroll et al. 2019; Le Blanc 2015; Pradhan et al. 2017; Weiland et al. 2021, p. 91.

[24] Brand et al. 2021; Allen 2018.

[25] Munro 2020; Nieuwenkamp R (2017) Ever heard of SDG washing? The urgency of SDG Due Diligence. OECD Development Matters Blog. https://oecd-development-matters.org/2017/09/25. Accessed 16 August 2023.

[26] E.g., Malay 2021. See also Proposal for a Directive on the substantiation and communication of explicit environmental claims (Green Claims Directive), COM(2023) 166 final.

[27] Orbie J (2020) SDG's: wie wil er nog wat oude wijn in een nieuwe zak? Waarom de duurzame ontwikkelingsdoelen de wereld niet zullen redden. https://www.mo.be/opinie/waarom-de-duurzame-ontwikkelingsdoelen-de-wereld-niet-zullen-redden. Accessed 21 October 2023.

[28] Adelman 2018.

well-being. Other worldviews and visions which typically provide a more eco-centric value orientation, such as *Ubuntu* and *Buen Vivir*, are not represented.[29] This brings us to the distinction between a "weak" and "strong" approach towards sustainability.[30] These two approaches reflect a more anthropocentric versus eco-centric worldview and different views on how to weigh the different sustainability dimensions (environmental, social, economic). According to the proponents of "weak sustainability" it is possible to protect nature in combination with economic growth. They interpret the concept of sustainable development to include green growth. This approach is anthropocentric, as it advocates a balance of the three sustainability pillars that focuses on the interests of people rather than nature. In contrast, the proponents of "strong sustainability" explicitly reject the link between sustainability and economic development in the form of economic growth. This view criticizes the impact of capitalism and emphasizes the need for a more eco-centric or bio-centric approach.[31] It starts from an awareness that we are crossing so-called "planetary boundaries". According to a study published in 2009, there are 9 planetary boundaries that define the biological and physical systems of the planet.[32] By 2009, three of those limits had already been exceeded (i.e., global warming, biodiversity loss and nitrogen). The strong sustainability movement argues that these changes have brought us into a new geological era, the Anthropocene, which requires us to abandon the definition of sustainable development linked to economic growth. Instead, we need to start thinking about "degrowth", which can be understood as planned reductions in energy and resource use designed to rebalance the economy to the living world in a way that reduces inequality and improves human well-being.[33] In other, more simple words, this view thus emphasizes the importance of environmental and social sustainability over economic sustainability.

Reassessing SGIs from a sustainability perspective is, thus, not a simple policy direction. It first requires a clarification of the approach towards sustainability one is adopting and the explicit acknowledgement of the complexities in view of the wicked nature of the services itself and the interconnection with other policy fields. Providers of SGIs that refer to the SDGs on their website without full engagement with the notion and operational challenges, risk being accused of SDG washing. Nonetheless, we should not forget that this reassessment happens in a context of extreme uncertainty—scientific uncertainty, political uncertainty and legal uncertainty. In this respect, it is interesting to explore how the law can be designed in

[29] E.g., van Norren 2020.

[30] De Moerloose 2021, p. 280.

[31] See, e.g., Salleh 2016; Adelman 2018.

[32] Rockström et al. 2009: in particular climate change, ocean acidification, stratospheric ozone depletion, nitrogen and phosphorus cycle, global fresh water use, change in land use, loss of biodiversity, atmospheric aerosol loading and chemical pollution. More recently, this approach has been developed into a quantification of "safe and just Earth system boundaries" (ESBs). See Rockström et al. 2023.

[33] E.g., Hickel 2020.

such a way to trigger a more resilient and adaptive law and governance framework to respond to contemporary wicked problems.[34]

7.4 Designing Law to Enable Adaptive Governance of Contemporary Wicked Problems

The literature on adaptive law and governance focuses on the question of whether laws and legal systems can become more "resilient" and "adaptive" to non-linear changes in complex interconnected systems.[35] Whereas the adaptive law framework has been developed in the context of ecology and climate change and has mainly been applied to US environmental and urban planning law, interesting lessons can be learnt from this framework for other jurisdictions and for other areas of the law as well, including for instance for SGIs.

Resilience is generally understood as the capacity of a system to withstand or adapt to "disturbances" or disruptions while maintaining the same basic structures and functions.[36] Resilient legal frameworks have a high level of adaptive capacity and have enough flexibility, redundancy and learning capacity to adapt to disturbances or changes without collapse or flipping into fundamentally different systems.[37] Achieving an appropriate balance between stability and flexibility is, however, not easy.[38] Moreover, one might argue that it requires a more dynamic approach towards the concept of legal certainty.[39]

The adaptive law framework can be used as a kind of a "diagnostic tool" to identify the maladaptive or adaptive features of our legal frameworks and to strengthen their resilience. Arnold and Gunderson distinguish four key elements, which are described here in a nutshell:[40] (1) adaptive goals: multiplicity of well-articulated goals; (2) adaptive structure: polycentric, multimodal and integrationist structure; (3) adaptive methods: methods based on standards, flexibility, discretion and regard for context; and (4) adaptive processes: integrative legal-pluralist processes with feedback loops, learning and accountability. To illustrate how these elements can be assessed, below I refer to some examples concerning the European Green Deal.

First, adaptive legal systems explicitly identify and list the rationale and a multiplicity of adaptive goals underlying the legal instruments. The European Green Deal provides a very ambitious framework listing indeed a multiplicity of goals. In the

---

34 This sentence refers the title of a fascinating article by Cosens et al. 2020, which is part of a gradually emerging literature on adaptive law and governance.

35 Arnold 2014.

36 Walker and Salt 2006, p. 8; Holling 1973.

37 Arnold 2014.

38 Craig et al. 2017.

39 Popelier 2008.

40 Arnold and Gunderson 2013.

Commission's communication of December 2019, the following objectives were stated:

> It is a new growth strategy that aims to transform the EU into a fair and prosperous society, with a modern, resource-efficient and competitive economy where there are no net emissions of greenhouse gases in 2050 and where economic growth is decoupled from resource use. It also aims to protect, conserve and enhance the EU's natural capital, and protect the health and well-being of citizens from environment-related risks and impacts. At the same time, this transition must be just and inclusive. It must put people first, and pay attention to the regions, industries and workers who will face the greatest challenges. Since it will bring substantial change, active public participation and confidence in the transition is paramount if policies are to work and be accepted. A new pact is needed to bring together citizens in all their diversity, with national, regional, local authorities, civil society and industry working closely with the EU's institutions and consultative bodies.[41]

The communication also presented an initial roadmap of the key policies and measures needed to achieve the European Green Deal. In the meantime, many of those policies and measures have been adopted and updated again. In the communication the Commission recognized that all EU actions and policies need to contribute to the European Green Deal objectives, acknowledging explicitly that the societal challenges addressed by the Green Deal are complex and interlinked. Nonetheless, the Commission is seeking "to maximise benefits for health, quality of life, resilience and competitiveness" all at the same time.[42]

Second, adaptive legal systems have a polycentric, multimodal and integrationist structure. No single governance actor, no single unit, no single law and no single mode or method can tackle complex, wicked problems.[43] There are no panaceas, blueprints or optimal solutions.[44] A central task of adaptive law and governance is to make linkages between and integrate governance scale and function, ecosystem scale and function. The multilevel nature of the EU context may appear to some as an extra complication that needs to be taken into consideration when examining the adaptive nature of the European Green Deal. However, one may also argue that the multilevel EU governance system already embraces a polycentric multimodal structure with multiple centres and sources of authority. It has a multiplicity of governmental sources of law with strong roles for local, regional and national governments and EU institutions with exclusive and shared competences. In addition, hybrid and quasi-public governance organizations collaborate with non-governmental actors and citizens and mixed forms of multilevel dispute resolution exist. These actors can rely on a mix of formal and informal tools, soft and hard law, regulatory and contract-like instruments. Intense coordination and integration is necessary to exploit the available synergies across all policy areas for the European Green Deal. Non-hierarchical vertical and horizontal networks also play an important role here. In 2019 the EU showed great

---

[41] Communication from the Commission of 11 December 2019 to the European Parliament, the European Council, the Council, the European Economic Aid and Social Committee and the Committee of the Regions. The European Green Deal, COM(2019) 640 final, p. 2.

[42] Ibid.

[43] Arnold and Gunderson 2013, p. 10434.

[44] Ostrom et al. 2007.

leadership with the launch of the policy package. Yet, coordination, integration and strong persistent commitment to the initial goals remain difficult and challenging, in particular in view of the existing geopolitical tensions. Similar opportunities and challenges arise in terms of operationalizing this dimension of adaptivity within the context of SGIs in a multilevel EU governance system involving a multiplicity of actors.

The third element of adaptivity, adaptive methods pose another difficulty: determining the kind of flexibility that is permissible or desired: what is the right balance in terms of stability that helps society to absorb shocks and changes and to prevent collapse while allowing for flexibility that helps society to adapt to shocks and changes in a resilient and sustainable manner. The way this balance should be achieved is context-dependent. The fourth element regarding adaptive processes is closely related to the third element regarding methods. Adaptive processes require feedback loops among multiple stakeholders, effective learning cycles and accountability mechanisms. More traditional approaches to law and policy making processes envision linear processes. Understandings of legal processes as linear may, however, conflict with the more complex modern reality. The complex and uncertain dynamics related to policy frameworks such as the European Green Deal and SGIs require a certain amount of discretion for decision-makers. Decision-makers should take into account the ecological and social impacts, short-term and long-term intergenerational impacts. Scientific knowledge plays a role in the decision-making process, but this knowledge is constantly evolving and thus the learning process, space for experiments and the possibility to remain flexible and adapt to uncertainty are very important.[45] However, it should also be possible to hold decisionmakers accountable on the basis of appropriate standards governing the exercise of this discretion (e.g. subsidiarity and proportionality principle) and when they continue to postpone their decisions or are inactive.

In many jurisdictions, the last decade examples of experimental or experimentalist governance have been emerging.[46] Various EU institutions and local and national authorities and governments in the EU Member States have been experimenting with more collaborative trajectories for policymaking in different policy fields, including for instance co-creation contexts, regulatory sandboxes, citizen's initiatives, communities of practice and a conference on the future of Europe. The multilevel context hence accommodates various "laboratories" for experimentation. Nonetheless, many of these initiatives occur in a specific policy field and do not necessarily account for the interdependent wicked nature of the policy problems. It goes beyond the scope of this chapter to evaluate to what extent these initiatives have been successful. However, it is interesting to note here that the legal literature on SGIs related to experimentalist governance appears to be quite limited, which could be an interesting topic for further

[45] Arnold and Gunderson 2013, p. 10436.

[46] E.g. Rangoni 2023 (examining five policy domains, including electricity, natural gas, communications, finance, and pharmaceuticals); Sabel and Zeitlin 2008; Wolfe 2018.

research. Experimentalist governance can provide a framework for developing policies to ensure the provision of high-quality SGIs by allowing for continuous learning and adaptation to diverse national contexts.

Legal innovation such as those proposed by the adaptive law framework must overcome several dilemmas to facilitate adaptation: (1) encouraging collaborative problem-solving between different heterogeneous actors; (2) garnering social acceptance and commitment; and (3) cultivating a culture of trust and tolerance for change and (legal) uncertainty.[47] As indicated by Arnold and Gunderson, although the change slowing effect of law may give the impression that it "helps society to absorb shocks and disturbances up to a point, law can be brittle and maladaptive if it cannot keep up with the pace, scale and direction of eco-social change".[48] Attention for trust-building mechanisms and a more systemic reconsideration of the meaning of legal (un)certainty may thus be other fascinating issues to explore further for legal researchers, including for SGIs.

7.5 Conclusions

Systems for SGIs are subject to continuous societal disturbances. The question is to what extent these systems can be (re)designed in such a way that they can absorb such unexpected, unpredictable disturbances while still retaining their basic function and structure (resilience), and without eroding the potential to meet future needs (sustainability).[49] The legal institutional framework is one of the building blocks to ensure that such systems are "Resilient and Sustainable by Design".[50] But how can we make the complex systems that we depend on resilient and sustainable? Models for optimization of systems focused on increasing efficiency and based on the assumption that changes are generally incremental and linear are inadequate, as we are confronted with extreme, non-linear events,[51] such as a global pandemic. Such linear models do not account for the dynamic, interdependent, wicked nature of our real-world challenges. The need for a more adaptive legal system is clear. But what would a more adaptive law that accommodates this dynamic complex reality look like and what would be its primary features?

In my opinion, the literature on adaptive law and governance provides an interesting diagnostic tool that could also be used for rethinking the law regarding SGIs to design a more resilient and sustainable legal framework. For certain areas of the law and some jurisdictions, this may be a large stretch, whereas other areas of

[47] DeCaro et al. 2017.

[48] Arnold and Gunderson 2013, p. 10427.

[49] Walker and Salt 2006, p. 1.

[50] This concept is inspired by the notion in the General Data Protection Regulation: "privacy by design". The underlying idea is that data protection in data processing procedures is best adhered to when it is already integrated in the technology when created.

[51] Walker and Salt 2006, pp. 9–11.

the law already to a certain extent employ adaptive goals, structures, methods, and processes. The European Green Deal is an ambitious framework, which already mobilizes several elements of adaptiveness, but safeguarding a more adaptive approach throughout legal systems, including in SGIs, is challenging. Strengthening those elements further is important, but will require strong leadership and community involvement and mutual trust from the Member States in the EU to continue to pursue that leadership, from the EU in Member States and between Member States.

References

Adelman S (2018) The sustainable development goals, Anthropocentrism and Neoliberalism. In: French D, Kotzé LJ (eds) Sustainable Development Goals: Law, Theory and Implementation. Edward Elgar, Cheltenham, pp 15–40.

Allen C (2018) Initial progress in implementing the Sustainable Development Goals (SDGs): a review of evidence from countries. Sustainability Science 13:1453–1467.

Allen C (2021) Priorities for science to support national implementation of the sustainable development goals: A review of progress and gaps. Sustainable Development 29(4):635–652.

Arnold CA (2014) Resilient Cities and Adaptive Law. Idaho Law Review 50:245–264.

Arnold CA, Gunderson L (2013) Adaptive Law and Resilience. Environmental Law Reporter 43:10426–10443.

Bocquillon P (2025) Climate and Energy Transitions in Times of Environmental Backlash? The European Union 'Green Deal' From Adoption to Implementation. Journal of Common Market Studies 62(S1):124–134.

Brand A et al. (2021) Promoting Policy Coherence within the 2030 Agenda Framework: Externalities, Trade-Offs and Politics. Politics and Governance 9(1):108–118.

Breakwell G (2020) In the Age of Societal Uncertainty, the Era of Threat. In: Jodelet D et al. (eds) Societies Under Threat - A Pluri-Disciplinary Approach. Springer, Cham (Switzerland), pp 55–71.

Cosens BA et al. (2020) Designing Law to Enable Adaptive Governance of Modern Wicked Problems. Vanderbilt Law Review 73(6):1687–1732.

Craig RK et al. (2017) Balancing stability and flexibility in adaptive governance: an analysis of tools available in US environmental law. Ecology and Society 22(2).

De Moerloose S (2021) Sustainability. In: De Feyter K et al. (eds) Encyclopedia of Law and Development. Edward Elgar Publishing, Cheltenham (UK), pp. 279–282.

DeCaro DA et al. (2017) Understanding and applying principles of social cognition and decision-making in adaptive environmental governance. Ecology and Society 22(1).

Fehling M et al. (2013) Limitations of the Millennium Development Goals: a literature review. Global Public Health 8(10):1109–1122.

Filipović S et al. (2022) The green deal – just transition and sustainable development goals Nexus. Renewable and Sustainable Energy Reviews 168 112759:1–12.

Hagan H (2022) Legal Design as a Thing: A Theory of Change and a Set of Methods to Craft a Human-Centered Legal System. Design Issues 36(3):3–15.

Hickel J (2020) What does degrowth mean? A few points of clarification. Globalizations 18(7):1105–1111.

Holling CS (1973) Resilience and Stability of Ecological Systems. Annual Review of Ecology and Systematics 4:1–23.

Kroll C et al. (2019) Sustainable development goals (SDGs): Are we successful in turning trade-offs into synergies? Palgrave Communications 5 140:1–11.

Le Blanc D (2015) Towards integration at last? The sustainable development goals as a network of targets. Sustainable Development 23(3):176–187.
Mair S et al. (2018) A Critical Review of the Role of Indicators in Implementing the Sustainable Development Goals. In: Filho WL (ed) Handbook of Sustainability Science and Research. Springer, Cham (Switzerland), pp 41–56.
Malay OE (2021) Improving government and business coordination through the use of consistent SDGs indicators. A comparative analysis of national (Belgian) and business (pharma and retail) sustainability indicators. Ecological Economics 184 106991:1–13.
Munro V (2020) CSR for Purpose, Shared Value and Deep Transformation: The New Responsibility. Emerald Publishing, Leeds (UK).
Nilsson M et al. (2016) Policy: Map the interactions between sustainable development goals. Nature 534:320–322.
Ostrom E et al. (2007) Going Beyond Panacea. Proceedings National Academies of Science USA 104(39):15176–15178.
Pollex J (2025) Is it all about distribution? - Debating the Green Deal in the European Parliament. Journal of European Integration 47(2):217–236.
Popelier P (2008) Five Paradoxes on Legal Certainty and the Lawmaker. Legisprudence 2(1):47–66.
Pradhan P et al. (2017) A systematic study of sustainable development goal (SDG) interactions. Earth's Future 5(11):1169–1179.
Rangoni B (2023) Experimentalist Governance: From Architectures to Outcomes. Oxford University Press, Oxford.
Rittel H, Webber M M (1973) Dilemmas in a general theory of planning. Policy Sciences 4:155–169.
Rockström J et al. (2009) A safe operating space for humanity. Nature 461:472–475.
Rockström J et al. (2023) Safe and just Earth system boundaries. Nature 619:102–111.
Ruhl J B et al. (2021) Resilience of Legal Systems: Toward Adaptive Governance. In: Ungar M (ed) Multisystemic Resilience. Oxford University Press, Oxford, pp 509–529.
Sabel CF, Zeitlin J (2008) Learning from Difference: The New Architecture of Experimentalist Governance in the European Union. European Law Journal 14(3):271–327.
Sachs JD (2012) From millennium development goals to sustainable development goals. The Lancet 379(9832):2206–2211.
Sachs JD et al. (2019) Six transformations to achieve the sustainable development goals. Nature Sustainability 2:805–814.
Salleh A (2016) Climate, Water and Livelihood Skills: A Post-Development Reading of the SDGs. Globalizations 13(6):952–959.
Vandemoortele J (2011) If not the millennium development goals, then what? Third World Quarterly 32(1):9–25.
Van Norren DE (2020) The Sustainable Development Goals viewed through Gross National Happiness, Ubuntu, and Buen Vivir. International Environmental Agreements: Politics, Law and Economics 20:431–458.
Van Zimmeren E (2023) Het concept 'duurzaamheid' ontrafelen – een begin, geen eindpunt [Untangling the concept of 'sustainability – a beginning, not an ending]. Tijdschrift voor Europees en economisch recht (SEW) 2023(7/8):305–318.
Waage J et al. (2015) Governing the UN sustainable development goals: Interactions, infrastructures, and institutions. The Lancet Global Health 3(5):e251–e252.
Walker B, Salt D (2006) Resilience Thinking: Sustaining Ecosystems and People in a Changing World. Island Press, Washington.
Weiland S et al. (2021) The 2030 Agenda for Sustainable Development: Transformative Change through the Sustainable Development Goals? Politics and Governance 9(1):90–95.

Wolfe D (2018) Experimental Governance: Conceptual approaches and practical cases, Background paper for an OECD/EC Workshop on 14 December 2018 within the workshop series "Broadening innovation policy: New insights for regions and cities". OECD, Paris. https://www.researchgate.net/profile/David-Wolfe-6/publication/342247057_EXPERIMENTAL_GOVERNANCE_CONCEPTUAL_APPROACHES_AND_PRACTICAL_CASES_1_Broadening_innovation_policy_New_insights_for_cities_and_regions_Experimental_Governance_Conceptual_approaches_and_practical_cases_A/links/5eea60bd458515814a672c98/EXPERIMENTAL-GOVERNANCE-CONCEPTUAL-APPROACHES-AND-PRACTICAL-CASES-1-Broadening-innovation-policy-New-insights-for-cities-and-regions-Experimental-Governance-Conceptual-approaches-and-practical-cases.pdf

World Commission on Environment and Development (1987) Report of the World Commission on Environment and Development: Our Common Future. https://sustainabledevelopment.un.org/content/documents/5987our-common-future.pdf. Accessed on 12 April 2023.

Esther G. H. M. van Zimmeren is professor of Intellectual Property Law and Governance at the University of Antwerp. She is also one of the coordinators of the GOVTRUST Centre of Excellence and partner of the Jean Monnet Centre of Excellence STRATEGO at the University of Antwerp. She is a visiting professor at the University of Copenhagen (CeBIL) and Vilnius University. This contribution was finalized in August 2023 and only small modifications and updates were added in August 2025.

Chapter 8
SGEI and Sustainability: Preventing (Over) Compensation Issues in the Transportation Sector

Pieter S. Wesselius

Contents

Abstract This chapter deals with the compensation of SGEIs in the transport sector. It discusses the recent *Lux Express Estonia* case, and its broader implications concerning the difference between the public procurement procedure and regulation through national legislation. It argues that the public procurement procedure brings forth fewer risks with respect to potential compensation of the provided public service. This is especially relevant in light of sustainability requirements, because compensating for 'sustainable SGEIs' may result in compensating unsustainable companies and thus breaching the polluter pays principle, as this chapter demonstrates.

Keywords SGEI · Sustainability · Transport sector · Overcompensation · *Altmark Trans* · Net financial effect · Procurement procedure

---

P. S. Wesselius (✉)
University of Groningen, Groningen, The Netherlands
e-mail: pietersjoerdwesselius@gmail.com

N. Ghazaryan et al. (eds.), *Services of General (Economic) Interest and EU Law*, Legal Issues of Services of General Interest, https://doi.org/10.1007/978-94-6265-723-6_8

8.1 Introduction

Sustainability regulations are becoming increasingly strict in order to achieve the European Union's (hereafter: EU) ambitious goals of 2030 (reducing the EU emissions by 55%) and 2050 (climate neutrality).[1] Throughout the EU economy, Member States are looking for methods to maximise sustainability and minimise pollution. One area that could see improvements in terms of sustainability is the SGEI: Service of General Economic Interest.[2] This chapter discusses potential complications that arise with increased sustainability standards in the transport sector.[3] It does so, largely on the basis of two Court of Justice of EU (hereafter: CJEU) judgments: *Lux Express Estonia*, and *Concordia Bus Finland*.

When market forces do not generate the most desired outcome, the solution may be to establish a SGEI, and task a company with the execution thereof.[4] The added costs that arise from performing this service, however, have to be compensated. In the area of transportation, Regulation 1370/2007 stipulates that performing a SGEI requires compensation, but not above the net financial effect.[5] This is in line with one of the *Altmark Trans* criteria for compensating SGEIs: the third criterion stipulating that there may be no overcompensation.[6] Such overcompensation would lead to the company obtaining an advantage which distorts competition, and subsequently requires notification to the European Commission under Article 108(3) TFEU.

In the recent *Lux Express Estonia* case, (over)compensation of a transport SGEI came to light. This case revolved around the compensation of service provision under an Estonian law which obliges transport operators to transport children and people with severe disabilities free of charge. An operator of this service claimed that it

---

[1] About the EU's 'Fit for 55 package': https://www.consilium.europa.eu/en/policies/green-deal/fit-for-55-the-eu-plan-for-a-green-transition/#:~:text=Fit%20for%2055%20refers%20to,line%20with%20the%202030%20goal. Accessed on 27 February 2023.

As Pouikli rightly emphasises: '[T]he EU Green Deal, which constitutes the new EU policy roadmap for the upcoming years, stressed once again the predominant role of the public procurement in achieving the ambitious EU environmental policy goals'. Pouikli 2020, p. 719.

[2] For more information about SGEI and environmental protection, see Nowag 2016, pp. 203–214; Sommerdahl 2017; Ølykke and Møllgaard 2016. For a more general (and historical) overview, see Schweitzer 2011.

[3] For more information about SGEI and the transport sector, see Zhu 2020, pp. 235–241.

[4] See Craig and De Búrca 2008, pp. 1071–1072.

[5] Regulation (EC) No 1370/2007 of the European Parliament and of the Council of 23 October 2007 on public passenger transport services by rail and by road and repealing Council Regulations (EEC) Nos 1191/69 and 1107/70, Regulation 1370/2007, published on 3 December 2007. Notably in light of the topic addressed in this chapter, the Preamble (para 17) of Regulation 1370/2007 mentions that 'competent authorities are free to establish social and qualitative criteria', for example with regard to environmental protection. Also, Regulation 1370/2007 actually targets Public Service Operators (PSO), and not SGEI. Within the context of this book, however, I shall speak of SGEI rather than PSO. After all, the famous *Altmark Trans* case also concerned PSO, even though it is practically intertwined with the concept of SGEI. About the compensation, see Regulation 1370/2007, Article 3(2).

[6] CJEU, *Altmark Trans*, Judgment, 24 July 2003, C-280/00, para 92.

performed an SGEI in light of Regulation 1370/2007, and demanded compensation for its performed services. Estonia rejected this claim, stating that there is no SGEI involved, and thus no need for compensation. The case is illustrative, because a SGEI (and thus the need for compensation) can exist regardless of it being clearly defined beforehand—by accident, to put it bluntly.

Against this background, this chapter suggests for Member States to use the public procurement procedure as an alternative method to achieve sustainability goals.[7] By using the public procurement procedure, Member States can avoid the 'SGEI-label' and compensating the service operators. In light of this, the *Concordia Bus Finland* is illustrative, and used to substantiate the argument.[8] In this case, a runner-up in a procurement procedure complained about the outcome of the procedure, because it was impossible for them to meet the sustainability requirements established by the local administration.

In addition to this, this chapter argues that providing compensation—and preventing overcompensation—for an SGEI may become complex when sustainability is involved.[9] Regulation 1370/2007 refers to 'no compensation above the net financial effect', which boils down to a different level of compensation for different companies. For sustainability measures this may entail compensating unsustainable companies more than sustainable ones: a direct conflict with the polluter pays principle.

As such, this chapter presents an overview of developments in issues relating to (over)compensation of an SGEI in the transportation sector, and adds a sustainability narrative. Its layout is as follows: Sect. 8.2 discusses the *Lux Express Estonia*, followed by a reflection thereupon in Sect. 8.3. Then, Sect. 8.4 introduces the sustainability factor, and suggests public organisations to use the public procurement procedure as an alternative method to achieve sustainability goals without the requirement of compensation. After this, Sect. 8.5 reflects on the previous sections, and approaches both *Lux Express Estonia* and *Concordia Bus Finland* cases from another angle. The chapter is summarised with a section on conclusions (Sect. 8.6).

---

[7] About the increased importance of public procurement in light of the EU Green Deal, see Pouikli 2020. More generally, on selecting a public service obligation provider, see Szyszczak 2013, pp. 21–22. About the relationship between public procurement and sustainability, see Sjåfjell and Wiesbrock 2015.

[8] CJEU, *Concordia Bus Finland Oy Ab and Helsinki kaupunki*, Judgment, 17 September 2002, C-513/99.

[9] On overcompensation, see Klasse 2013, pp. 43–44. See also the Commission Decision in *Busverkehr Wittenberg* about compensation to a local passenger transport company: Commission, May 16, 2006, State Aid N 604/2005, *Busverkehr Landkreis Wittenberg*.

8.2 *Lux Express Estonia*

Estonian law, Paragraph 34 of the *ühitranspordiseadus* (§34 ÜTS) to be more specific, stipulates that transport operators are obliged to carry free of charge several categories of passengers, among whom young children and people with severe disabilities. The law applies to all transport operators equally, and is applicable since 2000.[10] Lux Express Estonia is a transport operator active in Estonia, and adheres to §34 ÜTS. It opened a procedure at the Estonian administrative court about the compatibility of §34 ÜTS with European law, specifically Regulation 1370/2007 and Article 108 TFEU, arguing that it deserves to be compensated for additional costs made in its obeyance to the law.[11]

The referring court requests for a preliminary ruling, asking the following questions—paraphrased and summarised:[12] Does the situation in which transport services are obliged to transport free of charge children and people with severe disabilities constitute a SGEI within the meaning of Regulation 1370/2007? If so, can compensation be excluded by national law? And, if compensation cannot be excluded by national law, which conditions must Member States meet in order to comply with the State aid rules?

The CJEU ruled that, even though it was not explicitly referred to as such between parties, the obligation laid down in §34 ÜTS constitutes a SGE—and *Lux Express Estonia* deserves to be compensated for the extra costs it made—on the basis of Regulation 1370/2007, Article 2(e).[13] In light of this, it is important to note that Lux Express Estonia successfully argued that it would not have provided transportation services to children and people with severe disabilities free of charge, in the absence of the Estonian law. In addition to this, the Court of Justice stipulated that the Estonian law cannot exclude compensation for performing a SGEI; this would be at odds with Regulation 1370/2007, which states that the competent authority is required to compensate the SGEI for the net financial effect.[14] The phrasing of the Regulation: '[t]he competent authority *shall* compensate the public service operators…'[15] indicates that the competent authority enjoys no discretionary powers when it comes to compensation.

Thus, compensation is required for the SGEI, but to what extent? The SGEI can only be compensated for the so-called net financial effect, anything exceeding

---

[10] Even though in the case itself, the Court of Justice refers to 2015, another source (Lux Express itself) refers to the regulation being in force since 2000, see https://luxexpress.eu/en/news/the-estonian-state-is-obliged-to-pay-compensation-to-bus-carriers/.

[11] CJEU, *Lux Express Estonia v Majandus- ja Kommunikatsiooniministeerium*, Judgment, 8 September 2022, C-614/20, para 2.

[12] The referring court asked five questions; the three I have listed are most relevant in light of this chapter.

[13] CJEU, *Lux Express Estonia v Majandus- ja Kommunikatsiooniministeerium*, Judgment, 8 September 2022, C-614/20, para 47. See also Linke 2022.

[14] Regulation 1370/2007, Article 3(2).

[15] Regulation 1370/2007, Article 3(2), emphasis PSW.

this amount results in overcompensation which ought to be notified to the European Commission under Article 108(3) TFEU.[16] Where Advocate-General Campos Sánchez-Bordona leaves the amount of compensation to the referring court to decide, the Court of Justice makes an interesting remark about the calculation method. The Court of Justice says that

> the loss of revenue on the sale of tickets does not necessarily represent the effect of compliance with the obligation to carry certain passengers free of charge on the costs and revenue of the public service operator. The carriage of those passengers deprives the transport undertaking concerned of the possibility of carrying passengers who have to purchase a ticket only in cases where there is no longer any space for those passengers. The additional costs to the operator arising from the presence on board a coach of passengers who must be carried free of charge may also prove to be negligible.[17]

This phrase has important implications, which are discussed below.

8.3 Reflection: Several Implications

As a result of *Lux Express Estonia*, calculating the net financial effect of the obligation laid down in §34 ÜTS is potentially difficult. *Lux Express Estonia* is required to present a large amount of data, in order to satisfy the high threshold, set by the Court of Justice. Likely, the company argued that the calculation method should be more straightforward, for example counting the number of children and people with severe disabilities that make use of the transportation service, and multiplying this number by the cost of a bus ticket. Instead, Lux Express Estonia has to track its passenger inflow, and demonstrate that once a paying customer cannot enter the bus, a person exempted from paying by §34 ÜTS is occupying a place in the same bus.

Tracking the passenger inflow can be achieved through using digital cards, for example, but this system would require independent supervision in one way or another. The bus operators have both an incentive to 'fill buses' with persons that fall under §34 ÜTS, and an opportunity—by (for example) targeting this group with marketing schemes. Demonstrating that a paying customer cannot enter the bus due to its being packed with persons exempted from paying under §34 ÜTS is more difficult. A bus operator may claim that it denied its service to hundreds of paying customers, and without proper supervision it would be difficult to provide counterevidence and disprove such statements. Unlike the requirement of tracking the passenger inflow, there exists no (digital) travel data on paying customers that cannot use the transport service.

The Court of Justice's reasoning complicates matters, because it is unknown whether *Lux Express Estonia* has all the required data present for a successful damages claim (the compensation plus interest) over all the years it adhered to

---

[16] CJEU, *Altmark Trans*, Judgment, 24 July 2003, C-280/00, para 100.

[17] CJEU, *Lux Express Estonia v Majandus- ja Kommunikatsiooniministeerium*, Judgment, 8 September 2022, C-614/20, para 90.

§34 ÜTS. In theory the judgment may lead, however, to lower costs for regular bus passengers henceforth, since the compensation of adhering to the obligation laid down in §34 ÜTS can be passed on to them. For years, they have potentially paid an artificially high price for the transport service, so the judgment may be considered as good news to them.

Another interesting take from the judgment is that in order for a SGEI to be classified as one in light of Regulation 1370/2007, it does not necessarily have to be defined as such. In other words, despite the contents of the agreement between parties, if it is a SGEI, it is a SGEI, and therefore requires compensation.[18] Two roads lead to Rome, in this respect. Either, parties specifically declare the service as a SGEI, and sign a public service contract. Alternatively, it is a SGEI imposed by means of general rules.[19] In the case of *Lux Express Estonia*, a public service contract is absent, but the nature of §34 ÜTS is such that it 'appears to be defined with a view to guaranteeing public passenger transport services in the general interest.'[20] The existence of a SGEI in the legal sense appears technical or formalistic, but as the next section demonstrates, there may arise some practical complications with regard to environmental protection requirements.

8.4 SGEI and Environmental Protection Requirements

As pointed out in the introduction, it is likely that in the coming years sharper sustainability rules and regulations will see the light of day.[21] The consequence of this is that companies performing a SGEI will have to adhere to these rules and regulations, and may incur additional costs to do so. For example, bus transport operators may be required by national law to use hydrogen or electricity as a fuel. Transforming a diesel-powered bus fleet to one that is powered by a hydrogen or electricity is costly, and—when considered to be a SGEI which needs to comply with sustainability rules—requires compensation.[22] The question that remains is: to what extent?

---

[18] If it walks like a duck…

[19] Regulation 1370/2007, above n. 5, Article 3(2). See also CJEU, *Lux Express Estonia v Majandus- ja Kommunikatsiooniministeerium*, Judgment, 8 September 2022, C-614/20, para 46.

[20] CJEU, *Lux Express Estonia v Majandus- ja Kommunikatsiooniministeerium*, Judgment, 8 September 2022, C-614/20, para 41.

[21] See, for example, the EU Green Deal. https://ec.europa.eu/info/strategy/priorities-2019-2024/european-green-deal_en. Also, consider the 2014 Procurement Directives of the EU, in which it is stated that a major aim is 'to enlarge the possibilities for using public procurement in support of broader social and environmental goals'. See Sjåfjell and Wiesbrock 2015, p. 1 and Proposal of 20 December 2011 for a Directive of the European Parliament and of the Council on public procurement, COM(2011) 896 final, p. 2.

[22] Even though the parties (Member State and bus transport operators) have not agreed upon a PSO formally, it can be said that environmental arguments fall under the same 'general interest' category as did §34 ÜTS in the *Lux Express Estonia* judgment.

Integral compensation appears to be the simplest solution, at first glance. However, in practice this could lead to an undesired outcome directly opposite to the polluter pays principle. Imagine two bus transport operators, A and B, who both have a fleet of 50 buses. A has already invested in transforming its bus fleet towards more sustainability, and half of its fleet is powered by electricity or hydrogen. B has neglected to invest, and operates with 50 diesel-powered buses. If each company performs a SGEI in a separate region within the same Member State that requires 50 electric/hydrogen powered buses, A would need less compensation than B to meet the SGEI standards. In essence, A is being punished for its earlier investments, whereas B is rewarded for its negligence. A could rightly claim that the compensation rewarded to B constitutes an advantage in light of Article 107(1) TFEU, and needs to be notified to the European Commission based on Article 108(3) TFEU.

Calculating the amount of compensation is difficult and prone to discriminatory treatment between competing companies. For instance, taking the example of *Lux Express Estonia*: §34 ÜTS applies to every Estonian bus transport operator equally, although some companies may incur more costs, for example those that operate in crowded urban areas where buses are more likely to reach their maximum capacity than in rural areas. Sustainability regulations similarly apply to all companies equally, but might play out differently in practice due to dissimilarities in companies' investments towards sustainability. Important to note is that a SGEI should not become a way of escaping significant investment costs. Companies should be incentivised to invest in sustainability themselves, and only be compensated for the exceeding costs the SGEI requires of them. A differentiation between similar companies would directly conflict with one of the cornerstones of state aids: providing a selective advantage over companies that are in a similar factual and legal situation.[23]

EU regulations may incentivise companies to adjust their behaviour, and subsequently change the counterfactual analysis and thus the compensation required. If EU law requires a certain minimum level of sustainability, for example a hypothetical requirement that at most 50% of an operator's bus fleet is allowed to consist of diesel-powered buses, the amount of compensation is affected. Because of the regulation, transport operator B can no longer claim the integral costs of transforming its bus fleet, because under normal market conditions it would have to transform at least 50% thereof itself. Because of the supranational regulation, the Member State's law has less impact, because in the absence thereof bus transport operators are required to invest in sustainability regardless.

Either way, although integral compensation appears to be the logical option, it introduces the risk of discriminating between similar operators. How, then, should the compensation be calculated when a company incurs costs in order to adhere to certain sustainability standards? A solution could be to alter the definition of the SGEI to the extent that it does not cover the fleet transformation costs, and focus on sustainability during the procurement process instead. For example, a competent authority may design a procurement procedure where sustainability elements account for 75% of

[23] CJEU, *Ministero dell'Economia e delle Finanze v Paint Graphos Soc. Coop. arl*, Judgment, 8 September 2011, C-78/08 to C-80/08, para 49.

the total score. By doing so, the most sustainable operator is likely to be selected, and has to incur the 'sustainability costs' itself; in other words, it is rewarded for previous investments. It merely receives compensation for the actual performance of the public service obligation (hereafter: PSO)[24] or SGEI: the transport service itself, for example driving through an isolated, rural area of the bus route—or transporting young children and people with severe disabilities free of charge. The next section builds on this potential that procurement procedures offer in terms of sustainability standards, by covering the CJEU's *Concordia Bus Finland* judgment.[25]

8.4.1 Public Procurement and Sustainability Standards: **Concordia Bus Finland**

It speaks for itself that sustainability standards can be included in a procurement procedure. It is interesting to note, nevertheless, that the Court of Justice placed the threshold extremely low already in 2002, with its *Concordia Bus Finland* judgment.[26]

The case concerned a procurement procedure for a contract for the operation of a route in the urban bus network of Helsinki.[27] The issue was whether under Article 36(1) of Council Directive 92/50/EEC—amongst other criteria—extra points could be awarded on the basis of environmental factors.[28] In the *Concordia Bus Finland* case, points were awarded based on three factors: the overall price, the quality of the bus fleet, and the operator's quality and environment management.[29] Under environment management, additional points were awarded for various certified quality criteria and for a certified environment protection programme.[30] HKL won the tender, with Concordia coming in second. The latter appealed to the Finnish Competition Council, arguing that HKL was the only undertaking actually capable of satisfying the environment management criterion.[31] 'At the date of the invitation to tender, there was only one service station in the whole of Finland supplying natural gas. Its capacity enabled it to supply about 15 gas-powered buses. Shortly before the invitation to tender, HKL placed an order for 11 new gas-powered buses, which meant that the station's capacity was fully used and it was not possible to supply

---

[24] See above, n. 6.

[25] On 'green' or sustainable public procurement from an international trade law perspective, see Koch 2020. See also Halonen 2021.

[26] In his annotation, Kunzlik provides an exceptional overview of the case at hand. See Kunzlik 2003.

[27] CJEU, *Concordia Bus Finland Oy Ab and Helsinki kaupunki*, Judgment, 17 September 2002, C-513/99, para 2.

[28] Ibid.; See also Council Directive 92/50/EEC of 18 June 1992 relating to the coordination of procedures for the award of public service contracts, published on 24 July 1992.

[29] CJEU, *Concordia Bus Finland Oy Ab and Helsinki kaupunki*, 17 September 2002, C-513/99, para 21.

[30] Ibid., para 24.

[31] Ibid., para 72.

fuel to other vehicles'.[32] In addition to this, Concordia argued that the procurement procedure breached the principle of equal treatment, as HKL was owned by the city of Helsinki, i.e. the competent authority, itself.[33]

The Court of Justice disagreed, and noted that the principle of equal treatment does not preclude the taking into consideration of criteria connected with protection of the environment, such as those at issue in the main proceedings, solely because the contracting entity's own transport undertaking is one of the few undertakings able to offer a bus fleet satisfying those criteria.[34] As regards the environmental criteria, these may be taken into consideration provided that they are linked to the subject-matter of the contract, do not confer an unrestricted freedom of choice on the authority, are expressly mentioned in the contract documents or the tender notice, and comply with all the fundamental principles of Community law, in particular the principle of non-discrimination.[35]

8.5 Turning the Tables

So far, this chapter has demonstrated the complexity of (over)compensating a SGEI and offered a possible solution: to target the procurement procedure rather than the formulation of the SGEI. In *Lux Express Estonia*, the Estonian government (laudably) wanted to safeguard children's and people with severe disabilities' bus transport usage. Understandably, it did so by implementing §34 ÜTS, but it turned against itself, because unknowingly, the Estonian government, created a SGEI for which the operators require compensation under Regulation 1370/2007. As regard the *Concordia Bus Finland* case, even though it does not refer to compensation of the service, the municipality of Helsinki achieved its environmental objective without apparent complications.

To substantiate the argument that from the Member State perspective it is better to target the procurement procedure rather than implementing nationwide legislation, a counterfactual analysis is performed of both the *Lux Express Estonia* and *Concordia Bus Finland* cases. This hypothetical exercise aims to shed light on the subtle differences between both paths.

In the case of *Lux Express Estonia*, it must be assumed that the Estonian government, rather than introducing §34 ÜTS, conferred to its municipalities that each organises its public transport procurement in such way that it increases accessibility for children and people with severe disabilities. Companies that apply for the procurement procedure are awarded points on (amongst other economic criteria) the amount of discount or accessibility they offer to these groups in particular. This chapter argues that this would not constitute a SGEI in itself, because companies themselves

[32] Ibid., para 71.
[33] Ibid., para 70.
[34] Ibid., para 86.
[35] Ibid., para 69.

choose the extent to which they favour this group above regular customers. As such, no compensation is required for the lost profit. The downside of this is that it does not guarantee that the desired outcome of children and people with severe disabilities using the bus free of charge is reached, however. Depending on the extent to which the actual outcome (i.e. the best tender offer) differs from the desired one (transport free of charge for selected groups), the government can always intervene by implementing a PSO (and thus offer compensation).

In the case of *Concordia Bus Finland*, it must be assumed that the municipality of Helsinki requires of its transport operator to use gas-powered buses instead of diesel-powered ones. In this situation, the initiative comes from the municipality rather than the company—HKL—itself, and results in potential compensation for the latter company if the switch is regarded as a SGEI in light of Regulation 1370/2007. This is likely, as the applicable criterion is whether it is imposed by means of general rules. The nature of §34 ÜTS was such that it 'appears to be defined with a view to guaranteeing public passenger transport services in the general interest'.[36] It is not odd to think that a Finnish law stipulating that transport operators must use gas-powered buses instead of diesel-powered ones would meet this standard, too. Another complication arises when such a requirement applies to the whole of Finland, and not merely the city of Helsinki where HKL operates. Then, also less-sustainable companies, such as Concordia, have to be compensated for the shift from diesel-powered buses. These companies require more compensation than the already sustainable HKL. As such, a situation would arise which neglects the polluter pays principle.

8.6 Conclusions: Green Light for Sustainability Standards, but Beware of (Over)Compensation

The coming years will likely bring forth farther-and-farther-reaching laws to protect the environment and support sustainability. This chapter revolved around the transport sector, and discussed the (over)compensation of SGEIs. It centralised the recent *Lux Express Estonia* judgment, in which the Court of Justice makes some valuable remarks. National legislation cannot exclude compensation from performing a SGEI; there can be no compensation above the net financial effect, otherwise the notification obligation of Article 108(3) TFEU is triggered. In addition to this, the judgment clarifies that—in line with Regulation 1370/2007—a public service contract is not needed for a service to be declared a SGEI, which is required to receive compensation. It can also follow from the 'general interest', a phrase that might gain significant traction over the coming years.

Member States may try to incentivise a sustainable transition in the transport sector. As this chapter illustrates, however, by doing this, they may trigger Regulation

[36] CJEU, *Lux Express Estonia v Majandus- ja Kommunikatsiooniministeerium*, Judgment, 8 September 2022, C-614/20, para 41.

1370/2007 and (as in the case of Estonia's §34 ÜTS, accidentally) develop a SGEI, which demands compensation to the net financial effect. Contrary to §34 ÜTS, where by and large all transport operators are treated equally, sustainability regulations may provide additional implications due to vastly different situations on the side of operating companies. A Member State law stipulating that all bus fleets ought to be hydrogen/electricity powered, for example, risks invoking a SGEI on operators, who have to be compensated. The problem is that this conflicts with the polluter pays principle, as those who have previously invested in sustainability bear the burden and receive scant compensation compared to their adversaries who have neglected to invest. This may, too, spur interesting State aid appeals, but that is for another research to examine.

This chapter suggests that the solution may lie in the sphere of procurement procedures, where Member States enjoy a very wide margin of discretion when it comes to selecting sustainability criteria.[37] By arranging the intended sustainability objectives in the procurement procedure, the SGEI becomes not the sustainability investment itself, but rather the actual service. Instead, the initiative lies with the companies themselves. It also removes the risk of rewarding unsustainable operators, as these stand little chance of obtaining the contract.[38]

References

Craig P, De Búrca G (2008) EU Law, Text, Cases, and Materials, 4th edn. Oxford University Press, Oxford.

Halonen KM (2021) Is public procurement fit for reaching sustainability goals? A law and economics approach to green public procurement. Maastricht Journal of European and Comparative Law 28(4):535–555.

Klasse M (2013) The Impact of Altmark: The European Commission Case Law Responses. In: Szyszczak E, Van de Gronden JW (eds) Financing Services of General Economic Interest. T.M.C. Asser Press, The Hague, pp. 35–51.

Koch R (2020) Green Public Procurement under WTO Law, Experience of the EU and Prospects for Switzerland, EYIEL Monographs 9. Springer, Cham (Switzerland).

Kunzlik P (2003) Making the Market Work for the Environment: Acceptance of (Some) 'Green' Contract Award Criteria in Public Procurement. Journal of Environmental Law 15(2):175–201.

Linke B (2022) Transport Companies Are Entitled to Compensation for Public Service Obligations Imposed by General Rules – Case C-614/20 Lux Express Estonia, Annotation by Benjamin Linke. European State Aid Law Quarterly 21(4):419–424.

Nowag J (2016) Environmental Integration in Competition and Free-Movement Laws. Oxford University Press, Oxford.

Ølykke GS, Møllgaard P (2016) What is a service of general economic interest? European Journal of Law and Economics 41(1):205–241.

[37] Cf Wiesbrock 2015, p. 84: 'The use of award criteria relating to social, employment or environmental objectives can be a powerful tool for contracting authorities to promote sustainable development by giving preference to sustainable tenders.'

[38] For more about the potential of public procurement for achieving sustainability ambitions, see Wiesbrock and Sjåfjell 2015.

Pouikli K (2020) Towards Mandatory Green Public Procurement (GPP) requirements under the EU Green Deal: reconsidering the role of public procurement as an environmental policy tool. ERA Forum 21:699–721.
Schweitzer H (2011) Services of General Economic Interest: European Law's Impact on the Role of Markets and of Member States. In: Cremona M (ed) Market Integration and Public Services in the European Union, Collected Courses of the Academy of European Law. Oxford University Press, Oxford, pp. 11–62.
Sjåfjell B, Wiesbrock A (2015) Why should public procurement be about sustainability? In: Sjåfjell B, Wiesbrock A (eds) Sustainable Public Procurement under EU Law. Cambridge University Press, Cambridge, pp. 1–22.
Sommerdahl J (2017) A Public Service to Provide Renewable Energy: an Unexplored Possibility for the Member States of the EU? LLM thesis, Helsingfors Universitet, Helsinki.
Szyszczak E (2013) Introduction. In: Szyszczak E, Van de Gronden JW (eds) Financing Services of General Economic Interest. T.M.C. Asser Press, The Hague, pp. 1–32.
Wiesbrock A (2015) Socially responsible public procurement. In: Sjåfjell B, Wiesbrock A (eds) Sustainable Public Procurement under EU Law. Cambridge University Press, Cambridge, pp. 75–98.
Wiesbrock A, Sjåfjell B (2015) Public procurement's potential for sustainability. In: Sjåfjell B, Wiesbrock A (eds) Sustainable Public Procurement under EU Law. Cambridge University Press, Cambridge, pp. 230–242.
Zhu L (2020) Services of General Economic Interest in EU Competition Law. Legal Issues of Services of General Interest. T.M.C. Asser Press, The Hague.

Pieter S. Wesselius wrote this chapter during his PhD research at the University of Groningen. Thanks to the organisers of the 6th Radboud Economic Law Conference. Special thanks for M.S.E. Herz for his valuable feedback on this chapter.

Bibliography

ACM (2017) Explanatory Notes – Intensified attention for anticompetitive risks of hospital mergers'. https://www.acm.nl/sites/default/files/documents/2018-01/explanatory-notes-merger-control-hospitals_1.pdf. Accessed 7 May 2023.
Adelman S (2018) The sustainable development goals, Anthropocentrism and Neoliberalism. In: French D and Kotzé LJ (eds) Sustainable Development Goals: Law, Theory and Implementation. Edward Elgar, Cheltenham, pp 15–40.
Ahmadi A (2023) Fees for primary care: passion and emotion are integral to the conversation. British Medical Journal 380:596.
Allen C (2018) Initial progress in implementing the Sustainable Development Goals (SDGs): a review of evidence from countries. Sustainability Science 13:1453–1467.
Allen C (2021) Priorities for science to support national implementation of the sustainable development goals: A review of progress and gaps. Sustainable Development 29(4):635–652.
Andersen J (2018) Archiving, ordering, and searching: Search engines, algorithms, data- bases, and deep mediatization. Media, Culture & Society 40(8):1135–1150.
Angumuthoo M et al. (2020) Public Interest in Mergers: South Africa. The Antitrust Bulletin 65(2):312–332.
Arnold CA and Gunderson L (2013) Adaptive Law and Resilience. Environmental Law Reporter 43:10426–10443.
Baeten R and Palm W (2013) Preserving General Interest in Healthcare Through Secondary and Soft EU Law: The case of the Patients' Rights Directive. In: Neergaard U et al. (eds) Social Services of General Interest in the EU. T.M.C. Asser Press, The Hague, pp 385–412.
Barnard C (2020) Are social 'Rights' rights? European Labour Law Journal 11(4):351–363.
Bauby P and Similie MM (2012) Providing High-Quality Public Services in Europe Based on the Values of Protocol 26 of the Lisbon Treaty on Services of General Interest. CESI Europe Academy, Brussels.
Beetz J (2018) A two-tier conception of European Union peoplehood: A realist study of European citizens' bonds of collectivity. European Law Journal 23(6):467–481.
Belhaj S and Van de Gronden J (2004) Some room for competition does not make a sickness fund an undertaking. Is EC competition law applicable to the health care sector? (Joined cases C-264/01, C-306/01, C-453/01 and C-355/01 AOK). European Competition Law Review 25(11):682–687.
Berki G (2019) Patient Mobility in the EU: A Playground for All of Us? La Revue belge de sécurité sociale 1:65–80.
Biondi A and Ştefan O (2020) EU Health Union and State Aid Policy: With Great(er) Power Comes Great Responsibility. European Journal of Risk Regulation – Beyond COVID-19: Towards a European Health Union 11(4):894–902.
Boeger N (2007) Solidarity and EC Competition Law. European Law Review 32:319–340.

N. Ghazaryan et al. (eds.), *Services of General (Economic) Interest and EU Law*, Legal Issues of Services of General Interest, https://doi.org/10.1007/978-94-6265-723-6

Bradford A (2019) The Brussels Effect: How the European Union Rules the World. Oxford University Press, Oxford.

Brand A et al. (2021) Promoting Policy Coherence within the 2030 Agenda Framework: Externalities, Trade-Offs and Politics. Politics and Governance 9(1):108–118.

Breakwell G (2020) In the Age of Societal Uncertainty, the Era of Threat. In: Jodelet D et al. (eds) Societies Under Threat - A Pluri-Disciplinary Approach. Springer, Cham (Switzerland), pp 55–71.

Brightedge Research (2019) Organic Search Improves Ability to Map to Consumer Intent: Organic Channel Share Expands to 53.3% of Traffic. https://videos.brightedge.com/research-report/BrightEdge_ChannelReport2019_FINAL.pdf.

Brooks G and Stiernstedt P (2022) The Private Healthcare Insurance sector: A victim of fraud. Journal of Criminology 55(1):125–139.

Burke JM (2018) A Critical Account of Article 106(2) TFEU – Government Failure in Public Service Provision. Hart, Oxford.

Canoy M and Sauter W (2009) Hospital mergers and the public interest: recent developments in the Netherlands. TILEC Discussion Paper DP 2009-035. https://pure.uvt.nl/ws/portalfiles/portal/1112247/Sauter_hospital_mergers_SSRN_090910.pdf Accessed 16 July 2022.

Clark D (2022) Public Interest in Merger Control: Lessons from the end of the world. LLM thesis, Radboud University, Nijmegen.

Conference on the Future of Europe (2022) Report on the Final Outcome. https://futureu.europa.eu/en/pages/reporting?format=html&locale=en.

Cosens BA et al. (2020) Designing Law to Enable Adaptive Governance of Modern Wicked Problems. Vanderbilt Law Review 73(6):1687–1732.

Craig P and De Búrca G (2008) EU Law, Text, Cases, and Materials, 4th edn. Oxford University Press, Oxford.

Craig RK et al. (2017) Balancing stability and flexibility in adaptive governance: an analysis of tools available in US environmental law. Ecology and Society 22(2).

Cremer H et al. (2001) Universal service: an economic perspective. Annals of Public and Cooperative Economics 72(1):5–43.

Cseres KJ and Reyna A (2021) EU State Aid Law and Consumer Protection: An Unsettled Relationship in Times of Crisis. Journal of European Competition Law & Practice 12(8):617–629.

Davis D (2019) Public Interest, Industrial Policy and Competition Law Remedies: The South African Experience. In: Da Silveira PB and Kovacic WE (eds) Global Competition Enforcement: New Players, New Challenges (International Competition Law Series, Volume 79). Wolters Kluwer, Alphen aan den Rijn, pp 1421–1476.

DeCaro DA et al. (2017) Understanding and applying principles of social cognition and decision-making in adaptive environmental governance. Ecology and Society 22(1).

De Cecco F (2012) State Aid and the European Economic Constitution. Hart, Oxford.

De Ruijter A and Greer SL (2020) EU health law and policy in and after the COVID-19 crisis. European Journal of Public Health 30(4):623–624.

De Vries SA (2011) *BUPA*: A Healthy Case, in the Light of a Changing Constitutional Setting in Europe? In: Van de Gronden JW et al. (eds) Health Care and EU Law. T.M.C. Asser Press, The Hague, pp 289–311.

Den Exter A et al. (2015) One Year after the EU patient Mobility Directive: A Three-Country Analysis. European Law Review 40:278–292.

Dreyfus M (2009) Experience in the Member States: France. In: Krajewski M et al. (eds) The Changing Legal Framework for Services of General Interest in Europe. Between Competition and Solidarity. T.M.C. Asser Press, The Hague, pp 269–290.

European Commission (2016) Special Eurobarometer 447 on Online platforms. Publications Office of the European Union, Luxembourg.

European Commission (2020) Shaping Europe's digital future. Publications Office of the European Union, Luxembourg.

European Commission (2022a) Study on Greening Cloud Computing and Electronic Communications Services and Networks: Towards Climate Neutrality by 2050. Publications Office of the European Union, Luxembourg.

European Commission (2022b) Evaluation of the State subsidy rules for health and social services of general economic interest ("SGEIs") and of the SGEI de minimis Regulation {SWD(2022) 389 final}.

Filipović S et al. (2022) The green deal – just transition and sustainable development goals Nexus. Renewable and Sustainable Energy Reviews 168 112759:1–12.

Finger M and Finon D (2011) From the "public service" model to the "universal service" obligation. In: Finger M and Kunneke RW (eds) International Handbook of Network Industries. Edward Elgar Publishing, Cheltenham (Edward Elgar Publishing 2011) pp 54–69.

Frantziou E (2014) Case C-176/12 Association de Médiation Sociale: Some Reflections on the Horizontal Effect of the Charter and the Reach of Fundamental Employment Rights in the European Union. European Constitutional Law Review 10(2):332–348.

Friederiszick HW et al. (2007) European State Aid Control: An Economic Framework. In: Buccirossi P (ed) Handbook of Antitrust Economics. MIT Press, Cambridge, pp 625–671.

Gallo D and Mariotti C (2017) The Public Financing of Belgian Hospitals and EU Law: A Core Development in the Field of State Aid. In: Mastroianni R, Arena A (eds) 60 Years of EU Competition Law. Editoriale Scientifica, Naples, pp 173–198.

Garben S (2020) From sneaking to striding: Combatting competence creep and consolidating the EU legislative process. European Law Journal 26:429–447.

Gerbrandy A and Phoa P (2022) The Power of Big Tech Corporations as Modern Bigness and a Vocabulary for Shaping Competition Law as Counter-power. In: Bennett M et al. (eds) Wealth and Power. Routledge, New York City and Abingdon (Oxon), pp 166–185.

Giosa P (2022) The crucial role of the Single Market in tackling the COVID-19 pandemic: the case of State Aid. Work-in-progress presented at the UACES Annual Conference in September 2022.

Greaney T and Odudu O (2022) Introduction to Antitrust and the Provision of Healthcare in the United States and European Union. In: Orentlicher D and Hervey TK (eds) The Oxford Handbook of Comparative Health Law. Oxford University Press, Oxford, pp 311–315.

Greer SL and Sokol T (2013) Rules for Rights: European Law, Health Care and Social Citizenship. European Law Journal 20(1):66–87.

Gregory WR et al. (2021) The Role of Artificial Intelligence and Data Network Effects for Creating User Value. Academy of Management Review 46(3):534–551.

Griffiths M and Gumbie W (2015) The public interest test in the South African merger control regime. Journal of Antitrust Enforcement 3(2):408–424.

Guy M (2019) Competition Policy in Healthcare – Frontiers in Insurance-Based and Taxation-Funded Systems. Intersentia, Cambridge.

Guy M (2020a) Can COVID-19 change the EU competition law framework in health? Observatoire Social Euroṕeen Brussels Opinion Paper No. 25, September 2020.

Guy M (2020b) Towards a European Health Union: What Role for Member States? European Journal of Risk Regulation – Beyond COVID-19: Towards a European Health Union 11(4): 757–765.

Guy M (2023) Dealing with "unworkable ideas in primary legislation": Juridifying and dejuridifying competition in the English National Health Service. Public Law 57–80.

Hagan H (2022) Legal Design as a Thing: A Theory of Change and a Set of Methods to Craft a Human-Centered Legal System. Design Issues 36(3):3–15.

Haider J and Sundin O (2019) Invisible Search and Online Search Engines: The Ubiquity of Search in Everyday Life. Routledge, Abingdon (Oxon).

Halonen KM (2021) Is public procurement fit for reaching sustainability goals? A law and economics approach to green public procurement. Maastricht Journal of European and Comparative Law 28(4):535–555.

Hancher L and Sauter W (2012) EU Competition and Internal Market Law in the Health Care Sector. Oxford University Press, Oxford.

Hancher L and Sauter W (2013) This Won't Hurt A Bit: The Commission's Approach to Services of General Economic Interest and State Aid to Hospitals. In: Szyszczak E and Van de Gronden JW (eds) Financing Services of General Economic Interest – Reform and Modernization. T.M.C. Asser Press, The Hague, pp 249–272.

Haque SM (2001) The Diminishing Publicness of Public Service under the Current Mode of Governance. Public Administration Review 61(1):65–82.

Helberger N et al. (2021) EU Consumer Protection 2.0: Structural Asymmetries in Digital Consumer Markets. BEUC (The European Consumer Organisation), Brussels.

Hickel J (2020) What does degrowth mean? A few points of clarification. Globalizations 18(7):1105–1111.

Holling CS (1973) Resilience and Stability of Ecological Systems. Annual Review of Ecology and Systematics 4:1–23.

Kanavos P et al. (1999) Cross border health care in Europe. British Medical Journal 318(7192):1157–1158.

Klasse M (2013) The Impact of Altmark: The European Commission Case Law Responses. In: Szyszczak E and Van de Gronden JW (eds) Financing Services of General Economic Interest. T.M.C. Asser Press, The Hague, pp 35–51.

Koch R (2020) Green Public Procurement under WTO Law, Experience of the EU and Prospects for Switzerland, EYIEL Monographs 9. Springer, Cham (Switzerland).

Krajewski M (2009) Conclusions. In: Krajewski M et al. (eds) The Changing Legal Framework for Services of General Interest in Europe. Between Competition and Solidarity. T.M.C. Asser Press, The Hague, pp 499–506.

Krajewski M (2011) Grundstrukturen des Rechts öffentlicher Dienstleistungen. Springer, Heidelberg.

Krajewski M et al. (2009) The Changing Legal Framework for Services of General Interest in Europe. Between Competition and Solidarity. T.M.C. Asser Press, The Hague.

Kroll C et al. (2019) Sustainable development goals (SDGs): Are we successful in turning trade-offs into synergies? Palgrave Communications 5 140:1–11.

Kunzlik P (2003) Making the Market Work for the Environment: Acceptance of (Some) 'Green' Contract Award Criteria in Public Procurement. Journal of Environmental Law 15(2):175–201.

Le Blanc D (2015) Towards integration at last? The sustainable development goals as a network of targets. Sustainable Development 23(3):176–187.

Linke B (2022) Transport Companies Are Entitled to Compensation for Public Service Obligations Imposed by General Rules – Case C-614/20 Lux Express Estonia, Annotation by Benjamin Linke. European State Aid Law Quarterly 21(4):419–424.

Mair S et al. (2018) A Critical Review of the Role of Indicators in Implementing the Sustainable Development Goals. In: Filho WL (ed) Handbook of Sustainability Science and Research. Springer, Cham (Switzerland), pp 41–56.

Malay OE (2021) Improving government and business coordination through the use of consistent SDGs indicators. A comparative analysis of national (Belgian) and business (pharma and retail) sustainability indicators. Ecological Economics 184 106991:1–13.

Marshall TH (1950) Citizenship and social class. Cambridge University Press, Cambridge.

Ministry of Economic Affairs and Climate (2022) Kamerbrief over nieuw vergunningsbesluit voor concentratie PostNL – Sandd. https://www.rijksoverheid.nl/documenten/kamerstukken/2021/04/09/nieuw-vergunningsbesluit-voor-concentratie-postnl---sandd. Accessed 17 July 2022.

Ministry of Health, Welfare and Sport (2020) Kamerbrief over aanscherping fusietoezicht in de zorg. https://www.rijksoverheid.nl/documenten/kamerstukken/2020/02/18/kamerbrief-over-aanscherping-fusietoezicht-in-de-zorg.

Ministry of Health, Welfare and Sport (2022) Kamerbrief over Besluit verlaagde omzetdrempels zorg. https://www.rijksoverheid.nl/documenten/kamerstukken/2022/07/15/kamerbrief-over-besluit-verlaagde-omzetdrempels-zorg.

Morton AJB (2021) European Health Care Systems and the Emerging Influence of European Union Competition Policy. Journal of Health Politics, Policy and Law 46(3):468–486.

Morton AJB (2022) Re-establishing needed limits: European competition policy's role in European healthcare systems and the lessons of the *Dôvera* case. Social Policy Administration 56(3):472–484.

Mossialos E et al. (2010) Health Systems Governance in Europe: the role of European Union law and policy. Cambridge University Press, Cambridge.

Munro V (2020) CSR for Purpose, Shared Value and Deep Transformation: The New Responsibility. Emerald Publishing, Leeds (UK).

Neergaard U (2009) Services of General Economic Interest: The Nature of the Beast. In: Krajewski M et al. (eds) The Changing Legal Framework for Services of General Interest in Europe. Between Competition and Solidarity. T.M.C. Asser Press, The Hague, pp 17–50.

Nikolić B (2021) Applicability of European Union Competition Law to Health Care Providers: The Dividing Line between Economic and Noneconomic Activities. Journal of Health Politics, Policy and Law 46(1):49–70.

Nilsson M et al. (2016) Policy: Map the interactions between sustainable development goals. Nature 534:320–322.

Nowag J (2016) Environmental Integration in Competition and Free-Movement Laws. Oxford University Press, Oxford.

Ocello et al. (2015) What's Up with Merger Control in the Digital Sector? Lessons from the *Facebook/Whatsapp* EU merger case. Competition merger brief 2015(1):1–7.

Odudu O (2022) Health Care Services and EU Competition Law. In: Orentlicher D and Hervey TK (eds) The Oxford Handbook of Comparative Health Law. Oxford University Press, Oxford, pp 316–348.

OECD (2013) Government at a Glance 2013. OECD Publishing, Paris.

OECD (2016) Big Data: Bringing Competition Policy to the Digital Era. OECD Publishing, Paris.

Ølykke GS and Møllgaard P (2016) What is a service of general economic interest? European Journal of Law and Economics 41(1):205–241.

Ostrom E et al. (2007) Going Beyond Panacea. Proceedings National Academies of Science USA 104(39):15176–15178.

Pan B et al. (2007) In Google We Trust: Users' Decisions on Rank, Position, and Relevance. Journal of Computer-Mediated Communication 12(3):801–823.

Panara C (2022) Subsidiarity v Autonomy in the EU. European Public Law 28(2):269–296.

Piris J-C (2010) The Lisbon Treaty: A Legal and Political Analysis. Cambridge University Press, Cambridge.

Popelier P (2008) Five Paradoxes on Legal Certainty and the Lawmaker. Legisprudence 2(1):47–66.

Pouikli K (2020) Towards Mandatory Green Public Procurement (GPP) requirements under the EU Green Deal: reconsidering the role of public procurement as an environmental policy tool. ERA Forum 21:699–721.

Pradhan P et al. (2017) A systematic study of sustainable development goal (SDG) interactions. Earth's Future 5(11):1169–1179.

Prosser T (2005) The Limits of Competition Law – Markets and Public Services. Oxford University Press, Oxford.

Prosser T (2010) EU competition law and public services. In: Mossialos E et al. (eds) Health Systems Governance in Europe – The Role of European Union Law and Policy. Cambridge University Press, Cambridge, pp 315–336.

Purnhagen K et al. (2020) More Competences than You Knew? The Web of Health Competence for European Union Action in Response to the COVID-19 Outbreak. European Journal of Risk Regulation 11:297–306.

Rangoni B (2023) Experimentalist Governance: From Architectures to Outcomes. Oxford University Press, Oxford.

Revi B (2014) T.H. Marshall and his critics: reappraising 'social citizenship' in the twenty-first century. Citizenship studies 18(3–4):452–464.

Rittel H and Webber M M (1973) Dilemmas in a general theory of planning. Policy Sciences 4:155–169.

Rockström J et al. (2009) A safe operating space for humanity. Nature 461:472–475.
Rockström J et al. (2023) Safe and just Earth system boundaries. Nature 619:102–111.
Röling IMC (2012) Services of General Economic Interest within the Dutch healthcare system. LLM thesis, Tilburg University.
Roos A-F (2018) Mergers and Competition in the Dutch Healthcare Sector. PHD thesis, Erasmus University Rotterdam.
Rosenboom N (2018) Hospital Mergers and the Incorporation of Non-Competition Concerns. European Competition and Regulatory Law Review 2:271–279.
Ross M (2007) Promoting Solidarity: From Public Services to a European Model of Competition? Common Market Law Review 44(4):1057–1080.
Ross M (2009) A healthy approach to services of general economic interest? The *BUPA* judgment of the Court of First Instance. European Law Review 34(1):127–140.
Ruhl J B et al. (2021) Resilience of Legal Systems: Toward Adaptive Governance. In: Ungar M (ed) Multisystemic Resilience. Oxford University Press, Oxford, pp 509–529.
Sabel CF and Zeitlin J (2008) Learning from Difference: The New Architecture of Experimentalist Governance in the European Union. European Law Journal 14(3):271–327.
Sachs JD (2012) From millennium development goals to sustainable development goals. The Lancet 379(9832):2206–2211.
Sachs JD et al. (2019) Six transformations to achieve the sustainable development goals. Nature Sustainability 2:805–814.
Sambrook R (2012) Delivering Trust: Impartiality and Objectivity in the Digital Age. Reuters Institute for the Study of Journalism, Oxford.
Sánchez Graells A (2015) New rules for health care procurement in the UK: a critical assessment from the perspective of EU economic law. Public Procurement Law Review 1:16–30.
Sauter W (2008) Services of general economic interest and universal service in EU law. European Law Review 33(2):167–193.
Sauter W (2014) Public services in EU law. Cambridge University Press, Cambridge.
Schirato T and Webb J (2003) Understanding globalization. Sage, London, Thousand Oaks (USA) and New Delhi.
Schultheiß S et al. (2018) We still trust in Google, but less than 10 years ago: an eye-tracking study. Information Research 23(3).
Schweitzer H (2011) Services of General Economic Interest: European Law's Impact on the Role of Markets and of Member States. In: Cremona M (ed) Market Integration and Public Services in the European Union, Collected Courses of the Academy of European Law. Oxford University Press, Oxford, pp 11–62.
Sjåfjell B and Wiesbrock A (2015) Why should public procurement be about sustainability? In: Sjåfjell B and Wiesbrock A (eds) Sustainable Public Procurement under EU Law. Cambridge University Press, Cambridge, pp 1–22.
Skovgaard Ølykke G and Møllgaard P (2016) What is a Service of General Economic Interest? European Journal of Law and Economics 41:205–241.
Sommerdahl J (2017) A Public Service to Provide Renewable Energy: An Unexplored Possibility for the Member States of the EU? LLM thesis, Helsingfors Universitet, Helsinki.
Sundin O and Carlsson H (2016) Outsourcing trust to the information infrastructure in schools: How search engines order knowledge in education practices. Journal of Documentation 72(6):990–1007.
Szyszczak E (2009) Modernising Healthcare: Pilgrimage for the Holy Grail? In: Krajewski M et al. (eds) The Changing Legal Framework for Services of General Interest in Europe – Between Competition and Solidarity. T.M.C. Asser Press, The Hague, pp 191–214.
Szyszczak E (2013) Introduction. In: Szyszczak E and Van de Gronden JW (eds) Financing Services of General Economic Interest. T.M.C. Asser Press, The Hague, pp 1–32.
Unkel J and Haas A (2017) The effects of credibility cues on the selection of search engine results. Journal of the Association for Information Science and Technology 68(8):1850–1862.
Van Damme E (2019 De overname van Sandd door PostNL. Markt & Mededinging 22(5):160–174.

Van de Gronden JW (2004) Purchasing care: economic activity or service of general (economic) interest? European Competition Law Review 25(2):87–94.
Van de Gronden JW (2011) The Treaty Provisions on Competition and Health Care. In: Van de Gronden JW et al. (eds) Health Care and EU Law. T.M.C. Asser Press, The Hague, pp 265–294.
Van de Gronden JW (2018) Services of General Interest and the concept of undertaking. Does EU competition law apply? World Competition 41(2):197–224.
Van de Gronden JW (2021) Grensoverschrijdende zorg: vrij verkeer van patiënten in een oerwoud van regels. In: de Graaf KJ et al. (eds) Grensoverstijgende rechtsbeoefening Liber amicorum Jan Jans. Uitgeverij Paris, Zutphen, pp 149–156.
Van de Gronden JW and Guy M (2021) The role of EU competition law in health care and the 'undertaking' concept. Health Economics, Policy and Law 16(1):76–89.
Van de Gronden JW and Rusu CS (2013) The Altmark Update and Social Services: Towards a European Approach. In: Szyszczak E and Van de Gronden JW (eds) Financing Services of General Economic Interest – Reform and Modernization. T.M.C. Asser Press, The Hague, pp 185–216.
Van de Gronden JW and Rusu CS (2017) EU competition law and policy and health systems. In: Hervey TK et al. (eds) Research Handbook on EU Health Law and Policy. Edward Elgar, Cheltenham, pp 267–290.
Van de Gronden JW and Rusu CS (2024) Competition law in the EU, 2nd edn. Edward Elgar, Cheltenham.
Van de Gronden JW and Szyszczak E (2011) Conclusions: Constructing a 'Solid' Multi-Layered Health Care Edifice. In: Van de Gronden JW et al. (eds) Health Care and EU Law. T.M.C. Asser Press, The Hague, pp 481–495.
Van de Gronden JW and Szyszczak E (2014) Introducing Competition Principles into Health Care Through EU Law and Policy: A Case Study of the Netherlands. Medical Law Review 22(2):238–354.
Vandemoortele J (2011) If not the millennium development goals, then what? Third World Quarterly 32(1):9–25.
Van Eijken H (2014) European Citizenship and the Constitutionalisation of the European Union. Europa Law Publishing, Zutphen.
Van Norren DE (2020) The Sustainable Development Goals viewed through Gross National Happiness, Ubuntu, and Buen Vivir. International Environmental Agreements: Politics, Law and Economics 20:431–458.
Van Zimmeren E (2023) Het concept 'duurzaamheid' ontrafelen – een begin, geen eindpunt. Tijdschrift voor Europees en economisch recht (SEW) 2023(7/8):305–318.
Von der Leyen U (2020) State of the Union Address by President von der Leyen at the European Parliament Plenary, 16 September 2020.
Waage J et al. (2015) Governing the UN sustainable development goals: Interactions, infrastructures, and institutions. The Lancet Global Health 3(5):e251–e252.
Walker B and Salt D (2006) Resilience Thinking: Sustaining Ecosystems and People in a Changing World. Island Press, Washington.
Wehlander C (2016) Services of General Economic Interest as a Constitutional Concept of EU Law. T.M.C. Asser Press, The Hague.
Weiland S et al. (2021) The 2030 Agenda for Sustainable Development: Transformative Change through the Sustainable Development Goals? Politics and Governance 9(1):90–95.
Wendt C et al. (2009) Healthcare System Types: A Conceptual Framework for Comparison. Social Policy & Administration 43(1):70–90.
Wiesbrock A (2015) Socially responsible public procurement. In: Sjåfjell B and Wiesbrock A (eds) Sustainable Public Procurement under EU Law. Cambridge University Press, Cambridge, pp 75–98.
Wiesbrock A and Sjåfjell B (2015) Public procurement's potential for sustainability. In: Sjåfjell B and Wiesbrock A (eds) Sustainable Public Procurement under EU Law. Cambridge University Press, Cambridge, pp 230–242.

Wolfe D (2018) Experimental Governance: Conceptual approaches and practical cases, Background paper for an OECD/EC Workshop on 14 December 2018 within the workshop series "Broadening innovation policy: New insights for regions and cities". OECD, Paris. https://www.researchgate.net/profile/David-Wolfe-6/publication/342247057_EXPERIMENTAL_GOVERNANCE_CONCEPTUAL_APPROACHES_AND_PRACTICAL_CASES_1_Broadening_innovation_policy_New_insights_for_cities_and_regions_Experimental_Governance_Conceptual_approaches_and_practical_cases_A/links/5eea60bd458515814a672c98/EXPERIMENTAL-GOVERNANCE-CONCEPTUAL-APPROACHES-AND-PRACTICAL-CASES-1-Broadening-innovation-policy-New-insights-for-cities-and-regions-Experimental-Governance-Conceptual-approaches-and-practical-cases.pdf.

World Commission on Environment and Development (1987) Report of the World Commission on Environment and Development: Our Common Future. https://sustainabledevelopment.un.org/content/documents/5987our-common-future.pdf. Accessed on 12 April 2023.

Zhu L (2020) Services of General Economic Interest in EU Competition Law. Legal Issues of Services of General Interest. T.M.C. Asser Press, The Hague.

FSC
www.fsc.org
MIX
Papier aus verantwortungsvollen Quellen
Paper from responsible sources
FSC® C105338

If you have any concerns about our products,
you can contact us on
ProductSafety@springernature.com

In case Publisher is established outside the EU,
the EU authorized representative is:
Springer Nature Customer Service Center GmbH
Europaplatz 3, 69115 Heidelberg, Germany

Printed by Libri Plureos GmbH
in Hamburg, Germany